Contents

MAKING COMMUNITY DESIGN WORK

A GUIDE FOR PLANNERS

Umut Toker

American Planning Association
Planners Press

Making Great Communities Happen

Chicago | Washington, D.C.

For my family – my sister, Sıdıka Mine Toker; my mother, Nedret Toker; and my father, Mithat Toker

In loving memory of my grandparents Sıdıka Toker, Ömer Toker, Türkan Usta, and Osman Usta

205 N. Michigan Ave., Suite 1200, Chicago, IL 60601-5927

1030 15th St., NW, Suite 750 West, Washington, DC 20005-1503

www.planning.org/plannerspress

ISBN: 978-1-61190-002-6 (pbk.)

Library of Congress Control Number 2012930446

Printed in the United States of America

List of Figures

Unless otherwise indicated, the photographs, graphics, models, and renderings are by the author.

List of Tables

Acknowledgments

I would like to thank the following individuals who made this book possible. I am grateful to Henry Sanoff for his constant guidance and trust throughout my career. I thank Bill Siembieda and Hemalata Dandekar for their support. I would like to thank Denis Gray for his mentorship and his continuing support. I thank Whit Blanton and Frederick Steiner for spending time to talk with me about their experiences in community design. Finally, my special thanks go to APA Planners Press editor Timothy Mennel, for his continuous support and encouragement throughout the writing process.

Introduction

Throughout history, people have shaped their built environment to benefit their individual and community lives. Deliberation over how to shape the built environment is embedded in our past. At different times and in different contexts, however, the participation of different groups in this process has ranged widely.

With the increasing complexity of issues surrounding human settlements, especially in the second half of the 20th century, participatory planning and design today occupies a central place on the agenda of many community groups and institutions. Political governments and built environment professionals have sought to generate technical solutions to problems of accommodating increasing populations and related urban issues, while developing ways to involve people in decision making about the environments in which they live and work. Involving individuals and groups in decisions about their built environments has proved to be a strenuous but rewarding effort. Although participatory decision making in planning and design requires specific techniques and time commitment, it yields environments that are well suited to the needs and wishes of their inhabitants.

This book is a guide to the participatory planning and design of the built environment at various scales. Its goal is to provide a concise but comprehensive overview of community design for professional planners, designers, and students in built environment–related disciplines. The book accomplishes this goal through four parts. In Part 1, the history of and social motivation for community design are presented. Part 2 focuses on steps in the process of participatory decision making in planning and design. In Part 3, conventional and contemporary community design methods are examined, and some applications are introduced. Finally, Part 4 focuses on applying community design processes and methods to the built environment at four scales: urban, community (the entire town or city), regional, and the individual site, such as parks or buildings. Examples of applications in communities of various sizes are provided to demonstrate the concepts discussed.

Although this book is intended primarily for professionals and preprofessionals working in city and regional planning, architecture, and landscape architecture, the concepts, processes, and methods are presented in lay rather than discipline-specific language to the extent possible. This way, those receiving planning and design services may also find it a resource in working with professionals providing services. Those outside the ambit of the profession are encouraged to review the material in Chapters 4, 5, and 6 in particular and to apply it to the advantage of their projects.

PART 1
History and Social Motivation

Part 1 of this book introduces the historical background of and social motivation for current trends in community design. Chapter 1 explores the concept of participatory decision making and reviews the legal background that has prompted the turn to participatory decision making in planning and design. Chapter 2 introduces the objectives, stages, and outcomes of community design. Chapter 3 looks back to the origins of community design in the grassroots human-rights movements of the mid-20th century and forward to the role of social forces in fine-tuning participatory design practices and the role of the community designer.

1 Working with People for Their Future

It is pragmatically and psychologically beneficial for people to shape their environments to benefit their individual and community lives. In the case of a house, pragmatic concerns such as privacy or room proximity could define the benefit. In the case of a neighborhood, the location of commercial services in relation to major circulation axes could benefit all residents and business owners. In antiquity, people found efficacy in locating a temple dedicated to the veneration of a deity in a spot considered sacred.

The individual and community benefits to be derived from shaping the built environment, especially the urban environment, have usually accrued to those in power, however. In ancient Greek cities the agora, the city square where male landowners (but not slaves or females) gathered, would be situated prominently for exchange of political information and commercial goods. In cities of the Roman Empire, the building and location of stadiums, public baths, and other civic structures were understood to be part of the incumbent emperor's display of power. The medieval cities of Europe were not very different. While the ruling class and important personalities were centrally located in cities, sometimes residing in fortified structures for protection, field laborers usually had to work outside the walls of the city to grow food crops. From antiquity to the present day, moreover, uprisings by people against power have always included attacking the physical structures that symbolized and upheld the social system people were fighting against.

In the 19th and 20th centuries, the social and political implications of shaping neighborhoods and cities were more complex. In 19th-century Paris, the shaping of streets and plazas was influenced by efforts to minimize uprisings against the emperor while generating visual axes that reified grandiose governmental power. Perhaps one of the most dramatic examples of the shaping of urban environments is Berlin, where for decades, families and neighbors were separated by a wall and lived under two different political regimes. In one of the most celebrated episodes of people expressing their wishes concerning the built environment in which they live, the Berlin

Wall was demolished by the people and against the will of those who wanted to preserve it as a physical manifestation of their power.

Starting in the 1960s, the principle of people having a voice in the shaping of their built environment has been observed in many societies and through many design movements. But even as professionals and politicians have applauded the concept of participatory planning and design, a tension has remained between the concept of participatory decision making and the fact of power, whether that power is the hard power wielded by politicians or the soft power of planning and design professionals. In both cases there are individuals on one side who are deemed to have authority to make decisions about the built environment and, on the other side, individuals who must live in those built environments and who are the ones most affected by the decisions.

Evidently, the concept, process, and outcomes of participatory decision making concerning the built environment are complex. In this day and age, participatory planning and design sounds great: we live in a democratic society, and all should have a say in how our environment is shaped. In terms of process, however, everyone having a say has implications for those responsible for translating ideas into decisions about the built environment. It also has implications for those who express opinions about how their environments are shaped: participatory planning and design means exchanging information, ideas, opinions, and positions with those people who live near you. This may turn into lengthy discussions, even confrontations. So, participatory decision making for the built environment is not simple. As an introduction to community design, we can start by examining attitudes toward citizen participation over the past few decades.

1.1. THE CONCEPT OF PARTICIPATORY DECISION MAKING

> The idea of citizen participation is a little like eating spinach: no one is against it in principle because it is good for you. (Arnstein 1969, 216)

The concept of participatory decision making, that people should deliberate together over issues that affect their future and make decisions accordingly, is age-old. As Sherry Arnstein put it, participatory decision making by its very nature is good since it gives people who will be affected by certain decisions a say in those decisions (Arnstein 1969). It helps groups and individuals understand one another's point of view, and it facilitates decision making for the common good.

In a group of individuals trying to reach agreement, participatory decision making takes the power of making decisions away from any one individual and distributes it to everyone. In professional terms, participatory decision making means that the professional or the source of political power is not the sole decision maker but rather someone who works with people to help them reach decisions. In planning and design terms, participatory decision making means that the planner or designer works with people, helps them reach decisions about planning and design issues, and translates these decisions into planning and design language throughout the decision making process.

But if participation is "inherently good" (Sanoff 2000), why did Arnstein liken it to eating spinach, suggesting that it is good for you but perhaps slightly unsavory? We can approach this question from the point of view of various role players in the decision scenario.

Let us start with those who have the right to make decisions about the built environment, such as city officials, or those who are eligible to make decisions, such as professional planners and designers. If they want to hold on to that right or eligibility, participatory decision making may indeed be like eating spinach. Furthermore, participatory decision making may be perceived by such individuals as a process that needs more time and budget—yet another reason to think of spinach. On the other hand, members of the community will live in the planned and designed spaces. For them, the idea of participatory decision making may generate the impression that they will need to participate in more discussions and perhaps have to oppose the wishes of their fellow community members. Finally, might this process in fact go nowhere? After all the talk, might decision makers simply go ahead with what they had in mind in the first place?

Over the years, participatory planning and design has had its share of opposition. Some planning and design professionals have perceived the participatory approach as undermining the value of expertise and turning decision-making power over to uncredentialed individuals. Others have insisted that participatory planning and design consumes too much time and resources, and that professionals can reach the same decisions faster and more efficiently.

On the other hand, the advantages of community design are widely acknowledged, too. Community design puts everybody's issues on the table, builds mutual understanding, and enables decision making for the common good rather than for the sole benefit of particular individuals or parties. In this sense, participatory planning and design is inherently democratic. How, then, can communities, planners, designers, and civil servants overcome the concerns raised above? Here is where the various participatory decision-making methods and instruments developed by community planners over the decades come into play. They have demonstrated worth in overcoming such potential problems and in giving everyone who stands to be affected by planning and design decisions a voice in the decision process.

Over the past five decades, participatory decision making has thrived, and more and more people have had a chance to voice their opinions about the environments that surround them. Since the 1960s both professional providers and users of planned and designed environments have learned from project experiences and have contributed know-how to participatory planning and design. They have learned from each other and from going through the process the advantages of participatory decision making. Community design formats, methods, and instruments have been developed to achieve the following:

1. To let professionals become facilitators in the decision-making process and maximize the use of their technical expertise by hearing about issues.
2. To efficiently design, manage, and analyze community design events.
3. To move toward consensus building and away from compromise.
4. To help reach planning and design decisions collaboratively, with the least time and budget expenditure possible.
5. To guide parties that will contribute to and manage implementation so that the decisions made are implemented as desired by the community.

This book is about the experience of participatory decision making in planning and design. The primary objective is to summarize the community design experience of the recent half century and build on it by systematically introducing community design activity formats, methods, and instruments. Because experience has shown that participatory decision making can be used at a variety of project scales, a second objective is to investigate the use of participatory decision-making tools and processes in regional plan development, urban planning, urban design, and site-specific design and development. Case materials for each kind of site are introduced to show participatory planning in action.

There are, of course, certain principles that underlie community design. They are enumerated here and referenced again in discussions of examples from the field:

1. As receivers of planning and design services, the users of planned and designed environments should have the right to specify the desired aspects of the product they will receive.
2. The planner or designer working on a built environment–related project has a responsibility to provide planning and design services that will ensure that the product meets the users' needs and wishes.
3. By planning and designing together, users, planners, and designers simultaneously learn from one another. This process contributes to an overall increase in the quality of environments created for people.

4. The evaluation of environments created for people should be based on the users' experiences.

Through evaluations of the existing built environment and research, planning and design professionals can contribute to the body of professional planning and design knowledge and increase the quality of their work, as well as the overall quality of the services provided by their profession. The more planners and designers know about the qualities of the physical environment that will satisfy people, the better their products will be.

1.2. THE LEGAL BACKGROUND OF PARTICIPATORY DECISION MAKING IN PLANNING AND DESIGN

Participatory decision making takes place in a legal and regulatory framework. Many states require that decisions that affect people be made with their knowledge and input. Professionals who believe in maximizing the quality of their services choose participatory decision making for that reason, and not to meet legal requirements only. However, it is important that we look into the sources and current examples of legal requirements for participatory decision making.

Participatory decision making is embedded in the Constitution. The Fifth Amendment, Trial and Punishment, Compensation for Takings, states:

> No person shall be held to answer for a capital, or otherwise infamous crime, unless on a presentment or indictment of a Grand Jury, except in cases arising in the land or naval forces, or in the Militia, when in actual service in time of War or public danger; nor shall any person be subject for the same offense to be twice put in jeopardy of life or limb; nor shall be compelled in any criminal case to be a witness against himself, nor be deprived of life, liberty, or property, without due process of law; nor shall private property be taken for public use, without just compensation.

The due process clause establishes individuals' right to be heard in matters that affect them. While this is an overarching principle that can be implemented in a variety of ways, states have adopted laws that provide precise guidance on transparency and participation in decision making. California's Ralph M. Brown Act, for example, applies to legislative bodies of local agencies such as city councils and planning commissions and requires that such agencies enable the involvement of the public. Enacted in 1953, it states:

> Public commissions, boards, councils and other legislative bodies of local government agencies exist to aid in the conduct of the people's business. The people do not yield their sovereignty to the bodies that serve them. The people insist on remaining informed to retain control over the

> legislative bodies they have created. (California Government Code, § 54950, Ch. I, Preamble)

The Brown Act requires public notice of meetings, as well as public posting of meeting agendas. The Brown Act also allows people attending such public meetings to record and broadcast the event over radio or television (unless recording would disrupt the meeting).

Several other states have similar laws. The State of Massachusetts' Open Meeting Law, adopted in 1958, is applicable to governmental units at the state, county, and municipal levels. It requires that all meetings of a quorum of a governmental body be announced by public notice and that any individual be allowed to attend such meetings (with exceptions as defined by law). The states of New York, Nevada, Minnesota, Arizona, and Michigan, among others, have similar open meeting laws.

Over the course of the past five decades, planners and designers have developed innovative participatory decision-making formats, methods, and instruments not only to meet the legal requirements but also to ensure that people are involved in decisions that will affect them. While legal requirements for open decision making in some contexts and some jurisdictions exist, however, they do not guarantee that involvement will actually take place. Depending on how the law is implemented, public involvement may range from one-way, public hearing–style "respond to the ongoing discussion" activities to interactive community meetings.

2 What Is Community Design?

Objectives, Stages, and Outcomes

"Community design" is a term widely used in planning and design disciplines, and it has a variety of definitions. In the contemporary planning and design world, understandings of community design generally fall into one or the other of two main purviews. The first focuses on the *act of making* as a response to a group of people's needs and aspirations: making *for* people. The second focuses on the *act of decision making* in collaboration with a group to meet that group's needs and aspirations: making *with* people. The next section adds a bit more detail to these two views; then the chapter moves on to the objectives, stages, and outcomes of community design.

2.1. WHAT IS COMMUNITY DESIGN?

One available definition of community design is the act of designing the physical attributes of a community:

> Community design is the art of making sustainable living places that both thrive and adapt to people's needs for shelter, livelihood, commerce, recreation, and social order. (Hall and Porterfield 2001, 3)

Implicit in the "physical attributes" definition are the assumptions that a community is defined by, or at least related to, a locale and that the planning and design principles brought by the professionals will respond to people's needs. Some go further and propose that these planning and design principles may affect people's ways of doing things (Lennertz 1991). This approach is based on the following logic: (1) a planner or designer makes decisions with people's interests and the planner's own professional background in mind, (2) people occupy the product, and (3) people adapt to the product while the product adapts to people's needs.

The second definition considers community design as an act of decision making with people:

> How to make it possible for people to be involved in shaping and managing their environment is what the community design movement has been exploring over the past few decades. (Sanoff 2000, x)

Implicit in this definition is the assumption that community design is a process in which professionals work with the people who will be using the space and make decisions with them. The underlying premise is that people are experts on their own needs and aspirations and professionals need to work with them to translate those wishes and aspirations into reality, using professional expertise. By this definition community design is working *with* people, not *for* people (Hester 1990). Therefore, this approach is based on the following logic: 1) a planner or designer works with people and facilitates a process during which people and professionals learn from each other; (2) the planner or designer translates the wishes and aspirations of the people gathered during this process into plan or design proposals, using his or her expertise; and (3) the product, as an outcome of those plans or proposals, is adapted to the people.

This book subscribes to the second approach: it considers community design the process of making planning and design decisions in collaboration with the people who stand to be affected by those decisions. The process includes translating the decisions made collaboratively into planning and design language and formats, such as plan documents, sketches, three-dimensional renderings, architectural drawings, and vision documents. The professional planner or designer must fill multiple roles during this process:

1. as a facilitator, organizing the discussion environment for decision making,
2. as a student, learning from people about their day-to-day relationship with their environment,
3. as a teacher, sharing with people the planning and design implications of the decisions they are considering, and
4. as a professional, translating people's decisions into planning and design language and documents.

Now that we have briefly defined community design and the role of the professional in the process, let us look into the founding principles of community design in more detail.

2.2. OBJECTIVES OF COMMUNITY DESIGN

Community design, then, is participatory decision making with people. But beyond legal requirements, why participate? Don't professionals who have degrees from accredited planning and design schools know what works? Common questions planners and designers ask when they are first introduced to the idea of community design are:

"What is the professional's role going to be if we let people design for themselves?"

"What if people support decisions that we, as professionals, know would not be good for them?"

"What if people make terrible design decisions?"

To answer such questions, it helps to consider the objectives of community design. Community designers advocate participatory decision making for the following underlying objectives.

Objective One: Understanding People's Needs

As in every profession, planners and designers carry the responsibility of providing services that will answer to people's needs. In industry, testing is common to ensure a good fit. Automobile manufacturers conduct safety tests before introducing products to consumers to ensure their safety in the case of a collision. Chain restaurants have research-and-development departments that ask focus groups to test their foods and provide feedback. Technology companies such as cell phone manufacturers test prototypes of their products before product launch to make sure the devices function properly. Testing how well a product or service meets needs and performs its intended functions is a universal practice.

This effort is to ensure one thing: that people are satisfied with the services provided by professionals, which they have paid for. This simple notion is good for two reasons. First, it would be unethical for professionals to charge for a service and not provide a service that lived up to the level of payment. Second, if people are happy with the service they receive, they are more likely to return for more.

The concept is very similar for planners and designers. Unfortunately, professionals working in disciplines related to the built environment often do not have available to them the sorts of test mechanisms in the examples from industry discussed earlier. Structural engineers can test the versatility of an I-beam, but the day-to-day functioning of public spaces and buildings is much too complicated to be tested to ensure the satisfaction of those using the space. There are simply too many changing variables. Culture, use, background, context, the natural setting, people's choices at any time, and many other factors directly contribute to how well a public space or building functions.

Consequently, planners and designers must acquire a rich understanding of people's needs, wishes, and aspirations, for which they will create plans or design proposals. Developing this understanding is the safest way for planners and designers to craft proposals tailored to their clients' needs. How does one develop such an understanding? This is where participatory decision making enters the picture.

It would be very hard to build a billion-dollar building or plaza and test whether it worked or not. Through participatory decision making, however, planners and designers can understand people's needs and convert ideas into plan and design proposals that will meet those needs. By spending time with the future users of the spaces to be created, planners and designers increase their local knowledge and use their expertise to develop proposals based on that knowledge.

Objective Two: Practicing Good Design

What is good design? There is no easy answer to that question. In light of the professional's responsibility to provide services that are satisfactory to the client, however, good design can be considered that which responds to the needs and issues in each individual case. For example, good design could provide solutions that work with the local climate, so that the client does not need to resort to, say, air conditioning, to cool off, and pay beyond the services already paid for. Or in the case of a highly interactive cultural environment, good design could allow people to sit in front of their shops and greet passersby. The more unique solutions one can provide for unique social, physical, and environmental conditions, the closer one gets to good design.

Participatory decision making, by involving the ultimate users of the built environment, brings planners and designers closer to unique solutions, and thus good design (as we have limned it). The more time a planner or designer spends with the target clients, such as residents of a neighborhood or town or the future users of a building, the more knowledge she or he gathers about the unique conditions of that particular solution. The more questions the professional asks, the more knowledge of the unique conditions present the professional acquires. The more knowledge the professional acquires, the more customized the proposal is likely to be.

Objective Three: Learning

Knowledge empowers, and not only immediately but also in the long term. Planners and designers spend years acquiring professional degrees and training, harnessing incredible amounts of knowledge. Such discipline-specific expertise needs to be supplemented by on-the-job local knowledge gained from each individual challenge. The more planners and designers spend time with their clients, the larger their professional toolkit becomes. The larger the professional's toolkit, the easier it is to find unique solutions.

Participatory decision making provides an unparalleled opportunity for planners and designers to tap into an endless source of knowledge and expand the skills they acquire in formal training. It is a unique professional opportunity that is available to professionals throughout their professional careers. Planners and designers must feel the responsibility to tap into this knowledge resource.

Therefore, questions like the ones introduced at the beginning of this section are addressed by considering the objectives of community design. Ultimately, what is good for clients depends on their needs and wishes. It is the responsibility of the professional to understand the issues underlying those needs and wishes through participation and translate them into professional solutions that will not be "bad" for the people. This is by no means "making people design for themselves." On the contrary, it is a genuine effort to understand issues and provide quality responses to them.

Finally, what constitutes a poor design decision? Once again, what is good design? Sanoff states, "There is no 'best solution' to a problem. Each problem has a number of solutions" (2000, 13). The ultimate goal of community design is to provide planning and design solutions responsive to the unique needs of those who will be affected by the solution.

2.3. STAGES OF COMMUNITY DESIGN

Depending on the scale of the project, community design processes may involve many or few individuals, have small or large budgets, and be of short or long duration. For example, the development of a collective vision for a city will likely involve a larger group of individuals, consume more resources, and have a longer timeline than the redesign of a pocket park. Despite these differences in projects' scale and scope, the basic stages of community design processes are similar. We discuss each stage in detail in section 2. Here we look at some of the basics to gain a better understanding of what community design entails.

Problem Definition: What does the community want to get out of the process? The community design process involves many people in many roles, among them the individuals who will be affected by the project, local property owners, and local public service institutions. With so many players on the scene, it is important for the community designer to clearly define the problem. Often, individuals or groups that approach a community designer do not themselves have a clear notion of the problem to be addressed. Developing a clear definition of the problem at the outset also affords a safety net for the duration of the project. With the large number of players involved in the process, it is easy to get sidetracked and lose sight of the target. Having a clear problem definition helps the community designer and the community stay focused on the goal and move forward.

Timeline Development: When and by what steps does the community achieve the outcomes? Once the problem is defined, it is necessary to create a project timeline. What steps in what order will be taken to achieve the desired outcomes? At this point, the community designer may provide guidance on how to achieve the desired outcomes within a manageable process and timeline. The tasks at this stage include talking to community members and the individuals leading the project effort and designating meeting times, deliverables, and completion times for the deliverables. Developing the project timeline often goes hand in hand with identifying methods to achieve the project goals.

Identification of Methods: What types of activities and tools will be helpful for achieving the desired outcomes? In conjunction with drawing up a timeline, the community designer begins identifying methods to achieve the project's stated ends. Will community meetings be held? If a survey is to be carried out, what is the best survey technique for the particular community? Will online techniques help expand the outreach effort? The methods identification process is more likely to yield good results if the community designer consults representatives from the community or individuals who are advocates for the project. Local residents are likely to know better how the community will respond to a particular method, and this knowledge will inform the choice of methods. For example, conducting an online survey would not be efficacious in a community where people do not spend much time online. Ultimately, the objective is to gather the community's ideas efficiently through a clear, easy process that does not take an inordinate amount of community members' time.

Identification of Outreach Techniques: How will community members be informed about the process and invited to provide input? The outreach process is one of the most challenging and amorphous stages in the community design process. In many communities, simply creating an open process will not necessarily elicit ideas from the community. Active recruitment of ideas in a systematic manner is crucial. For this, the community designer needs to select the methods by which the community members will be informed about the process and invited to provide input. Common methods include mailing flyers to households, using television announcements, recruiting online, contacting active community organizations such as local school districts, and walking through the project area disseminating information by talking and handing out media. Section 2 provides an in-depth discussion of several outreach techniques, along with the advantages and disadvantages of each.

Interaction with the Community: Outreach and receiving input. Following problem definition, methods identification, and identification of outreach techniques, the community designer moves into closer interaction with the community. The first step in the interaction process is to conduct outreach. During outreach, the community designer explains what the project is about and invites community members to provide input. At this point the boundaries between conducting outreach and gathering input start to blur. During the outreach effort the community designer will start hearing about issues, concerns, wishes, and examples of what the community likes. This community input should be recorded since it not only informs upcoming community meetings but is also invaluable for the entire process.

The initial outreach effort then broadens into systematic interactions with the community in the form of community meetings, surveys, workshops, and other methods. Throughout this process the community designer gathers input, translates the ideas into planning and design language, shares this work with the community, and receives feedback. For example, the community designer assembles initial ideas developed from a first meeting and works out planning or design concepts in the form of images and sketches, then shares these with the community. Community members respond to the sketches and provide input on ideas, which enables the community designer to refine, develop, or edit the concepts. With each pass the plan or design proposal comes closer to a product that responds to the issues and ideas developed by the community members.

The Nonlinear Nature of the Community Design Process. At this point it is important to pause for a moment and reflect on the fact that community design processes in most cases are nonlinear. That is, the progression through the stages outlined here does not necessarily happen sequentially. In most cases the boundaries are not distinct, and the community designer may need to visit other stages to customize the process to the progression of events. Therefore, the process resembles more a spiral, but one with discontinuities between stages. In some cases the process may turn back to earlier stages, such as problem definition, or look forward briefly to upcoming stages, such as identification of outreach techniques. As idea development continues, it is not uncommon to visit stages nonsequentially.

As a basic example, let us say the community designer has completed the definition of the problem and moved into timeline development. Both of these tasks may have involved certain assumptions. Depending on how accurate these assumptions turn out to be, it may be necessary to revise the problem definition or the timeline. The reasons for revisiting these stages may be conceptual or practical. For example, underlying the request for the design of a neighborhood park may be a larger scale issue of the need for more greenery in a neighborhood, which leads to revisiting the problem definition. Or the original timeline may need to be changed if it becomes clear that some community members cannot be involved at particular times (perhaps they cannot meet on Saturdays because of other commitments).

The same is true for identifying community design methods and outreach techniques. Despite the best intentions of the community designer and the community members, the community design methods and outreach techniques chosen may prove to be less efficient than expected once the process is under way. For example, some community members may be reluctant to write their ideas on a plan view of their neighborhood. In such cases the community designer should devise a method that will ensure input from those community members. Or it may become apparent at a community meeting that the outreach techniques used were not effective—perhaps only a small number of community members showed up to provide input. In that case, the community designer will need to go back and choose different media to inform community members and invite their input.

Finally, throughout the interaction process with the community, whether it occurs in meetings, through informal methods, by surveys, or by online methods, the community designer will spend time gathering ideas, translating them into planning and design language, and going back to community members to receive feedback after each iteration. With this general event sequence in mind, we move into the proposal development and implementation stages, which with luck require less revision.

Proposal Development: Translating the community's ideas into plan and design proposals. The community designer starts developing more tangible plan or design proposals toward the end of the process. Tangible proposals are important so that community members can see their ideas translated into professional language—as documents, sketches, images, or mockups—and view the expected outcomes of their effort. The community designer should show progress to the community so that the process can move forward. The community designer therefore must specify a point where community input is temporarily paused and the translation into a visible artifact occurs. Once the proposal is developed, based on the project's needs and progression, it may be necessary for the community designer to solicit feedback about the proposal and edit it based on this feedback.

Implementation: Translating the plan and design proposals into tangible products. Implementation of a plan or design proposal may take varying amounts of time based on the scale and initiators of the project. In the case of larger scale plans or specific plans, the plan proposals likely will have to proceed through regulatory channels before being implemented, which may take a long time. In the case of smaller scale plans or design proposals, projects may get the green light and be implemented relatively quickly, depending on the complexity of the proposals and the number of players. A smaller scale does not guarantee a faster implementation, however. For example, community members may divide into opposing groups, which may delay the entire process beyond the expected completion time.

The community designer must introduce possible sources of delay to the community. Community members need to understand that providing input on processes or plans does not guarantee implementation. The community designer's role is to facilitate the process and help the community develop a unified voice. To this end, it may be very useful to conduct action planning exercises with the community, asking individuals to suggest who could implement their ideas and who might fund the implementation. Such exercises help people think realistically about the implications of their wishes. Figure 2.1 summarizes the stages of community design discussed in this section and shows their nonlinear progression.

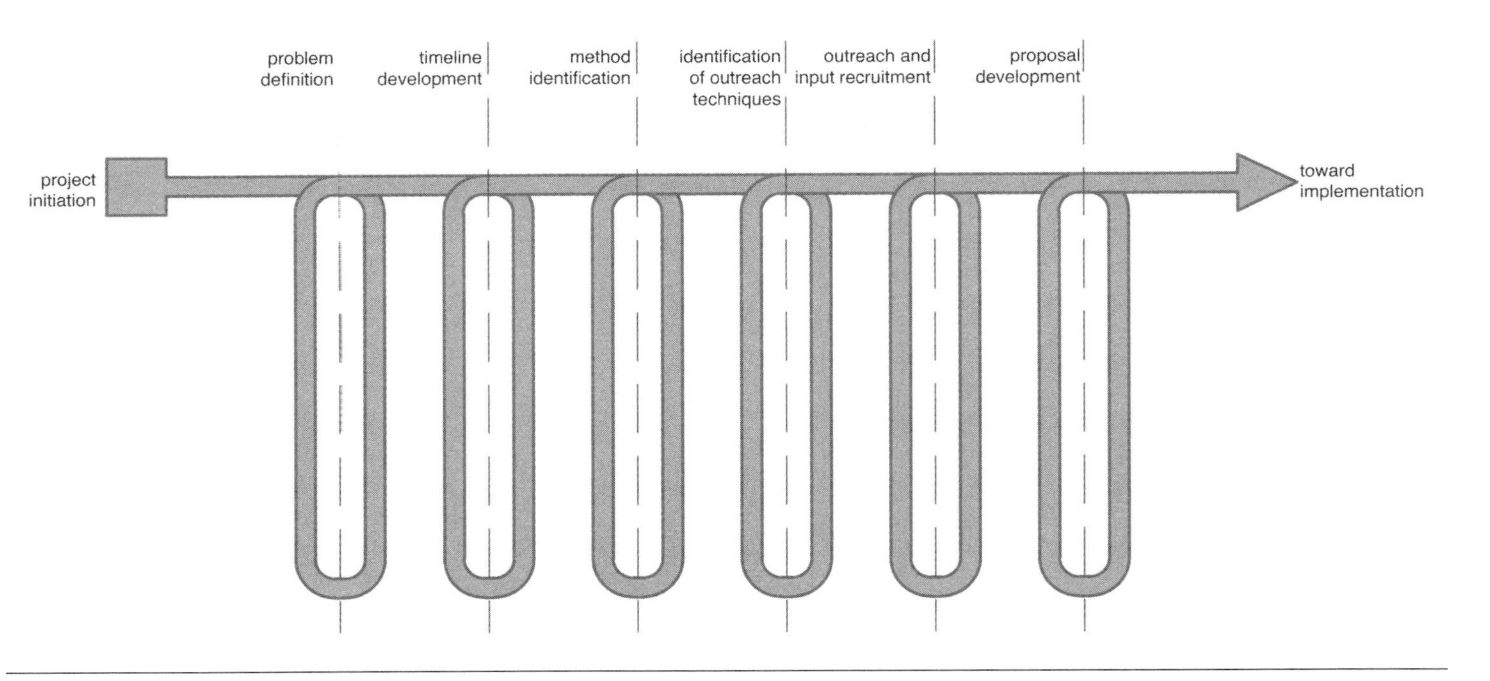

2.1. A visual summary of the stages of community design and their nonlinear progression

2.4. OUTCOMES OF COMMUNITY DESIGN

Community designers go through systematic idea generation processes with groups of people and translate the resulting ideas into professional proposals. Such processes require a good amount of coordination, organization, and collaboration. Do community members and community designers gain any advantage from going through these processes? What are the outcomes of community design processes beyond the development of plan or design proposals? A summary of the most common outcomes suggests the many advantages to be had.

Learning from Each Other. The community design process provides a unique venue for community members and designers to learn from each other. When people come together to discuss ideas for the future of their communities, they start talking about the reasons behind their ideas. It is not uncommon to hear statements such as "Let's put some lights in those alleyways, I don't think they're safe at night" in community meetings. A statement of this sort helps community members understand each other's concerns or wishes and the underlying reasons. People get to know each other, and the community designer acquires valuable local information about why people have certain preferences. In this way the solution moves beyond a physical change such as installing lighting fixtures to a change that is more sophisticated and to the point, such as procuring nighttime safety in alleys.

Empowerment. The community design process, through the close interaction of the professional and community members, removes the traditional barriers between the two parties. Rather than a professional tell people what is good for them, individuals speak for themselves. In this way, many individuals who would not be consulted in a conventional planning or design process become integrated into the decision-making process and given a voice. The community design process thus reaches beyond planners and designers and the party who hired them to engage all parties who might be affected by the outcomes.

Bringing Design and Planning Expertise to Everyday Environments. Since community design is concerned with people's needs, the spaces people live and work in on a day-to-day basis are natural arenas of interest for community designers. The projects that receive the most publicity tend to be those that touch on spaces and environments cherished by the community. Community designers, however, are interested in people's needs regardless of locale. By bringing design and planning expertise to environments and spaces that might not traditionally attract planners and designers, community designers also have an opportunity to introduce state-of-the-art knowledge into environments that would not typically be the first to receive such knowledge.

Developing Unique Solutions for Each Project. We live in a world in which people increasingly talk about the staleness or sameness of their environments. Whether this is true of any given environment or not, community design emerges as a liberating approach. By definition, community design develops unique solutions for each project. In the process, it acknowledges and embraces the multiple backgrounds and ideas of people who would be affected by the project, and it develops an approach that includes multifaceted input. As a result, the products are highly customized.

2.5. COMMUNITY DESIGN: MAIN PRINCIPLES

The objectives, stages, and outcomes of community design provide a platform on which to mount a set of community design principles.

1. Start with a Clean Slate That Recognizes Existing Facts

Community design is concerned with the needs and wishes of the people who are ultimately affected by the process and its outcomes. As professionals with expertise in planning and design issues, however, community designers might feel moved to recommend solutions, approaches, or methods to solve problems at the outset of a project. This is problematic for two reasons. First, it introduces the danger of not being able to hear adequately what the community members are saying. Second, if people realize the community designer harbors certain preconceived notions, they may lose faith in the process. It is useful, therefore, to start every project with a clean slate, though one that recognizes existing facts. As individuals educated in planning and design disciplines, we tend to know what worked previously. It is tempting to propose similar solutions when faced with a similar problem definition. As community designers, however, we should avoid this end-game and hear the people first.

2. Accept and Acknowledge People's Expertise on Their Own Lives and Environments

To take the position in principle 1 one step further, it is important to accept and acknowledge people's expertise on their own lives and environments. People who experience what community designers see as "the project area" have an irreducible amount of knowledge about the day-to-day function of the place and how people use it. Although community designers are educated as planners and designers, it is important to establish this as a principle at the outset and accept a community's experience as a form of expertise. Further, verbalizing this acceptance will help build trust in the process.

3. Focus on People's Needs and Preferences First

Another trap community designers easily fall into is discussing aesthetic issues at the outset of a project. Once again, community designers are proficient in this area. Nevertheless, the main concern of community design is people's needs and preferences. The last thing people want to hear when they are trying to communicate their day-to-day practical issues is some expert taking about the aesthetic qualities of their environments. People's needs and preferences should be focused on first, and once those are addressed, aesthetic issues can be raised for discussion.

4. Work to Provide a Level Playing Field

In any group, some members will be more active in generating ideas, or will talk louder, or will simply be more efficient in communicating. Moreover, different communities are likely to exhibit different power relationships. In one community the elderly may have a greater say in public meetings than younger individuals. In another community there may be an organized group of outspoken individuals that commandeers the meeting. Or some individuals may be precluded from participating in the process because of conflicting work schedules.

Community designers need to pay attention to such issues. Ultimately, the objective is to provide solutions that will work for people. Not being able to hear some community members' concerns will undermine the validity of any solution. Therefore, it is important for community designers to establish as a principle working toward a level playing field, during outreach *and* interaction processes. When inviting individuals to provide input into a discussion, community designers should strive to reach every individual that could be affected by the subject. Similarly, during discussions, community designers must ensure all voices are heard.

5. Focus on Underlying Interests, Not Positions

When working with a group of people to tackle a problem or develop a proposal, the community designer should accept that people state their positions on issues first. However, every position reflects an underlying interest of some kind. For example, a position statement formulated as "Let's plant trees on Main Street's sidewalks" may reflect an interest in having a shaded, more walkable summer environment. It is important for the community designer to hear that interest. By understanding the underlying interest or reason, the community designer can work with the community to develop an answer that will work best in that particular situation. Eliciting a concern rather than just a position deepens a community design discussion and ultimately will increase efficacy and productivity.

6. Keep the Process Flexible

As the community design process progresses, there may be times when people and planners need to be flexible. For example, community participants may need more time than anticipated to absorb certain types of information, or they may need to reschedule a progress meeting. They may ask the community designer to meet with them on a specific date to discuss ideas. Since community design is a customized effort, it is important to be flexible. Flexibility on the planner's part will not only engender trust from the community, it will also help in developing a customized proposal.

In the following chapters we return to these principles for detailed analysis, along with examples from field-based cases.

3 Community Design

Origins, Development, and Current Views

How did practitioners of community design come to the conclusion that participatory decision making is a better way to go about planning and designing places? What led to the definition of community design used in this book? This chapter looks at the historical processes that helped shape community design and reviews contemporary developments in the field.

3.1. GRASSROOTS MOVEMENTS

The grassroots movements of the 1960s had a major impact on the development of community design. This era was marked by important social movements such as the civil rights movement, the women's rights movement, and the anti-war movement. Although these movements had distinct goals, they emerged as part of a larger struggle for social justice (Sanoff 2000). Sherry Arnstein (1969) describes this as a struggle by the "have-nots" to share in power. In search of stronger social justice, community groups organized around the principle of having a say in decisions that would affect them. Participatory decision making was front and center on the agenda.

The implementation of participatory decision making and its outcomes, however, were questioned by the very community groups that supported the process. It seems that participatory decision making alone did not necessarily lead to positive changes for a community. In 1969, Arnstein published a landmark article that critiqued efforts toward participatory decision making. An advocate of community participation, Arnstein sought genuine participation for America's communities. She developed a categorization of levels of participation from least to most, likening them to the rungs of a ladder: manipulation, therapy, informing, consultation, placation, partnership, delegated power, and citizen control.

Manipulation and Therapy. Arnstein considered manipulation and therapy, the two lowest rungs of the ladder, forms of nonparticipation. *Manipulation* she defined as giving participants the feeling they have participated in decision making, in a process that will not really yield any significant results. It is, in essence, a method of deflecting the quest to share power. *Therapy* she defined as interacting with community members with the goal of getting them to change their views.

Informing, Consultation, and Placation. Arnstein described informing, consultation, and placation, the next rungs on the ladder, as forms of tokenism and considered them empty, symbolic rituals. *Informing* she defined as a one-way information transfer in which the community does not get a chance to give feedback. For example, providing information late in a decision-making process precludes community members from using that information. *Consultation*, while having the potential to generate useful feedback, she believed still failed to provide genuine participation if conducted with limited means. For example, a surveying that provides respondents with few options to choose from may not uncover the real issues of concern to people. *Placation* takes interaction one step further, but not all power holders are included in the process. As an example, Arnstein pointed to decision-making committees whose members are hand-picked to discuss and make decisions without the involvement of the actual people who stand to be affected by those decisions.

Partnership, Delegated Power, and Citizen Control. With these top rungs of the ladder Arnstein moved firmly into the arena of citizen power. *Partnership* she defined as the collaborative work of community members (and their organizations) and conventional power holders. Implemented effectively, partnerships between conventional power holders and community organizations—such as neighborhood committees—approach genuine participatory decision making. *Delegated power*, on the other hand, she defined as community groups gaining the power to oversee decision-making processes through the organizations they form. For example, a neighborhood association may be assigned by the city the task of overseeing a decision-making process. Finally, *citizen control* she defined as a community's ability to initiate, develop, and manage decision making on issues that affect them. Arnstein considered these top three rungs of the ladder closest to genuine participation.

Arnstein's ladder is well known, and the conceptual framework it affords for understanding levels of citizen participation is still used by professionals and academics. The language of the article, however, tends to reinforce the view that community empowerment comes about through policy making. In the years after its publication, many progressive planners and designers developed models and methods that inserted an argument for genuine participatory decision making into planning and design processes. The question that arises now is why planning and design professionals wanted to introduce participatory decision making into their practice. What did they want to change?

3.2. PROMINENT PRE-1960S PLANNING AND DESIGN IDEAS

Although this book does not purport to give a historical account of planning and design, to understand where the ideas that influenced community design originated it is important to know something about the most influential ideas and practices since the Industrial Revolution.

By the end of the 19th century the Industrial Revolution, which took root in the United Kingdom in the 18th century and flourished into the following century, had begun to take its toll on European and American cities. Rapid industrialization had triggered the building of new factories, most close to existing city centers, to take advantage of proximity to transportation. This meant two major changes to the social and spatial structures of large cities such as London, Berlin, Chicago, and New York. First, the factories attracted large populations to work in the new industries, triggering an immense need for more residential units. Many major industrial cities grew eight to fifteen times in population in this time, including such cities as London, Manchester, Berlin, and New York (Frampton 1992). Second, industrialization adjacent to or within city centers inevitably brought pollution. The result was environmentally disastrous for many cities, which were overcome by air and water pollution and had housing units with unacceptable conditions by today's standards. Moreover, people were living together in unprecedented density, exacerbating issues of health and safety. Planners and designers struggled to develop solutions that would promote the health and safety of residents while efficiently managing the issues created by high population densities (Hall 2002). Three mainstream planning and design models emerged, all partly influenced by these conditions. The implementation of and responses to these models shaped many cities and neighborhoods around the world for the better part of the 20th century.

3.2.1. The City Beautiful Movement

The City Beautiful movement, a reform philosophy preoccupied with aesthetics and monumentalism, flourished in Paris during the reign of Napoléon III in the 1850s through 1870s. Paris had grown about six times in population over the course of the 19th century. Like other industrialized cities, it had serious housing and infrastructure problems; it also had a history of revolutionary street action in the medieval alleyways that cut through the city like a spider's web. In the first half of the 19th century the city suffered through two big cholera outbreaks because the main water source and the sewer outlets were the same, the Seine. Air pollution, population density, and lack of adequate housing worsened the conditions. Napoléon III assigned the Seine prefect, Baron Georges-Eugène Haussmann, the task of battling the city's existing infrastructure, open space, and circulation problems (Frampton 1992).

Haussmann's response was to develop a new network of broad avenues and large open spaces that would provide better circulation, more open air, and better infrastructure to the city. During his tenure, Haussmann oversaw projects that cut through the existing organic mesh of streets, creating wide, axial boulevards that connected neighborhoods and converged on broad plazas. The reconstruction destroyed the old city, slicing buildings in half and leveling neighborhoods. While these projects created the scenic axial corridors for which Paris is known today, the planners were not particularly concerned with the individuals whose lives were disrupted.

Although Haussmann wanted to be the "neutral" engineer, the transformation was dictated by the interests of those in power. The architects of the plan were very much civil functionaries. Buildings were ruthlessly appropriated, including structures on avenues that existed only in drawings. According to Kenneth Frampton, Haussmann "was finally broken by an ambivalent bourgeoisie, who throughout his tenure supported his 'profitable improvements' while at the same time defending their proprietorial rights against his intervention" (Frampton 1992, 24).

The City Beautiful movement in the United States was an outcome of the transformation of 19th-century European capitals—Vienna and Barcelona had followed Paris in devising their own transformation schemes—and its starting point was Chicago. Daniel Burnham marked the start with his 1909 Plan of Chicago, which proposed integrating streets, open parks, rail facilities, and harbors in a unified vision for the city. Spatially, the City Beautiful movement placed a strong emphasis on monumentality, which was achieved through axial streets and boulevards radiating from landmarks—the city hall, a central plaza, a museum in the grand style. The sculptural quality sought by the movement was a response to the worsening physical and health conditions of the time, just as in Paris (Hall 2002). And, as in Paris, mostly upper-middle-income groups developed an interest in the movement, hoping to restore the pre-industrial city conditions—the former "social order"—and catalyze an urban economy. Hall writes,

> For many among the civic-minded bourgeoisie, faced with increasing ethnic and cultural heterogeneity and escalating threat of disorder, the problem appeared to be the very preservation of urban social fabric. Henry Morgenthau, put it plainly enough at a conference of 1909: the planner's first aim was to eliminate the breeding places of "disease, moral depravity, discontent, and socialism." (Hall 2002, 190)

The movement's focus, therefore, was aligned with the interests of certain sectors of the population, and those groups supported it. Others criticized it as a "municipal cosmetic" for ignoring day-to-day problems such as public health, education, and housing (Hall 2002).

The City Beautiful movement was influential in shaping some industrial cities in the United States, including Seattle and Kansas City. The concern of the planners and architects working in the movement, however, was never with the masses that had to live in congested conditions but with "cleaning up" the city for the bourgeoisie. Thus, this early response to unprecedented urban problems came down heavily on the side of aesthetics and the interests of the well-to-do and paid scant attention to the working classes, which, needless to say, were not consulted about the form and function of spaces in which they lived and labored.

3.2.2. The Modern Movement and Modernism

In the early 20th century, along with industrialization there came technological developments of various forms. Major breakthroughs, such as Henry Ford's assembly line, began having broad social impacts. Materials could now be produced faster and cheaper. Transportation became easier and faster. Large parts of the population could access mass-produced products easily. In 1911, Frederick Winslow Taylor wrote his landmark *Principles of Scientific Management*, in which he defined systematic standardization of organizational processes, in the office and on the production line. His principles of efficiency and productivity became well known under the rubric "Taylorism." Intellectually, principles of rational organization, speed, and efficiency began to diffuse across society. Progress and the scientific method became early 20th-century hallmarks. The rationalization of life marked the condition of modernity. Essentially, through the modern movement, societies were redefining themselves in the day-to-day operations of life. As the philosopher Jürgen Habermas observed,

> The concept of Modernization refers to a bundle of processes that are cumulative and mutually reinforcing: to the formation of capital and mobilization of resources; to the development of the forces of production and the increase in the productivity of labor; to the establishment of centralized political power and the formation of national identities; to the proliferation of rights of political participation, of urban forms of life, and of formal schooling; to the secularization of values and norms; and so on. (Habermas 1990, 2)

The impact of the modern movement on planning and design was significant. Beginning in the 1920s, architects and planners started introducing concepts of efficiency, rationalization, and mass production into their professional work. One of the arguments behind the rationalization of planning and architecture was the need to address conditions in increasingly crowded and polluted cities. Le Corbusier, the Swiss-born French architect, developed one of the best-known proposals, to improve the conditions of the city he lived in at the time, Paris. Peter Hall summarizes the conditions of Paris at the time:

> The history of Paris has been one of constant struggle between the forces of exuberant, chaotic, often sordid everyday life and the forces of centralized, despotic order. In the 1920s and 1930s, it was clear that the former were winning. . . . Behind the facades, the city was racked by slums and disease. (Hall 2002, 222)

Le Corbusier's grand idea was to start with a clean slate and design a city of neatly organized rectangular blocks spaced far enough apart to allow clean air, greenery, and sunlight into the city. This was his rational answer to the problems he observed. Le Corbusier was strongly influenced by the technological achievements of the time, and he wanted a rational basis for his work. In *Toward an Architecture* (*Vers une architecture,* 1923), he pointed to industrial buildings, ocean liners, automobiles, and airplanes as sources of inspiration, and emphasized that the chaos of the cities was a problem to be tackled through planning and architectural design:

> It is time that we should repudiate the existing lay-out of our towns, in which the congestion of building grows greater, interlaced by narrow streets full of noise, petrol fumes and dust; and where each storey the windows open wide on to this foul confusion. The great towns have become too dense for the security of their inhabitants and yet they are not sufficiently dense to meet the needs of "modern business." (Le Corbusier 1931, 57)

Le Corbusier's ideas reflected his interpretation of the modern movement in planning and architecture. While the intent was to respond to the urban problems of the day, the attitude was that of an expert, without much empirical evidence on whether or not the ideas proposed would in fact help alleviate the problems. The technological developments of the time were based on engineering experimentation, trial-and-error, and evidence, but planning and design lacked such a foundation. Further, the implementation of design ideas directly affected the lives of real people, whereas experiments in technological development could stop the production of a product before it reached its audience.

Le Corbusier was not alone. The modern movement in architecture and planning step by step developed interpretations of modern thought. New construction techniques, new materials, and an interest in principles of economy helped create a new visual language. In an effort to maximize construction efficiency and residential unit production, standardization of floor plans became common practice, resulting in interchangeable modules and units. As standardization became the norm, designers had to accept certain assumptions about their clients' ways of living. Room sizes and the configuration of living space were sometimes defined by the square footage one would need to function in a kitchen, sometimes by a particular height of window that, it was thought, would help minimize costs and maximize construction efficiency (Brolin 1976).

The principles of modern thought, originally oriented toward liberating individuals, were reinterpreted and became modernism in planning and architecture. Planners and architects around the world, in both developing and developed countries, experimented widely with this model. Standardization, and therefore construction efficiency, made the model particularly attractive in developing countries.

The main trouble with modernism was the inability of many communities to adapt to its products, and conversely, modernism's failure to accommodate these communities' needs. The interpretation of modernist ideals generally meant starting with a clean slate and often independence from the local context—visually, socially, and culturally. Communities with hundreds of years of a building tradition, closely connected to their social structures, found themselves in urban environments that were increasingly alike. Especially in the post–World War II period, it became common to see rectangular mid- to high-rise residential blocks on all continents (Figure 3.1).

In the 1960s, many planners and designers also contributed to modernism with objectives different from those of the founders of the movement. Particularly in the UK, socially conscious planners and designers implemented the techniques of the modern movement to minimize the cost of residential production so that the numbers of housing units produced per unit of time could be increased (Russell 1981). Similar techniques were used in the United States to provide public housing for the masses. There was now an additional problem: not only could the residents of these buildings not adapt to the new high-density, urban lifestyle offered but cheap construction led to maintenance problems.

The best-known example is the Pruitt-Igoe residential complex built in St. Louis during the 1950s. Although the complex won awards, its construction reflected an extension of the urban renewal efforts of the time. Its residents, coming from well-established, mostly rural neighborhoods, could not adapt to the new lifestyle. Increasing numbers of vacant units in the

3.1. Examples of modernist residential blocks from two continents. Left: London; right: San Francisco

complex made it easier for criminal elements to move into the complex. Cheap construction was followed by rapid decay of the structures and the architectural details. The wide open spaces provided between the buildings became a no-man's land, then hot spots of crime. Sixteen years after it was completed the project was demolished (Hall 2002).

Similar experiences with the Corbusian residential model across the Western world triggered a backlash. A landmark study of the phenomenon was conducted by Oscar Newman, who demonstrated through empirical research that variables such as site planning and building form could be related to the formation and sustenance of criminal elements (Newman 1996). Such studies and the visual connotations between the Corbusian form and problematic residential areas led to a widespread rejection of the model that accelerated in the 1990s.

The misinterpretation of modern ideals, therefore, initiated the imposition of certain aesthetic and economic principles on many communities around the world. The disparity between planning and design principles and communities was similar to that of the City Beautiful movement. Its impacts, however, were felt across a much greater geographic area.

3.2.3. Mainstream American Modern

A third planning response to the improvidential urban conditions of the 19th century was conceived in the UK to address problems in London, but in its American form it shaped the conventional American suburb. As industrialization and its effects proceeded apace, Ebenezer Howard proposed one solution to the congestion problems of London in *Garden Cities of To-morrow*, which he originally self-published as *To-morrow: A Peaceful Path to Real Reform* in 1898, then reissued under a publisher's imprint in 1902. Howard's concept was simple: develop small towns in the countryside and provide their residents with jobs through the relocation of industrial plants from London to these towns. These "Garden Cities" would have greenbelts around them, which would limit their growth. They would be connected to big cities through a network of railroads and would be economically self-sufficient since the industries that were expected to relocate near them would provide jobs.

The Garden City concept was realized with varying degrees of success in the United Kingdom, thanks to the advances brought about by industrialization. In some cases influenced by the City Beautiful movement and shaped accordingly, Garden Cities provided access to jobs, nature, and, through the railway networks, to the big cities (Figure 3.2). During implementation, however, glitches did appear, such as the construction of railway networks initially making more people homeless than providing homes, or the Garden Cities eventually becoming upper-income residential clusters in the form of Garden Suburbs adjacent to big cities (Hall 2002).

The concept of decentralizing the congested city utilizing new technologies was a strong one, however, and the young, resource-rich United

3.2. The Garden City concept. Top: Hampstead Garden Suburb; bottom: Letchworth Garden City

States was ideally poised to capitalize on it. By the beginning of the 20th century, major U.S. cities were already utilizing the concept. New York City constructed a sophisticated subway network that ferried people into and out of the downtown areas, and Los Angeles became the hub of a complex rail network connecting distant cities. People could now live in lower density areas and commute to city centers. The greatest independence, however, came with the automobile. The United States was the first country in which mass-produced automobiles were affordable by a large proportion of the population, thanks to Henry Ford's mass production line. Developers and local governments realized that residential development did not have to be within walking distance from a railway station anymore. It was time for suburban development (Hall 2002).

In New York, Robert Moses would help support the creation of the first American suburbs. Parkways were built to convey city residents to the city's beaches, and residential developments sprang up in locations close to parkways (Ballon and Jackson 2007). Los Angeles followed a similar trajectory, offset by a few decades. At the beginning of the 20th century more than 50 communities around Los Angeles were served by a complex railway system. As in New York, with mass automobile ownership, the highways that snaked through Los Angeles started to serve as tools for real estate development and inspired the formation of residential suburbs. In the process, the rail system was gradually replaced by highways (Hall 2002).

The American architect Frank Lloyd Wright, a contemporary of Le Corbusier, supported the development of 20th-century American suburbia with his own interpretation of modernism. Like Corbusier, he took advantage of the new technologies. He was not, however, interested in high-density residential settings. Rather, he saw technology, particularly the automobile and highways, as a means of giving people freedom. His concept of Broadacre City—the apotheosis of suburban development—envisioned freedom: freedom in the form of single-family homes and families living an agrarian life, growing their own crops (Wright 1945). With his celebrated architectural language and his detailed plans for Broadacre City, Wright lent strength and support to the newly appearing American suburbia. Suburbs indeed developed, but without Wright's envisioned agrarian life. Broadacre City's influence was ultimately limited to the physical form and density of new neighborhoods, not the lifestyle.

Mainstream American modern, therefore, was shaped by the forces of real estate development and was not particularly interested in people's wishes and preferences unless those wishes related to profits. Moreover, particularly after World War II such development involved differential treatment of communities and sectors of communities. Lower income communities were usually disadvantaged by the decisions made about physical development, such as the selection of sites for infrastructure, or the policies that shaped development. The heavy social hand lying over development is evident in this example from New York:

> But there were limits to public spirit: deliberately, [Robert] Moses built the parkway bridges too low not only for trucks, but also for buses. The magnificent bathing beaches that he built at the ends of the parkways would thus be strictly reserved for middle-class car owners. (Hall 2002, 298)

Moreover, policies for financing new development put certain portions of the community at a disadvantage. The best-known and most controversial policy was in force for urban renewal. To clear away blight, many American cities used federal aid to purchase and redevelop existing properties in mainly residential areas. The policy, however, made this aid available for purchasing property and building new residential developments, not for maintenance. Consequently, maintenance had to be supported by the rent paid by the residents, which meant those who could afford the rental rate; the lowest income members of the community would not even be eligible to live in these new developments. The land purchased, however, would be the cheapest possible, which in many cases turned out to be land already inhabited by the lowest income people. This structure turned into a mechanism for displacing the low-income residents of many American cities (Hall 2002). Obviously, these practices were not particularly aligned with the needs and preferences of existing communities.

3.2.4. Lessons from Pre-1960s Planning and Design Practices

The historical factors spurring the development of community design are now more clearly in view. None of the reactions to the congestion and overpopulation problems of the 19th-century industrial city were particularly advantageous for the masses. The City Beautiful movement ended up as an effort to beautify cities, and mostly connived in the interests of urban merchants and their profits. Modernism in planning and design urged new environments on people based on unfounded assumptions about new ways of living and ended up creating human-unfriendly environments. American modern was not only limited in the extent to which planning decisions could provide profit (like the City Beautiful movement), it also operationalized certain policies that could only result in the differential treatment of different parts of existing communities.

3.3. COMMUNITY DESIGN: THE BEGINNINGS

The pre-1960s picture shows that despite some good intentions, the planning and design disciplines remained largely disconnected from the needs and preferences of people even as they sought to respond to the new conditions wrought by social, economic, and technological change. It was this lack of connection between the people and planning and design practice that brought planners and designers to the idea of community design.

Community designers wanted to break the pattern of institutionalization of planning and design practices and use their expertise to create products that would not conflict with the lives of their clients. This introduced an ironic contradiction. In going back to the ideals of modern thought, community designers rooted for an expanded role for participation in their disciplines and the liberation of people from bureaucratic principles that disregarded the needs of actual communities. Therefore, community designers initiated a true modernization of the field: they reinitiated the modern project. Though modernism in planning and design has become so synonymous with practices disconnected from people that many professionals prefer not to be even remotely related to the rubric, it is important to recognize the true ideals of modern thought and how they differed from modernism as it was practiced in planning and design.

Owing to its flexible nature and the varied definitions it has enjoyed, community design has taken many shapes and forms. In addition, the anti-establishmentarian attitude of the practice has connected community design to ongoing social rights movements. Practitioners in the United States and abroad have pursued and led many projects with different objectives and scales. A few notable ones are described below.

3.3.1. Participatory Design and Environment-Behavior Studies: The Role of the Bay Area in California

One of the most significant "hot spots" of the participatory design movement was Berkeley, California. In the early 1960s two young academics who would later become internationally recognized design researchers were at work on the University of California–Berkeley campus, Henry Sanoff and Amos Rapoport. Their interest in people-oriented design would blossom into a new research area in planning and design known as environment-behavior studies. This interest also helped define community design. While Rapoport stayed on the environment-behavior research course and published many classics in the field (e.g., *The Meaning of the Built Environment*, 1982), Sanoff went on to teaching and practicing community design. He started the Community Design Group (CDG) at North Carolina State University (NCSU). His work covered many contexts and issues, from the design of educational facilities to farmworker housing. The CDG also defined the community outreach model in design education. Under the CDG banner, Sanoff's NCSU design studios would reach out to communities that could not afford design services and utilize participatory design methods to help these communities reach their objectives (Sanoff 2000).

Sanoff's community design model heavily utilizes community workshops. The process begins with outreach, which in many cases is conducted in collaboration with a key person in the community. A number of workshops—the exact number based on the scope and scale of the project—are then conducted to specify issues and recommendations. The process ends with a project proposal that the community can move forward on. The model provides expertise for the community and improves its abilities to achieve its objectives. Community designers do not take an active role in implementation or advocacy for that particular community.

On the West Coast, architect Michael Pyatok emerged as one of the leading practitioners of community design. Based in Oakland, California, he works with many communities. His firm specializes in affordable housing, which brings another level of complexity to the community design process. Pyatok and his colleagues utilize community workshops in their decision-making processes (Jones, Pettus, and Pyatok 1997).

Environment-behavior research has paralleled community design in the academic world. This branch of design research focuses on aspects of the built environment and their relationship to the day-to-day experiences of people in various contexts. Like community design, environment-behavior research concerns itself with everyday environments in an attempt to present empirical findings to planners and designers so that their proposals better serve their clients. As Rapoport has written, "design must be based on knowledge of how people and environments interact, i.e. on research (basic and applied) on environment-behavior relations (EBR); design becomes the application of research-based knowledge" (Rapoport 2005, 1).

Environment-behavior studies therefore provide the knowledge base for planners and designers. Over the past four decades, environment-behavior researchers have informed planning and design professionals about how characteristics of built environments at various scales relate to human behavior (Zeisel 2006).

3.3.2. Advocacy Planning

The community organization and advocacy model promotes more of a spokesperson role for the community designer. In this model, the community design process invests heavily in issues of social justice, the fair distribution of resources, and advocacy for the interests of that particular community. The role of the community designer goes beyond facilitation. Paul Davidoff provided a definition of this model in his landmark 1965 article, "Advocacy and Pluralism in Planning":

> The advocate planner would be above all a planner. He would be responsible to his client for preparing plans and for all of the other elements comprising the planning process. Whether working for the public agency or for some private organization, the planner would have to prepare plans that take account of the arguments made in other plans. Thus the advocate's plan might have some of the characteristics of a legal brief. It would be a document presenting the facts and reasons indicating the inferiority of counter-proposals. (Davidoff 1965, 331)

The community design and advocacy model materialized in the United States in Saul Alinsky's work (Sanoff 2000). A community organizer, Alinsky went beyond planning and design issues and got involved in the social and organizational aspects of community building. He focused mainly on lower income communities and worked with them for social change. His well-known *Rules for Radicals* (1971) provides guidance for proponents of this approach.

3.3.3. Self-Help and Self-Build Approaches

The self-help approach, by contrast, focuses on empowering communities by helping them develop the means and skills to effect incremental change. In 1972, John F. C. Turner published *Freedom to Build*, in which he endorsed individuals' and families' right to self-build. Turner was mainly interested in methods and processes of self-help in developing countries. His work detailed methods of making and using building materials within the existing conditions of such communities.

Elsewhere, while Nick Wates (2000, 2010) followed methods similar to those of Sanoff, professionals such as John Habraken and Lucien Kroll turned their attention more to the physical implications of self-building. At MIT, Habraken developed the concept of "Supports," in an effort to provide an alternative solution to residential development. The main thrust of the concept was to develop "support structures" that would provide the infrastructure needed for residential units but would allow the residents to arrange the spatial organization of units themselves on an as-needed basis. While the concept does not exactly argue for self-help, it does suggest that the users of such buildings should be able to decide the size and layout of their units (Habraken 1972). Today, this tradition is sustained in the "Open Building" concept.

A student of Habraken, Nabeel Hamdi put a version of the supports concept into practice in the United Kingdom. He developed methods that would allow residents to reconfigure and personalize the layouts of residential units as needed. He also developed a structural shell that would accommodate users' preferred layouts (Hamdi 1995). Hamdi went on to practice participatory methods in developing countries, working with the United Nations to help impoverished communities enhance their built environment incrementally in context-dependent ways (Hamdi 2004; Toker and Toker 2006a). With respect to context dependency and incremental development, his approach is similar to Turner's (1972). Hamdi is also one of the contemporary community designers who have helped shape a pragmatic understanding of community design, which we discuss in section 3.5.

In Belgium, architect Lucien Kroll utilized a concept similar to Habraken's and Hamdi's in the design and construction of student housing on the campus of Catholic University of Louvain Medical School (Hatch 1984). Employing a structural grid of varying dimensions, Kroll worked with students to develop a system that would allow them to change their room layouts. He also designed modular structural elements that permitted students to change floor levels and layouts in certain spaces with multifloor heights.

In addition, in an effort to provide the workers building the complex with a creative contribution, Kroll advocated incorporating builders' and workers' original additions to the complex, such as sculptural details on columns. Termed "anarchitecture," Kroll's approach was not well received by the university administration, primarily because it did not allow conventional methods of managing student housing. An ever changing floor plan and spatial structure heralded unforeseen challenges in space management, and the situation was further complicated by the financial implications of the structural elements (Kroll 1984). Nevertheless, Kroll's approach stands as a landmark of community design in the provision of university student housing.

3.3.4. Community Design Centers

A common but not heavily publicized model of community design in the United States emerged with the concept of community design centers (CDCs). The main objective of CDCs was to bring professional design and planning services to communities that could not afford them. This objective did not exclude social activism, since such communities often needed empowerment—socially, economically, and politically. As a natural extension of these objectives, CDCs did not exist in the mainstream planning, design, and development world but were established either in universities as educational units that practiced community design or as nonprofit entities that did not have direct contacts with universities (Curry 2004).

University-based CDCs sprang up on campuses where faculty interested in community design were active and could provide leadership. One example is Henry Sanoff's Community Design Group on the NCSU campus, discussed in section 3.2.1. In New York, the Pratt Institute Center for Community and Environmental Development (PICCED), led by Rex Curry, utilized a model similar to that of Sanoff's CDG. PICCED worked with communities distressed in various ways and engaged in community building, advocacy, and participatory design activities. Curry describes the early activities of PICCED this way:

> Among its first community projects were community leadership and training workshops in the 1960s and the early 1970s. PICCED planners literally translated deferral urban renewal legislation into terms people could understand and illustrated to them the probable impacts on their home turf. (Curry 2004, 65)

Essentially, PICCED provided community design services to such communities and brought its faculty expertise and student work to help them on various levels. In exchange, the university-based CDCs provided students with real-world experiences that would be difficult to replicate on campus. In rural Alabama, Samuel Mockbee implemented a similar model under Auburn University's Rural Studio (Mockbee 2004). In Chicago, the City Design Center of the University of Illinois–Chicago (UIC) provided similar services, with faculty and students drawn from multiple disciplines. As UIC's Roberta M. Feldman remarks in "Activist Practice," "Students participate in all our community design work, and, in the process, broaden their education to make the linkages among theory, practice, and social interests" (Feldman 2004, 111).

Nonprofit CDCs, on the other hand, focused on public service through advocacy, community building, community design, and training in an effort to empower distressed communities. Commonly known examples that followed this model include Asian Neighborhood Design in San Francisco and the Los Angeles Community Design Center (Curry 2004).

How does all this work relate to Sherry Arnstein's ladder of citizen participation? Closely connected to the social developments of the time, community designers in the 1960s and 1970s engaged in projects that enabled them to explore the top rungs of the ladder. While Alinsky, Davidoff, and Turner advocated for citizen power, Sanoff, Habraken, Hamdi, and Kroll were more interested in bringing it into their planning and design activities. In that sense, these designers were instrumental in working with communities on the partnership and delegated power rungs of Arnstein's ladder.

3.4. COMMUNITY DESIGN AND ITS TRANSFORMATIONS

About two decades after the start of the community design movement, in 1984, Randolph Hester conducted a U.S.-based survey of the values of community designers. This was an important development, since times had changed since the political turmoil of the 1960s. The survey asked practicing community designers (1) what they were trying to accomplish in their work, (2) what general principles guided their work, and (3) what the important personality traits of community designers were. The responses indicated that empowering the powerless, improving the environments of the poor, and achieving environmental justice were the top objectives. The respondents identified fostering user participation, creating environments meaningful to the community, and utilizing long-term processes to promote economic decentralization as the main principles of community design. Finally, having a strong ego without being egocentric, working well with people, listening, and a commitment to principles were traits the respondents deemed necessary for community designers (Hester 1990).

Hester's survey indicated that empowerment and working with lower income communities were still the top concerns in the field. The survey also revealed that the past two decades had taught community designers certain traits that would enable them to practice community design. While the advocacy idea was very much alive in community design practice, community organization to advocate for issues unrelated to design or planning did not surface in Hester's survey. This suggests that by the mid-1980s, community designers had internalized their experiences from the social movements and community organization activities in community design practice.

Around the same time, Sweden-based Frederik Wulz published a paper on the practice of community design and the varying levels of community involvement in the process (Wultz 1986). Wulz identified seven forms of participation: representation (depending on the designer's expertise), questionary (surveying user needs), regionalism (focusing on the local physical context), dialogue (consulting with the users), alternative (providing alterative solutions to users), co-decision (decision making with the users), and self-decision (the users making decisions about the plan or design proposal).

In contrast to Arnstein's ladder, Wulz's forms of participation show an emphasis on the professional's expertise and less emphasis on facilitating a process for the community. The concept of self-help is not in the picture, and with the exception of co-decision and self-decision, all forms of participation he proposed include considerable professional autonomy and the exercise of professional expertise. Furthermore, there is no mention of working with lower income communities or adopting advocacy approaches. Therefore, while Hester's 1984 survey provides one look at how community designers defined the field, Wulz's 1986 conceptualization of participation gives us indications about ways in which the field may have changed from the 1960s to the 1980s.

It was another two decades before a new study was published on how the community design field is defined by community designers. In 2007, Zeynep Toker published findings from a survey of 79 community design practitioners. The practitioners were asked (1) how they defined their community design practice, (2) who the most influential people in the community design field were, and (3) how they personally defined community design. The findings indicated that individuals like Sanoff, Pyatok, and Curry still were identified as the most influential people in the field. Newer names of individuals mentioned as influential included Andres Duany and Peter Calthorpe—professionals affiliated with new urbanism. Key concepts mentioned by the respondents in the definition of community design included participation, answering people's needs, involving local people, empowering people, the public realm, and sustainability. The new concept mentioned in the definition of community design was sustainability (Toker 2007).

Toker's research discovered that while most of the concepts used to define community design were the same, their rank order (frequency mentioned in the survey) had changed since Hester's 1984 survey. While Hester's survey indicated that empowering people and working with lower income communities were top concepts in the field, Toker's survey found that participation and answering people's needs were the top concepts: "The new trend is towards focusing on participation with decreasing emphasis on disadvantaged groups and empowerment" (Toker 2007, 320).

Contemporary community design, therefore, still has as strong an emphasis on people's needs and participatory decision making as it did in its early phases. It does not, however, consider empowering disadvantaged groups a priority as it used to. This does not mean that community design does not work with disadvantaged communities. As seen in the cases discussed in upcoming chapters, many community designers are still very instrumental in facilitating positive development for such communities. The specific intent to work with such communities, however, is not as central.

There may be a number of reasons for this development. First, the focus of the political turmoil is different from what it was in the 1960s. Some of the injustices of that decade have to some extent been addressed. For example, there have been efforts to ameliorate the adverse effects of urban renewal. Second, newer issues have appeared, such as the global environmental crisis. Now that communities around the world actually feel the effects of climate change, the discussion of related topics would be expected to dominate. The appearance of "sustainability" as a key issue in community design may relate to this experience, as may concerns about sustaining some of the social and economic advances communities have made since the 1960s.

Third, starting in the early 1990s, a new rubric has moved into the mainstream in planning and design circles: new urbanism. With its emphasis on walkability, mixed uses, and attention to local physical, social, and natural contexts, new urbanism moved into mainstream in the United States. These emphases and new urbanism's promotion of the charrette as a community involvement method may have contributed to its prominence in community design. Further, as discussed in Chapter 2, new urbanist literature tends to use the term community design frequently, but in reference to designing places and not the process. These factors inevitably trigger a certain amount of confusion and suggest new urbanism "is at odds with the original characteristics of community design, which included advocacy and empowerment" (Toker 2007, 320).

Later chapters discuss at greater length the differences between various community involvement methods and their advantages and disadvantages. The historical material summarized in this section serves as a useful introit to contemporary practices of community design, to which we now turn.

3.5. THE CONTEMPORARY COMMUNITY DESIGNER: ACCOMMODATING MULTIPLE PARTIES

What does the contemporary community designer do? Has practice changed since the 1960s? As we saw in the previous section, today the emphasis is less on empowering disadvantaged groups and more on participation. The past four decades of community design have taught practitioners that all parties to the process must be heard. In a recent interview, Nabeel

Hamdi described his experience in community design as one of bringing the agendas of multiple stakeholders together: the institution or organization funding the project, the local authority, and the local community (cited in Toker and Toker 2006b). A funding institution asks for the process as part of its own agenda, the local authority introduces its concerns, and the local community brings its issues to the table. "The question then is about entrepreneurial skills of practice: How do you bring those three agendas together?" (Hamdi, cited in Toker and Toker 2006b, 126).

Typically in a community design project, an institution or a local government approaches the community designer on behalf of a community and in search of solutions for a particular set of issues. For example, a city's community development department may want to initiate a process for a particular portion of the city (e.g., Downtown Delano, California, Concept Plan, discussed in section 8.5), or an institution concerned with the issues of a particular community may want to initiate a process to ensure its voice is heard (e.g., San Francisco, California, 4th/5th Streets SOMA study, discussed in section 7.7). Such processes require the community designer to be able to bring together multiple agendas and reconcile the objectives of the institution, the local government, and the community. As Hamdi points out,

> So, immediately in those three arrangements, as it were, we have three different agendas. We have the outsiders interested in privatization. The government is interested in water, for example, and the community is interested in education. (Cited in Toker and Toker 2006b, 126)

The contemporary social, economic, and political climate puts the community designer in the position of seeking genuine participation from all parties, particularly local communities, so that nobody's voice is lost. In reference to Sherry Arnstein's ladder, in cases with multiple role players, there may be a particularly high risk of getting stuck on the lower rungs of consultation or therapy. Consequently, the contemporary community designer also has the responsibility of analyzing the relationships among the local community, the local government, and the funding institution.

Hearing and accommodating multiple parties, both within and across groups of people, is the core task for the contemporary community designer, and it is a challenging one. How do community designers face this challenge?

Understanding people's positions and their underlying interests lies at the heart of facing the challenge of community design. Too often, individuals bring "compromise" into the picture and talk about finding a compromise that will make people comfortable with the decision under discussion. The notion of compromise, however, has negative connotations. The 2010 *Merriam-Webster's Collegiate Dictionary* defines *compromise* as "to adjust or settle with mutual concessions," indicating there is yielding involved. As a result, people do not see the participatory process as an advantage, they believe the goal can only be a compromise and nobody will be happy with the outcome.

Another commonly used term is "consensus." Despite its positive connotations, consensus worries a lot of people as a state difficult to impossible to reach. *Merriam-Webster's Collegiate Dictionary* provides two definitions of *consensus*: "general agreement, unanimity" and "group solidarity in sentiment and belief." Consensus is more popularly understood to mean unanimity, which many see as impossible to reach in a good number of cases. However, the second definition refers to a form of group solidarity, with an emphasis on sentiment and belief: an indication that the process of reaching consensus may be more sophisticated than reaching unanimity within or across groups. As Sanoff writes, "The process of consensus allows for the iterative dialogue of idea generation and debate toward decision making. The danger lies in limiting any access to the debate or considering any input more or less than others" (Sanoff 2000, 15).

In daily usage, however, the term somehow implies that people need to reach unanimity. But the core task of consensus building is finding underlying common interests and helping parties reach decisions that satisfy those interests. Viewed from this perspective, consensus becomes less the achievement of a concrete goal and more a process through which people understand each other's concerns and make decisions collaboratively based on common interests.

The contemporary community designer's role thus seems to be one of facilitating discussions in which multiple parties are brought to understand the underlying interests behind positions and discuss common community interests, with the goal of promoting decision making. The key in such discussions is to ask "why" when people share their positions, and to understand the reasons behind those positions. In many cases it will be possible to find shared underlying interests behind different positions in communities. The positions of people may look like two different icebergs over the water, but beneath the surface they may be connected through shared interests. From this perspective, real consensus can exist without compromise. Tom Atlee, for example, in *The Tao of Democracy* defines "real consensus" as "comfortably agreed-to outcomes achieved through real dialogue that creatively and collaboratively explores differences as well as noting common ground" (Atlee 2003, 238).

The contemporary community designer does face the challenge of accommodating multiple parties, and must bring clients to an awareness that shared interests exist in communities and that it is indeed possible to go beyond positions and reach decisions that will satisfy shared interests.

This may easily explain the contemporary focus of community design on participation and its decreasing emphasis on empowerment. The 1960s model of advocacy and empowerment involved groups with conflicting interests, and many of the socially conscious community designers did need to align themselves with particular interests and agendas. Such issues in the past were addressed through conflict management practices (Carpenter and Kennedy 2000), whereas community designers are dealing more and more with different role players (Toker and Toker 2006a).

Finally, what happens when there are conflicting interests? Conflicting interests in communities are not unusual. If unmanaged, it is easy for processes with conflicting interests to spiral out of control and approach a crisis state. Professionals and academics in many fields have been developing conflict management methods and strategies for such situations (Carpenter and Kennedy 2000). It is not the objective of this book to expand on conflict management techniques. It is important, however, to acknowledge that the contemporary community designer faces the challenge of making sure that multiple parties in community design processes are heard equally and sufficiently and their interests are accommodated through discussions that focus on those underlying interests, not on individual positions. In Part 2 we examine how to prepare for community design processes before going into the field.

PART 2

THE COMMUNITY DESIGN PROCESS

Part 1 introduced the historical and social background of community design. Part 2 moves into the contemporary community design process. Chapter 4 takes the reader through the steps involved in the initiation of a community design process and introduces the techniques available to the community designer to conduct outreach. Chapter 5 moves into the community design process in the field. It introduces the "V" process, which begins with a well-posed project statement to kick-start a preliminary exploration of issues, then takes the reader through the decision-making process. Specifically, it covers those decision-making stages of the community design process that follow the preliminary exploration phase: goal setting, strategy identification, action planning, and connecting the choices made during these stages to specific planning and design outcomes. With knowledge of these techniques and of how the participatory framework is constructed, we will be ready to discuss community design methods and their applications in the ensuing sections of the book.

4 Initiating the Participatory Planning and Design Process

A community design project is initiated when an entity or person—a department of local government, an organization, a community member—identifies a problem area affecting the community and requests help in resolving it. From the first contact, the different functions and roles of participants are put into play. The community designer needs to develop a project timeline at the outset, in consultation with the parties initiating the project. These measures, which occur in advance of any designing or planning, are the structural elements of the participatory framework within which the project will move toward its goals. This chapter will first introduce the key tasks and points involved in project timeline development. It will then introduce the key points in identification of individuals who should participate in the process, and outreach—the process of contacting those individuals and recruiting their participation.

4.1. CONSTRUCTING THE PARTICIPATORY FRAMEWORK

When the community designer receives a request for a project, the first task is to identify the key parties. These parties will differ depending on who initiated the contact with the community designer. The objective is to identify those who have the strongest insights into the community and its day-to-day workings and who also have a broad social network within the community. The insights provided by the key parties will help guide the first steps of the planning process and are invaluable in creating the project timeline.

4.1.1. The Players: Leading Group, Key Informants, and the Community Designer

In most cases, one of the four following *leading groups* will contact the community designer: (1) members of the community; (2) members of the community in a leadership position, such as a group of local business owners; (3) members of the local government; or (4) a nonprofit organization that would like to initiate change in the given community.

Once a project request is received from the leading group, the community designer develops questions about the process and about the community that will receive the designer's services. "Insider" information from *key informants*—members of the community with good insights into the community's functioning and with broad social connections—is fundamental to answering questions such as the following: What is the target completion date for the community design process? How many activities—meetings, workshops, interviews, site visits—need to be conducted to recruit participation? At what frequency? Would community members be more comfortable with frequent activities or would they prefer to be less frequently involved? The knowledge of the community's day-to-day workings sought through these questions is important for timeline development. This is where key informants are needed the most.

Key informants may infrequently come from the leading group. Several factors weigh against a joint role, however. Although the strongest insights are expected to come from members of the community, it would be unusual for regular community members to come to an agreement, organize a group of people willing to invest time and effort in the project, and seek help from a community designer on their own. Moreover, those in the group may not be experts on the community. A different set of circumstances arises when members of the local government or a nonprofit organization approach the community designer as the leading group. They may be less familiar with the inner workings of the community than its members or leaders. In fact, despite their best intentions, the local government or nonprofit organizations may be surprisingly disconnected from the day-to-day realities of the communities they serve. Members of local government and nonprofit organizations are hired (or elected) for their expertise in a subject area, not because they know the local community. Consequently, the community designer needs to uniquely identify key informants and make it clear to the leading group that the insights the key informants can provide are critical to developing a timeline for the project.

The *community designer* serves in multiple roles during the participatory process. To begin the process, the community designer frequently functions as a facilitator. Not all projects are well thought out when first presented to the community designer by the leading group. The project description may be well defined or vague and unorganized. It is not unusual to hear a project description along the lines of "We would like to do something about our downtown" or "We all want to make it better, we just need some guidance. We don't know how to." The community designer works with the leading group to craft a more narrowly defined project statement that will serve as the starting point of the design process. It is very important for the community designer to superimpose a conceptual framework on the process from the beginning by narrowing the subject through questions. This conceptual framework is also closely connected to the timeline that will be developed for the project.

4.1.2. The Players: Project Participants and the Project Champion

Project participants potentially include anyone who is likely to be affected by the outcome of the project. It is the community designer's responsibility to make sure all such parties are contacted and invited to participate. This practice enriches the project and generally works to create a smoother process. Once the process is under way, busy people are less likely to volunteer as participants and cannot be recruited to provide opinions.

Community members with no specific training in planning or who oppose the project could plausibly constitute a significant number of project participants. The leading group or project proponents may feel uneasy and urge a different participant makeup, believing that the project would otherwise turn out to be more onerous and time-consuming than necessary. The question of participation then turns into an ethical one that the community designer must confront. By hewing to the fundamental tenet of participatory design and planning, namely, those who are most affected by the outcomes should have a say, the community designer should be able to resolve the question and bring all interested parties to the table for discussion.

An important role player who may enter the picture somewhat later than the leading group or key informants is the *project champion*. A project champion is particularly interested in the success of the project and genuinely believes it is advantageous for the community. A community member who becomes particularly engaged after attending a participatory meeting may emerge as the project champion, as may a member of the leading group who finds her or his interest in the project evolving and deepening. The project champion advocates for the project in the community, assists with outreach, and makes efforts to demonstrate the benefits of the project to the community. The project champion also serves as a bridge between the designer and the community, and in future phases of the project can advise the designer on how the project is being received by the community or perhaps ease tensions that may arise. For this reason, it is advisable for the community designer to try to identify a project champion through personal observation, establish a relationship with that person, and work toward trust and collaboration.

ROLE PLAYERS IN THE COMMUNITY DESIGN PROCESS

Leading group: The group of people requesting the community design process. The leading group may be composed of (1) members of a community; (2) community leaders, such as a group of active local business owners; (3) members of the local government; or (4) members of a nonprofit organization who would like to initiate change in the given community.

Key informant: A community member who has strong insights into community functioning and a broad social network; someone who can provide the community designer with "insider" information.

Participant: Any individual who is likely to be affected by the outcomes of the community design process and the project; one who should be invited to participate in the community design process.

Project champion: An individual who is particularly interested in the success of the community design process and genuinely believes in the project to be advantageous for the community.

4.1.3. Developing a Timeline

All projects need a timeline established at the outset, to monitor progress and ensure efficiency. For community design projects, having a clear, step-by-step timeline is crucial. The number of people involved and their diverse roles mean the community designer must be able to explain the project clearly and describe its progress to any of the parties at any time. Consequently, the community designer strives to develop a project timeline, however rough, early in the process. Because elements of the timeline, such as meeting schedules, are coordinated with outreach efforts (to the parties who will be affected by the project), the timeline and outreach plan are usually developed with consideration for the other.

Turning to key informants for advice on timeline development has three distinct advantages for the community designer. Key informants can provide information on what time frame (i.e., process length) would elicit the most interest from the community, the history of the community and possible obstacles to the process, and community members' day-to-day lives, which can provide guidance on subschedules in the timeline.

4.2. IDENTIFYING TASKS AND INSTRUMENTS

Once the basic participatory design framework is in place, the next stages follow quickly. The project statement is reviewed and fine-tuned as needed, agreement is reached on the form the final design proposal will take, and the format and frequency of participatory decision-making activities are set out, with provisional dates added to the timeline. The decision-making meetings will require all project participants to be kept abreast of progress and informed of the issues that need to be discussed and brought to a consensus. Several instruments are available for education and outreach to the community; they are discussed in this section and the next.

The specification of goal statements takes place among the community designer, the leading group, and the key informants. The community designer then identifies the format and frequency of participatory activities as well as the participatory decision-making instruments. In doing so, she or he may receive input from the leading group and key informants. These tasks are usually more dependent on the community designer, however. Finally, before outreach, the community designer works with the leading group and key informants to organize the participatory decision-making activities.

4.2.1. Specifying Goal Statements

An important part of managing a project is clarifying goal statements: what is being sought, initially, and what kind of outcome is expected. The leading group and project participants may have a clear, tangible result or format in mind or may seek guidance in identifying a common target and putting it in writing. The community designer works collaboratively with the leading group and the project participants to craft these two important bookends of a project.

Fine-tuning the Project Statement. Not all requests as they are originally received by the community designer will be well posed. In such cases, people need to come to a shared vision prior to the development of more specific plan or design proposals (and they may seek only facilitation toward this end from the designer, whose role would end there). For example, the community may want to identify what types of activities would improve the vitality of a neighborhood, or the community may want input on the most appropriate uses for the project site. In such instances the community designer and leading group will take into consideration community demographics and patterns of social interactions in crafting a clear project statement.

Developing the Plan or Design Proposal. The question the community designer asks at this point is what the community expects as an outcome of the project. Depending on the progress made by community members prior to approaching the community designer, a concrete plan or design proposal may be expected. In that case, the community designer, working with the leading group and key informants, will need to specify what the final product will look like. Possibilities include a detailed, comprehensive plan proposal in document format, including the rationale for the project and graphic materials, or smaller scale booklets summarizing the target plan or design objectives, with visual support. The decision on proposal format will depend on how the community intends to proceed. If the plan is to be presented to a government agency for consideration for adoption, a formal plan document is necessary. If, however, the final product is intended to promote and explain an idea to the community and solicit community support for it, then smaller scale, easily comprehensible booklets are appropriate.

4.2.2. Specifying the Format and Frequency of Participatory Activities

Community design processes entail community members and the community designer coming together and engaging in participatory decision making. Drawing on personal expertise, and with consideration for the project description, community characteristics, and available resources, the community designer identifies the kinds of participatory decision-making activities and their number and frequency. The activities may be in the form of community workshops, charrettes, focus group interviews, street interviews, or task force meetings. Here the community's characteristics are key to choosing an appropriate format. For example, community workshops work well when many members of the community can spend a couple of hours together. Focus group meetings, on the other hand, work better when small groups of individuals can gather for shorter periods of time. The details, advantages, and disadvantages of each activity format are discussed in section 3 of this book.

Along with the format of upcoming activities, the community designer specifies their number and frequency, which again will be largely determined by community characteristics. A community of young working professionals may prefer to conduct a rapid process with many activities compressed into a short period of time, while a community with many retirees may be more comfortable with fewer activities and less frequent meetings. In a farming community, the number and frequency of activities will be affected by seasonal work commitments. Budget and time resources also weigh into the decision, for space may have to be found or rented, and the entire arc of the project may be time-sensitive. Close collaboration with the leading group and key informants will prove useful in such conditions. Some cases presented in upcoming chapters show how to incorporate participatory activities into timeline development within the constraints of resource availability, community characteristics, and project description.

4.2.3. Identifying Instruments

Instruments are tools that help project participants think systematically about the project. They may be as simple as posters or as sophisticated as wireless voting devices. Again, community characteristics will suggest which among the myriad available instruments are likely to capture the most useful ideas from the community, with minimal time and effort expenditure by both the community and the designer. For example, relying on instruments that use digital media may not be a good idea in a community that is known to be relatively independent of computers. Complex instruments that work well with a community composed predominantly of professionals could fail with a younger audience. Each instrument may need to be customized for the particular community and project, and different instruments will likely be needed for different stages of the project. It is important for the community designer to keep this in mind and allow sufficient time for instrument design and preparation while developing the project timeline. The advantages and disadvantages of several instruments available to the community designer are discussed in Part 3.

4.2.4. Organizing Activities

It is beneficial both for the community designer and for the project participants to discuss logistics before beginning the process. Organizing activities usually takes more time and effort than simply preparing instruments. Securing a venue will be necessary, for example. The leading group or key informants may be helpful not only for their knowledge of local venues but also for their possible help in securing them. If refreshments are to be offered at participatory gatherings, someone should be assigned to that task, and a budget line allocated. These and other logistical tasks, large and small, should be identified before the process gets under way, and responsibilities for executing the tasks should be shared among the role players—the community designer, members of the leading group, and community volunteers.

As the various logistical steps, tasks, and activities are added to the timeline of the community design project, the community designer can seize the opportunity to introduce the upcoming steps to the leading group as well as involved members of the community. Timeline development and the accompanying discussions afford the community designer a great opportunity to get more familiar with members of the leading group and the community in general.

4.3. OUTREACH

In the community design field, the term "outreach" is used to mean both (1) contacting individuals to participate in a community design project and (2) conducting community involvement for a project. Here, outreach is defined as the act of identifying, contacting, and recruiting community members to participate in a community design process. It is one of the most time-consuming processes in community design. The community designer must account for this effort when preparing the project timeline.

Outreach efforts may be kick-started by the community designer or the leading group but are usually more efficacious when done by people known to the community, which can put the leading group, especially if it is a government agency or organization, at a disadvantage in trying to conduct outreach. Key informants and others known to the community are usually best. Known, trusted individuals will also produce better results in the all-important face-to-face contacts, such as neighborhood meetings and personal phone calls. The advantage of familiarity is enormous in establishing relationships with the community and pays dividends at every turn in the community design process.

The purpose of outreach is to educate the entire community about the project and its objectives, and to create a means for community members to self-identify as project participants—those willing to spend more time in participatory decision making. Broad representation from across the community will help the process flow faster as matters needing decisions arise in the future and more community response is required. Outreach and education efforts may also be targeted to local groups representative of the community, such as school and church groups. The community designer, once familiar with the community, can assess which groups to target and initiate a stronger relationship with them if desired. There is a wide variety of outreach methods that have been developed in the field over the past few decades. An outreach method is the combination of activities to plan and contact parties and invite their participation in the project. Each method incorporates instrument(s) used to inform parties about the project.

4.3.1. Indirect Outreach Methods

Outreach methods are generally of two kinds, indirect or direct. Indirect methods typically use media to inform community members and invite their participation. A community newspaper, either printed or distributed online, is often an excellent means of getting the word out. Other examples of indirect methods are flyers and ads placed in newspapers, on the radio or television, and Internet advertising.

Flyers. Flyers can be posted in public places or mailed out to the community. One disadvantage of posting flyers in public spaces is that they are easily overlooked or deemed to be of no interest. Their size and design should therefore be attention-getting and the graphic language and message easily understood by the local community. Color schemes, figures, images, and typefaces must be selected to capture the community's attention. In communities where more than one language is spoken, it is imperative that multiple versions of the flyer be created in the different languages using the same information, images, and typefaces. Such a practice will convey that every person who is part of the community is welcome to participate and be heard.

Example: Cal Poly undergraduate students undertook the City of Delano, California, Strategic Plan development process under studio instructors' supervision. During this process, flyers and posters were designed based on the community's existing patterns of sign and poster design. Visits to the community confirmed that signage and posters in vibrant colors and forms were dominant on storefronts around the community. Posters and flyers were therefore designed using vibrant colors and forms and energetic slogans. Informal icons and symbols were used to make the graphic language attractive to all age groups in the community. Furthermore, since the community used both English and Spanish, posters and flyers were created in both languages (Figure 4.1). For more information on the City of Delano, California, Strategic Plan development process, see Chapter 9.

4.1. An example of the posters and flyers designed for outreach for the City of Delano, California, Strategic Plan development process

Flyers may also be mailed out to the community, though there are associated costs and the flyers may be lost among similar-appearing advertisements. A common practice is to send flyers out along with bills (i.e., water bill, power bill) to the community. However, these can easily end up in the trash.

Advertisements. Placing advertisements in local newspapers or on radio or television is another method that can be used for outreach. The effectiveness of this method depends on the extent to which these outlets reach the community. In many cases, a local television channel on which public meetings such as the planning commission's meetings or city council meetings are broadcast may help access a large cross section of the community since this medium tends to be a popular source of local information.

Online Methods. Sending notices electronically, through mass e-mails or by announcing the project on frequently accessed websites, is another common outreach method. If resources allow, developing a project webpage and using it to inform the community about the project and recruit participation may prove helpful. In the early days of the Internet, a common criticism was that it would exclude younger and older community members. As Internet access and use became widespread, however, the challenge has shifted to attracting attention and making the notice stand out among other electronic advertising. Therefore, combining electronic outreach with some form of traditional printed media will increase uptake.

If outreach is highly dependent on indirect methods, multiple methods should be used to reach the widest possible cross section of the community. Information should be provided in all the languages spoken in the community, and the graphic language of the instruments should be easily relatable by members of the local community.

No matter how many methods are used, however, indirect methods are limited in their ability to attract people to actually attend activities. Often,

Example: During the Madera Ranchos, California, Avenue 12 Concept Plan development process, outreach relied heavily on advertisements in the local newspaper, posters posted in popular local locations such as the public library, and flyers provided to community members. The local public planners had noted that the local community relied rarely on the Internet as an information source; consequently, printed materials—advertisements, posters, and flyers—were the main media used in outreach efforts. The turnout for community design activities was strong, indicating that the selected outreach methods were successful in recruiting community members for attendance. For more information on the Madera Ranchos, California, Avenue 12 Concept Plan development process, see Chapter 9.

people have specific questions about the project that are not addressed by indirect methods, and want to have a discussion regarding the project before they decide whether they will attend an upcoming activity. Consequently, community designers have developed more personal methods to ensure widespread participation of the community members they work with.

4.3.2. Direct Outreach Methods

Direct, personal outreach methods use many of the instruments used in indirect outreach but include the human element. The parties conducting the outreach introduce face-to-face or phone contacts and visits to potential participants' domains to make the process more accessible. For example, staffing an information booth at a local event or placing phone calls are among the methods often utilized in the field. Some form of printed media (an indirect method) is typically supplied at the event even as the staffer answers questions and provides information in person.

Visiting Local Businesses. Visiting local businesses can be an effective method to recruit participants. Local business owners are often familiar with the community and can be instrumental in informing community members about a project. Posting flyers in local businesses makes information broadly available and suggests the support of the businesses. A more efficient approach is to leave note card–sized versions of the flyer in multiple languages with the business. If they are made available on the counter, people can take them home to share with friends, family, and colleagues.

Example: During the Downtown Morro Bay, California, Enhancement Plan development process, three Cal Poly graduate student teams undertook the task of developing specific plan alternatives for the project area. The students conducted extensive outreach under the guidance of the studio instructors. One of the methods the students adopted was to visit local businesses, distribute flyers, and leave note card–sized versions of the flyers that featured English on one side and Spanish on the other. Throughout the outreach process the local business owners reported that the note card version of the flyers attracted strong attention, and members of the leading group repeatedly asked for more cards to distribute. The students disseminated hundreds of these cards through the local businesses (Figure 4.2). The turnout for community design activities organized by the studio was very strong, indicating that the selected outreach methods were successful in recruiting community members for attendance. For more information on the Downtown Morro Bay, California, Enhancement Plan, see Chapter 8.

4.2. During the Downtown Morro Bay, California, Enhancement Plan development process, local businesses received note card–sized versions of outreach flyers with the information in English on one side and Spanish on the other.

Visiting Local Organizations. Another direct outreach method is to attend activities sponsored by local business organizations, unions, and temples. Depending on the community, visiting such organizations may be an efficient way to access many community members. For example, visiting a church or attending a local school district meeting may provide access to a cross section of the community not readily available at other times and days. Similarly, attending a meeting of local business organizations may open up access to many owners. The goal is to find out the interests of the community and tap into organizations that pursue those interests.

Example: Cal Poly undergraduate students undertook the City of Delano, California, Strategic Plan development process under studio instructors' supervision. One of the outreach techniques utilized in this process was visiting local organizations. Under the studio instructors' supervision, students visited local organizations (such as local churches and a local farmworkers' union), requesting their members' attendance in the upcoming community design activities. As the community design process progressed, the number of participants attending the community design activities increased, indicating that in addition to other outreach efforts, visiting local organizations also supported participation. For more information on the City of Delano, California, Strategic Plan development process, see Chapter 9.

Telephone Calls. A less personal but also less time-consuming and potentially more effective direct outreach method is telephoning. A brief phone call to inform community members that they will receive a flyer about an ongoing community project can go a long way toward triggering interest. Telephoning first, then mailing a flyer, is much more effective than either activity alone in engaging the community.

Example: Cal Poly undergraduate students undertook the City of Delano, California, Strategic Plan development process under studio instructors' supervision. One of the outreach techniques utilized in this process was placing phone calls to local businesses and organizations. Under the studio instructors' supervision, students placed phone calls to local businesses and community organizations (such as local churches and a local farmworkers' union), requesting their members' attendance in the upcoming community design activities. As the community design process progressed, the number of participants attending the community design activities increased, indicating that in addition to other outreach efforts, placing phone calls also supported participation. For more information on the City of Delano, California, Strategic Plan development process, see Chapter 9.

Staffing Booths at Local Events. An effective outreach method is to staff a booth at a local event, hand out flyers, and talk to residents about the project. Such a booth can easily function as a preliminary data collection venue. While introducing the project and handing out flyers, booth staffers can solicit residents' opinions about the project and hear their concerns. Festivals and farmers markets are excellent venues for this form of direct outreach.

Example: During the Downtown Morro Bay, California, Enhancement Plan development process, three Cal Poly graduate student teams undertook the task of developing specific plan alternatives for the project area. The students conducted extensive outreach under the guidance of the studio instructors. One of the methods the students used was setting up a booth in the local farmers market. The farmers market was held within the project area. After the studio instructors received permission from organizers, the students set up a booth in Morro Bay farmers market on a Saturday morning. The booth (Figure 4.3) featured posters on both sides to attract attention, and a table for its visitors to write down ideas using a wish poem and a "have" poem (see Chapter 6). Throughout that Saturday morning the students invited local residents to attend the first community design activity, to be held at the local community center later that week. The students provided visitors to the booth with information on the project and the note card version of flyers announcing the upcoming community design workshop. Since the booth was staffed on the weekend before the first community design workshop, it had a strong positive impact on attendance: many of the individuals who stopped by the booth also attended the first workshop. For more information on the Downtown Morro Bay, California, Enhancement Plan, see Chapter 8.

4.3. During the Downtown Morro Bay, California, Enhancement Plan development process, Cal Poly students set up a booth at the Morro Bay farmers market on a Saturday morning. The booth featured posters on both sides to attract attention and a table for visitors to write down ideas using a "wish" poem and a "have" poem.

The advantage of direct, personal outreach methods is associating a face or a voice with the project. A personal invitation makes the project more accessible and allows people to ask questions or make comments about it. The outreach team can also learn what other paths to follow to reach more people. Community members reached using these methods can inform the outreach team about other outreach avenues that had not been considered originally.

4.3.3. Outreach Logistics: Time Frame and Consistency

When to initiate outreach and how long to sustain it are universal outreach concerns. Since people are busy going about their lives, it is easy for them to forget about the project. Therefore it is advisable not to leave too long a time between outreach and the first activity involving community participants. Conversely, people also need time to schedule upcoming activities, so that planning the first activity too close to the outreach moment is not recommended.

Sustaining the outreach effort is equally important. The community designer should ensure that participants hear about the outcomes of their efforts and receive regular updates on the project's progress. Indirect methods such as e-mail blasts and web page updates can be helpful in sustaining outreach and keeping the community updated.

Consistency over time in the type of information provided and the visual language used will add strength to the outreach campaign. The color schemes, typefaces, and types of images used become associated with project updates and serve as quick memory aids reminding community members that the process is ongoing and that they will have further opportunities to make known their opinions and ideas.

Example: During the Downtown Delano, California, Concept Plan development process, flyers and posters inviting community members to the upcoming community design activities were designed to sustain a shared language so that the community members could follow the progression of the project. For each community design activity conducted, a new poster or flyer was created to invite local residents to attend. A common visual language for the process was developed and used on all printed materials. The use of visually consistent materials communicated to residents that each event was part of a larger community design effort (Figure 4.4). For more information on the Downtown Delano, California, Concept Plan development process, see Chapter 8.

public invitation for planning our downtown

The City of Delano invites you to participate in the creation of the *'Concept Plan for Downtown Delano'*. We will be working with faculty and students from Cal Poly, San Luis Obispo in a series of workshops to strengthen and improve Downtown Delano!

workshop 1

AWARENESS WALK

SATURDAY, MARCH 1, 2008
WHERE: CIVIC CENTER, 1009 ELEVENTH AVE.
WHEN: 1:00PM.

Come tour and photograph the downtown with us!

We will begin with a Downtown Awareness Walk. Each household will be given two disposable cameras to record their likes and dislikes as we take a walk around our downtown.
The awareness walk will take about 1.5 hours.

We look forward to your participation in this exciting project as we build *a better and stronger Downtown Delano.*

LET'S WORK ALL TOGETHER TO MAKE OUR DOWNTOWN BETTER.

public invitation for planning our downtown

The City of Delano invites you to participate in the creation of the *'Concept Plan for Downtown Delano'*. We will be working with faculty and students from Cal Poly, San Luis Obispo in a series of workshops to strengthen and improve Downtown Delano!

workshop 2

OPPORTUNITIES IN DOWNTOWN DELANO

SATURDAY, MARCH 8, 2008
WHERE: Delano Union Elementary School District Boardroom
1405 12th Ave., Delano, CA
WHEN: 1:00PM.

Let's discuss what makes our downtown 'tick'!

Our workshop is expected to take about 2 hours.

LET'S WORK ALL TOGETHER TO MAKE OUR DOWNTOWN BETTER.

public invitation for planning our downtown

The City of Delano invites you to participate in the creation of the *'Concept Plan for Downtown Delano'*. We have been working with faculty and students from Cal Poly, San Luis Obispo in a series of workshops to strengthen and improve Downtown Delano!

workshop 3

OUR GOALS, AND STEPS TO TAKE

SATURDAY, MARCH 15, 2008
WHERE: Delano Union Elementary School District Boardroom
1405 12th Ave., Delano, CA
WHEN: 1:00PM.

Get ready to put those thinking caps on!

Our workshop is expected to take about 2 hours.

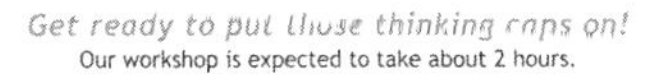

public invitation for planning our downtown

The City of Delano invites you to participate in the creation of the *'Concept Plan for Downtown Delano'*. We have been working with faculty and students from Cal Poly, San Luis Obispo in a series of workshops to strengthen and improve Downtown Delano!

workshop 4

DOWNTOWN PLANNING GAME

SATURDAY, MARCH 22, 2008
WHERE: Delano Union Elementary School District Boardroom
1405 12th Ave., Delano, CA
WHEN: 1:00PM.

Get ready to shape our Downtown!

Our workshop is expected to take about 2 hours.

LET'S WORK ALL TOGETHER TO MAKE OUR DOWNTOWN BETTER.

4.4. During the Downtown Delano, California, Concept Plan development process, flyers and posters inviting community members to the upcoming community design activities were designed to sustain a shared language so that the community members could follow the progression of the project.

5 The "V" Process

From Project Objectives to Plan Proposal

This chapter opens up the process of getting from project objectives to plan proposal, the two bookends of a participatory planning process. Between these bookends, much happens. It is up to the community designer to impose an orderly framework within which the process unfolds in steps.

The conceptual framework for the process resembles the letter V, in that it starts from a broad perspective and gradually focuses in on discrete action steps. Assuming a well-posed project statement (please see Chapter 4 for getting to that state), the process begins with a preliminary exploration, such as a walk-through of the project site, to gain knowledge about the current state of issues. The information gained from the preliminary exploration serves as the basis for setting goals. Strategies are identified to achieve those goals, and action steps are identified for each strategy. Finally, the goals, strategies, and action steps are connected to the specific planning and design outcomes desired. To summarize, the conceptual framework starts from the well-posed project statement and moves through

- preliminary exploration,
- goal setting,
- strategy identification,
- action planning, and
- connecting decisions to plan and design proposals,

which, once executed, yield the basic data that become the basis of the plan document.

As in any design process, these stages need not—and likely will not—occur sequentially. The community designer and project participants may find it necessary to revisit previous stages or look ahead to upcoming stages—for example, to consider some action steps simultaneously with sorting out strategies. The V analogy (Figure 5.1) is provided to help the reader organize the process logically, and the following discussion amplifies each part of the process.

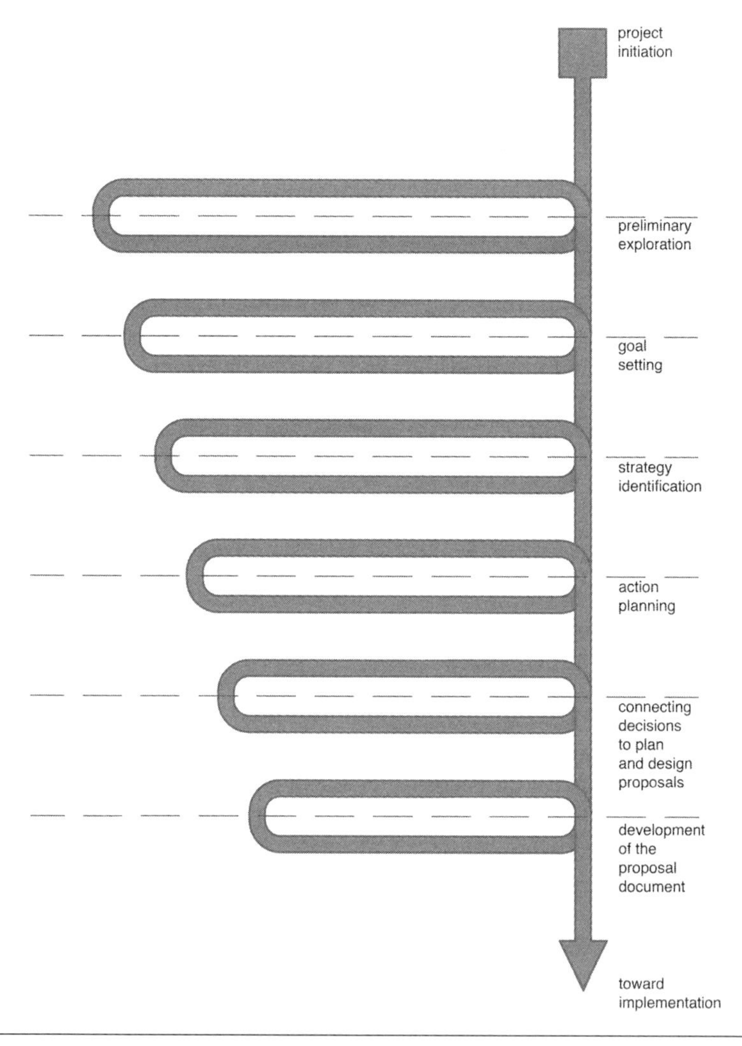

5.1. The "V" process of community design: preliminary exploration, goal setting, strategy identification, action planning, and connecting decisions to planning and design proposals. As in any design process, these stages need not occur strictly sequentially; the process may loop back or jump forward.

5.1. PRELIMINARY EXPLORATION—KNOWLEDGE ACQUISITION

We frequently take for granted spaces and places in our built environment. Once people start looking at a particular environment critically, much more is revealed. A critical look also suggests how random the information we keep in mind is. Because of the human tendency to retain only partial, incomplete, and perhaps unrepresentative bits of information about the built environment, it is often useful to conduct a preliminary exploration of existing conditions at the project site. This exploration is conducted with the community members and may focus on existing site data, examples of previously completed similar projects, or the local context.

Existing Data. Once a site is selected, and especially if the project is of large scale, community members may request information on existing conditions of the site. The data provided may be qualitative, such as visual representations of the site, or quantitative, such as traffic volumes of streets within the project site. Since a quantitative data-based exploration may require previous experience, it will need to be conducted by the community designer. And because not all community members will be able to make sense of the data, the community designer will need to present the data in an easily comprehensible format and language.

Examples of Previously Completed Similar Projects. Community members may also ask to see completed projects similar to theirs when asked about their wishes and preferences. At this point the community designer may wish to show similar examples or ask community members to provide photographs or descriptions of places they have visited. Once again, to make this information accessible to all community members, the community designer should sift through the examples so that they can be easily understood and compared by community members.

Local Context. Especially on smaller projects, a visit to the project site may be easily managed. In such cases, it is advisable for the community designer to arrange for a pre-activity tour of the project area or arrange for community members to visit the site on their own time. As an alternative to a site visit, the community designer may provide photographs of the site and its context at a community meeting.

A preliminary site exploration has advantages for both the community designer and community members. For the community designer, this exploration provides invaluable insight into the community and the project area. For the community members, a preliminary exploration is a better way to understand existing conditions and expand knowledge about conditions and issues they may have overlooked. Finally, for the community design process, a preliminary exploration makes the discussions better informed and thus more effective. We discuss the specific methods and instruments for conducting a preliminary exploration in the following chapters.

Example: During the Downtown Morro Bay, California, Enhancement Plan development process, a preliminary study was conducted by the community design team (composed of faculty and students), community members, and the leading group. The study entailed a walking tour of the project area during which community members took pictures of positive and negative aspects. The tour lasted about an hour and was followed by a goal-setting activity. For more information about this preliminary exploration, see the case "Downtown Morro Bay, California, Enhancement Plan" in Chapter 8.

5.2. GOAL SETTING

Once the preliminary exploration is completed, the larger goals for the project need to be set. At this stage the project participants are asked their preferences for the future direction of their community. This usually results in long venting sessions during which the project participants bring issues, hopes, preferences, and day-to-day experiences to the table. It is not uncommon to hear about items unrelated to the project. Some items may have strong but indirect connections to the project. All issues, wishes, and preferences brought up, however, must be heard. Regardless of how distant the discussion topics may be from the project, shutting down discussions sets a very negative tone and gives the impression that participants' time spent on the project is not worth anything.

As part of the goal-setting process the community designer needs to elicit answers to the following questions:

1. What longer-term goals does the community have, and what would the community members like to achieve with the current project?
2. What qualities of the project area and the community are participants satisfied with?
3. What kinds of changes would the community members like to see at the project site, as well as in their community in the future?
4. What kinds of changes at the project site and in the community are the community members against?

These questions ordinarily spark lively discussions among participants and help uncover issues that may not have surfaced earlier. They also help the participants organize their thoughts and identify collaboratively the general direction they would like their community to move in. For the community designer, this lays valuable groundwork for the next part of the process, strategy identification.

Goal setting has distinct advantages for the community design process. First, because community members are able to express their views and be heard in a public environment, they start trusting the process. Second, as a result of gaining trust in the process, the community begins to own the process. The project now advances beyond the more technical task description identified by the community designer and the leading group and starts belonging to the community. Third, the community starts shaping the process. The shaping occurs as the input provided by community members during goal setting helps the community designer modify the timeline and, using the same input, design the upcoming activities and instruments. Therefore, by participating in goal setting, community members start customizing the process for themselves. We discuss specific methods and instruments for goal setting in the following chapters.

5.3. STRATEGY IDENTIFICATION

Once community members identify the goals of the process, the next step is to identify strategies to achieve those goals. At this point the community designer closes the goal-setting discussion and channels community engagement toward identifying these strategies. The task is to narrow the discussion from the issue of large-scale community goals to what paths might be explored to move in that direction. During strategy identification the community designer learns more about the community's potential from the community members, and community members simultaneously begin to learn how to approach problem solving systematically.

Example: During the Downtown Delano, California, Concept Plan development process, community members, the leading group, and the community design team went through a goal-setting activity. Although the ultimate objective of the project was to generate a concept plan to help develop a specific plan, one of the longer term goals specified by the community members was "make Downtown a destination with character." As discussed in the text, the goals set by the community members at this stage often include relatively abstract, larger scale targets. This goal was strongly agreed upon and was acknowledged in the final plan document. Strategies and actions were specified in the plan document to help the community move toward achieving this goal. For detailed information about the goal-setting process, see the case "Downtown Delano, California, Concept Plan" in Chapter 8.

Strategies for achieving project goals most often include plan and design interventions in the physical environment of the community. Strategizing is not limited to the physical environment, however. Depending on the number and breadth of the goals set, strategies may include combining community resources to achieve the goals set, exploring strategies adopted for similar projects by other communities, and identifying potential parties responsible for executing strategies. In the following chapters we discuss specific methods and instruments for strategy identification.

Example: During the Downtown Delano, California, Concept Plan development process a relatively abstract, larger scale goal was identified by the community members: "make Downtown a destination with character." The community members later identified strategies to achieve this goal. The strategies they identified include "preserve historic buildings," "bring in public art," and "bring in a landmark and placeholders." Strategy identification helps specify the targets of the community beyond larger scale goals, as demonstrated by this process. Community members later proceeded to identify action steps to follow each strategy. For further information on this strategy identification process, see the case "Downtown Delano, California, Concept Plan" in Chapter8.

5.4. ACTION PLANNING

At the level of goal setting and strategy identification, the discussion and the resulting ideas are relatively abstract. Consequently, after setting goals and identifying strategies, the community designer needs to focus in on the action steps required to carry out the strategies and achieve the larger goals. Here the community designer works with the community members to answer the following basic questions for each strategy identified:

1. What first steps should be taken to execute each strategy?
2. Who, either inside or outside the community, can and should take the first steps?
3. Who, either inside or outside the community, can and should provide the necessary resources, monetary or otherwise, for taking the first steps?

Such basic questions will prompt other questions, such as what actions should follow the first steps and what additional resources are needed to initiate change. The action planning process essentially functions as a reality check on the ideas developed and lets the community members review their ideas for practicality.

Action planning is an essential task, especially for longer term projects, for several reasons. First, prior to action planning, many ideas will have been generated, not all of which will be realistic. Without action planning the community designer risks elevating the hopes of the community members beyond what can be achieved. By asking community members to think about these questions, the community designer can keep expectations realistic.

Second, action planning is important to develop and sustain a common understanding of issues among community members, as well as to avoid misjudgments. When discussing goals and strategies, it is easy for people to reach agreement, but at the level of action planning, community members begin discovering the practical impacts of these goals and strategies on their daily lives. Action planning thus helps filter out ideas that do not yield commonly preferred outcomes.

Third, action planning gives the community designer tangible input that will prove immensely helpful when the time comes to connect the process to physical planning and design decisions. Through action planning, not only are unrealistic expectations eliminated, but actions that can directly inform the planning and design decisions are identified.

Fourth, by making community members think about the practical implications of their ideas and decisions, action planning spurs a review of the process and of the decisions made since the beginning of the community design process. This review provides the community designer with a valuable foundation for the upcoming physical planning and design decisions.

Essentially, it strongly connects upcoming steps to the results of preliminary exploration, goal setting, and strategy identification. We discuss the specific methods and instruments for action planning in the following chapters.

Example: During the Downtown Delano, California, Concept Plan development process, community members identified first steps to take to follow strategies, as well as potential funding sources and potential individuals to take the first step. The goal, "make Downtown a destination with character," and its strategy, "bring in public art," was one of the items discussed by the community members. Community members identified "form an art foundation and hold a public art forum" as first steps to take, "impact fee for new businesses, Chamber of Commerce, and the City of Delano" as potential funding sources, and "local artists, art clubs, and Chamber of Commerce" as the parties to potentially take the first steps. Through this action planning process, community members were able to specify realistic actions to take to achieve their larger scale goal in the long run. For more information about this action planning process, see the case "Downtown Delano, California, Concept Plan" in Chapter 8.

5.5. CONNECTING DECISIONS TO PLANNING AND DESIGN OUTCOMES

Through the processes of preliminary exploration, goal setting, strategy identification, and action planning, the community designer works with community members to sort through issues, ideas, and decisions. After the action planning phase the community designer has sufficient tangible input from community members to start connecting the process to physical planning and design decisions. It is rare, however, that community members have the background or the expertise to relate planning and design decisions to previous discussions. Visual media have a strong effect, and one that is very different from that of written or spoken ideas. Bringing professional-level visual aids, such as sketches, drawings, or renderings, into the process may therefore be risky for the community designer. People may feel their ideas are not reflected in the visual aids and so may conclude they have not been heard.

For this reason, it is important to connect previous decisions to physical planning and design decisions together with the community members. It is advisable for the community designer to develop instruments and methods that will help community members think about the planning and design implications of their discussions. Broadly, community members' discussion and efforts should revolve around the following questions:

1. How should the physical environment change to help us move toward the goals we set?
2. Which of these changes would help preserve the qualities we are satisfied with?
3. Given the practical implications of our goals and strategies, what kinds of changes are likely to be implemented with minimal burden (monetary or otherwise) to the community?

The discussion that develops around these questions can continue through a number of activities and over different time periods, depending on the size of the project as well as the resources available. Through this process, the community designer starts translating community-based ideas into planning and design language. Feedback cycles for fine-tuning are strongly recommended to ensure the community's satisfaction with plan and design development. In the following chapters we discuss specific methods and instruments for connecting decisions to planning and design outcomes.

Example: A community design process to develop a new design proposal for a community center was undertaken in Sandhills, North Carolina. After goal setting, strategy identification, and action planning, a community workshop was organized to have community members generate design ideas. Through a design game developed by the community design team, participants generated their ideal floor plan layouts for a new community center. The community design team integrated the layout proposals into one common layout and mailed a feedback form to community members. The feedback form showed the common layout and provided space to write down opinions about the proposal. The feedback received was integrated into the final design proposal for the community center and presented to community members in a final meeting. The community members received the design proposal very positively and commended the community design team for the way in which the community's ideas were materialized in the design proposal. For detailed information on the process of connecting decisions to design ideas, see the case "Sandhills Family Heritage Association Community Center, Spring Lake, North Carolina" in Chapter 11.

PART 3
COMMUNITY DESIGN: METHODS AND APPLICATIONS

Part 2 covered the community design process and the concept of progressing toward plan and design proposals in stages that incrementally clarify the project. Part 3 introduces a toolkit the community designer can use in the field, and provides examples of its use on community design projects of different scales. We scrutinize specific community design methods and suggest instruments that can be used with each. We also discuss community design activity formats, such as community workshops or charrettes, in relation to community design process and methods. By the end of Part 3, readers will understand how to select the appropriate methods to use in specific planning and design problems.

6 Methods and Instruments for Community Design Activities

Over the years, community designers have developed a variety of formats, methods, and instruments with which to gather input from people in community design processes. Through exploration and experience, methods and instruments have been fine-tuned, and the opportunities and constraints of different activity formats have become apparent. This chapter reviews this toolkit and discusses the advantages and disadvantages of its use in different contexts and in different stages of the design process.

A few definitions of terms will help set the stage. A community design *activity format* has to do with the organization of the activity. Common activity formats include community workshops, charrettes, and information/reaction formats such as public hearings.

A community design *method* is the means by which information flows between the community designer and community members. Common community design methods include, but are not limited to, interviews, surveys and design games.

Finally, a community design *instrument* is the tool that makes information flow between the community members and the community designer possible. It allows ideas to be captured as they are developed through the interaction between the community members and the community designer. Commonly used community design instruments include maps, recording sheets, and game kits. With advances in digital technologies, instruments such as GIS-based devices and digital cameras have been increasingly used in recent years.

Depending on its format, a community design activity may use a variety of methods, each method associated with one or more instruments. Certain instruments may be used for more than one method. Similarly, a community design method may be used in different activity formats. Therefore, there is no one-to-one correspondence matching formats to methods and instruments, although some clusters are more common than others. The "V" process introduced in Chapter 5, whereby decision making in community design is systematically narrowed down, affords a framework for discussing community design methods by the stages of that process: preliminary exploration, goal setting, strategy identification, action planning, and making connections to design decisions. We then look at the activity formats available for the community designer and consider which methods and instruments are commonly used with each activity format.

GLOSSARY

Activity format: The way a community design activity is organized.

Method: A means by which the community designer collects information from community members.

Instrument: A tool that makes information flow between community members and the community designer possible.

6.1. METHODS AND INSTRUMENTS FOR PRELIMINARY EXPLORATION

In Chapter 5, three types of preliminary exploration were introduced: exploration of existing data, exploration of similar projects, and exploration of the local context. Exploration of existing data and exploration of similar projects rely on common information search and presentation techniques. For example, the community designer may need to check online databases or contact colleagues who have completed similar projects to collect information. This information is then presented to the community members through discussion or printed media. Exploration of the local context is conducted in person with the community members or members of the leading group, typically through a tour of the project area. The community designer may tour the area with community members, or the community members may be asked to tour the project area on their own time. The following discussion explores these methods and the instruments that can be used with them to acquire knowledge.

6.1.1. Awareness Walk

An awareness walk is a simple kind of exploration. It is essentially a tour of the project area by the community designer and community members or the leading group and is premised on the observation that people often take their immediate environment for granted. The awareness walk, which is conducted with project items in mind, gives participants an opportunity for a fresh look at the conditions of the project area. Participants are often surprised by how much of their environment they overlook or do not see. The awareness walk also helps instill a sense of excitement about the project and provides a good setting to kick off community design processes. It also acquaints the community designer with issues that might not arise in more formal, systematic discussion sessions such as meetings.

Instruments for Awareness Walks. Route maps, notepads, and pens are common instruments for awareness walks. Participants receive these items at the beginning of the walk, along with a briefing on the object of the activity. It is not unusual to conduct awareness walks without any instruments, however. Participants may simply tour the project area and share their observations with the community designer and fellow participants. In either case it is recommended that the community designer record participants' comments.

Example: During the Madera County, California, Avenue 12 Concept Plan development process, the community design team and members of the leading group conducted an awareness walk of the project area. During the walk, the community design team recorded the comments of the leading group members in a notebook. The community design team also visually documented the project area by taking photographs. For more information on the Madera County, California, Avenue 12 Concept Plan development process, see Chapter 9.

6.1.2. Awareness Camera Activity

The awareness camera activity is very similar to the awareness walk. Participants are provided with cameras to take photographs of project area elements that are significant to them, whether liked or disliked. This activity shares the advantages of the awareness walk and has the additional advantage of contributing to an inventory of images relevant to the project.

It is important to keep track of the reasons why project features are photographed. One way to systematize the tracking is to provide participants with color-coded cameras, such as green-tagged cameras for liked features and red-tagged cameras for disliked features. Participants may also be given recording sheets with spaces to note the photograph number, why it was taken, and any additional comments (Figure 6.1).

Both approaches have advantages and disadvantages. The color-coded camera approach is simple and easy to understand and implement by

Photograph No.	The reason this photograph was taken	Additional Comments

6.1. A record like the one shown here can be provided to participants using the awareness camera method. Participants record the photograph number, why it was taken, and any additional comments.

the participants. It creates an invaluable visual library about the project. When the photographs are organized and shown to the community, they can trigger in-depth discussions. However, since the reasons behind the photographing of project area elements are not systematically tracked, the community designer has to be constantly alert and questioning throughout the process. In addition, it is important to ask about participants' reasons for photographing elements in future steps in the process.

The recording sheet approach is much more accurate in terms of recording why participants are taking photographs but does require more effort by the participants. They need to write down the number of a photograph they take and why they took the photograph. This will detract from the discussion to some extent. A more important issue is whether people are interested in carrying around pencil-and-paper tablets while photographing the project area. The approach chosen by the community designer should match the project objectives and the community.

Instruments for Awareness Camera Activities. Film or digital cameras may be used in camera awareness activities. As long as photograph numbers can be effectively linked to comments on the photographs, participants may use their own cameras.

Example: During the Downtown Morro Bay, California, Enhancement Plan development process, Cal Poly graduate students and their studio instructors conducted an awareness camera exercise with community members. Participant groups of two to three were provided with two disposable cameras, one labeled green that read "Things we like about Downtown Morro Bay" and another labeled red that read "Things that we think can be improved in Downtown Morro Bay." The group toured the project area for about an hour, taking photographs and having discussions (Figure 6.2). Immediately after the awareness camera exercise the group met in a community workshop setting and continued on to identifying project goals. For more information on the Downtown Morro Bay, California, Enhancement Plan, see Chapter 8.

6.2. During the Downtown Morro Bay, California, Enhancement Plan development process, an awareness camera exercise was conducted with the community members. The group toured the project area for about an hour, taking photographs and talking about what they saw.

6.1.3. Awareness Walk or Awareness Camera Activity on Community Members' Own Time

For projects subject to time and budget limitations, awareness walks or awareness camera activities may be of secondary importance since the activities are exploratory in nature. As well, the characteristics of the community or weather conditions may undermine the advantages of these activities (e.g., rain, or a community of mostly elderly people facing a very hot summer). In such cases, the community designer may provide an opportunity for community members to do the exploration on their own time. It is advisable to have a brief informative meeting to give instructions and a timeline to the community members. In this meeting, community members are given a deadline and informed how to transmit their photographs and observations to the community designer (Figure 6.3).

The main advantage of organizing awareness walk or awareness camera activities on community members' own time is flexibility: participants may carry out the activity as their schedules allow. As a method, however, it is not as efficient, since it is not easy for the community designer to receive immediate, direct input from community members. This method also lacks the energizing kick-off effect of an awareness walk or awareness camera exercise. Finally, it is easy for participants to get distracted by their daily obligations and put off doing the activity.

Instruments for Awareness Walks or Awareness Camera Activity on Community Members' Own Time. This method shares the same instruments with awareness walk and awareness camera activities. An additional instrument providing written instructions to the participants may also be advisable.

6.3. During the Madera County, California, Avenue 12 Concept Plan development process, an awareness camera activity was conducted on participants' own time. Participants were provided with disposable cameras labeled with green ("Things I like about Avenue 12") or red tape ("Things that could be improved about Avenue 12").

6.2. METHODS AND INSTRUMENTS FOR GOAL SETTING

Once the preliminary exploration of the site has been completed, the community designer needs to select methods for goal setting. At this point many ideas have been broached already, and unsupervised discussions can take long periods of time without yielding any relevant results for specific targets. Goal setting puts in place the main structure of the project, and subsequent steps depend on the tone and quality established in this step. Therefore, selecting methods for goal setting is important. Goal-setting methods typically involve eliciting community members' opinions about existing conditions and what they think could be improved. The following paragraphs detail a range of methods and instruments used for goal setting.

6.2.1. Likes and Dislikes Analysis

A relatively simple method used for goal setting is to ask community members what they like and dislike about the existing conditions of the project area. It is advisable to ask community members to prioritize issues and focus on the highest priority ones. To generate a discussion and cover issues systematically, the following questions are useful:

- What are the top three things you like about this community?
- What are the top three things you think could be improved in this community?

Because these questions still ask for an overview of issues, as people tackle them they may forget to include issues important to them in the first instance. To overcome this proclivity, community members should be asked to think about these questions individually first, then share their answers with the rest of the participants.

In this approach, participants are asked to form small groups of five to eight and write down their answers individually. Then the participants take turns reading their answers to the rest of the small group. Once all the answers are read, a facilitator in the group starts the discussion to determine the likes and dislikes agreed on by members of the group. Finally, the facilitator of each group reads aloud to the whole assembly the answers that were agreed on in the small groups. The community designer records the answers on large sheets of paper on an easel or on a whiteboard, thus finalizing a list of likes and dislikes. During the process, the participants engage in extensive discussions of project area issues and the community designer receives a valuable education in local concerns.

Instruments for Likes and Dislikes Analysis. Instruments for conducting a likes and dislikes analysis are fairly simple. Often sheets of paper with the likes and dislikes questions and blank spaces for participants to write down answers are sufficient. To facilitate the discussion, larger sheets or printing of the answers could be recommended. By recording the participants' likes and dislikes on large sheets of paper, the facilitator not only sustains the discussion but also emphasizes that the ideas of the participants are being heard and recorded.

Example: During the Downtown Delano, California, Concept Plan development process, the community members were provided with letter-sized sheets of paper to note three things they liked in the project area and three things they would like to see improved. After all participants had written down their ideas, they were asked to form small groups of five to six and share their ideas with the small group. Each group developed lists of items they all agreed on. Group spokespersons then read the lists of agreed-upon items, and the results were discussed by the participants. Facilitators from the community design team made notes of the results throughout the discussion (Figure 6.4). For more information on the Downtown Delano, California, Concept Plan development process, see Chapter 8.

6.4. Facilitators Brian Barnacle (left) and Jennifer Venema (right) from the community design team noting the results of the likes and dislikes analysis

6.2.2. Wish Poems

Another method that is helpful for identifying goals is creating a wish poem. A wish poem includes the phrase "I wish (the project area) . . ." on every line, followed by a blank space to be filled in by the community members (e.g., "I wish my town . . .") (Sanoff 2000). This method provides the participants with a fun activity and yields a record of both preferred directions and aspects of the project area that need improvement. To complement the wish poem and record aspects of the area that the participants are happy with, a "have" poem can be added to the activity. The have poem includes the phrase "I am glad (the project area) . . ." on every line, followed by a blank space to be filled in by the community members (e.g., "I am glad my town . . .").

As in the likes and dislikes analysis, it is advisable to have the participants complete the wish poems and have poems individually first, then discuss them in five-to-eight-person groups. A facilitator in each group asks the participants to read aloud their answers. After each group comes to agreement on a list of wishes and haves, the facilitators read aloud to the whole assembly their group's lists. Wishes and haves from each group are recorded by the community designer on large-format wish and have poems. Once again, recording the ideas on large-format sheets of paper or on a whiteboard helps facilitate the discussion and emphasizes to the participants that their ideas are important.

Instruments for Wish Poems. Instruments for wish and have poems are sheets of paper with the phrases "I wish (the project area) . . ." and "I am glad (the project area) . . ." typed on every line, followed by blank spaces to be filled in by the participants (Figure 6.5). As in the likes and dislikes analysis, large-format means of compiling all the items mentioned in the wish and have poems are advisable for group decision making.

Example: During the Downtown Soledad, California, Urban Design Plan project, Cal Poly undergraduate students with their studio instructor conducted wish and have poem exercises. Participants first completed the wish and have poems on their own, then shared their ideas with the rest of the group. After this workshop, the findings were analyzed and recorded on large-scale posters for a prioritization exercise in a second workshop (Figure 6.6).

Madera Avenue 12 Concept Plan
Leadership Meeting, 07/09/2009

wish poem

I wish Avenue 12 ______________________________
I wish Avenue 12 ______________________________
I wish Avenue 12 ______________________________
I wish Avenue 12 ______________________________
I wish Avenue 12 ______________________________
I wish Avenue 12 ______________________________
I wish Avenue 12 ______________________________
I wish Avenue 12 ______________________________
I wish Avenue 12 ______________________________
I wish Avenue 12 ______________________________
I wish Avenue 12 ______________________________
I wish Avenue 12 ______________________________
I wish Avenue 12 ______________________________
I wish Avenue 12 ______________________________
I wish Avenue 12 ______________________________
I wish Avenue 12 ______________________________
I wish Avenue 12 ______________________________
I wish Avenue 12 ______________________________

Madera Avenue 12 Concept Plan
Leadership Meeting, 07/09/2009

have poem

I'm glad Avenue 12 ______________________________
I'm glad Avenue 12 ______________________________
I'm glad Avenue 12 ______________________________
I'm glad Avenue 12 ______________________________
I'm glad Avenue 12 ______________________________
I'm glad Avenue 12 ______________________________
I'm glad Avenue 12 ______________________________
I'm glad Avenue 12 ______________________________
I'm glad Avenue 12 ______________________________
I'm glad Avenue 12 ______________________________
I'm glad Avenue 12 ______________________________
I'm glad Avenue 12 ______________________________
I'm glad Avenue 12 ______________________________
I'm glad Avenue 12 ______________________________
I'm glad Avenue 12 ______________________________
I'm glad Avenue 12 ______________________________
I'm glad Avenue 12 ______________________________
I'm glad Avenue 12 ______________________________

6.5. Sample wish poem and have poem instruments

downtown sole‑dad urban design plan
what we heard in the community meeting

wish poem

I wish Downtown...

- had a plaza (possibly combined with parks)
- had a gateway
- had brighter streetlights
- had more mission style architecture
- had updated storefronts, enhanced facades
- was symmetrical (utilizing west of Front Street)
- had upgraded street conditions
- had trees, bike lanes on all streets
- had more disabled parking & accessibility
- had more trees & landscaping
- had a stronger link to the Mission
- was less windy
- had an information center on Pinnacles
- had more electricity power surges for festivals / community events
- had a link to the railroad
- could generate more traffic, had more activity, had something unique to attract travelers on Highway 101
- had more mixed use, more varied development form (2 & 3 story buildings)
- had more businesses
- had more variety of shops / commerce ("Mom and Pop" Stores, restaurants, a coffee shop, a multi-cultural book store, a music store, a hobby shop for kids, a shoe shop, drycleaners, more grocery stores)
- had more coffee shops / restaurants / outdoor dining / deli / In'n'Out
- had a train stop or transit station
- had a stronger connection with the train and railroad
- had a Convention Center, a Cultural Center
- had a hotel with a conference center
- had an International Theme (Steinbeck Village)
- had a movie theater
- had a performing arts center, or other entertainment options.
- had better nightlife (i.e. a brewery or pub, a sports bar)
- had a year-round Farmers Market
- had a sports complex
- had a wine store or wine tasting center
- had better connection to the wine industry.
- had a courthouse
- had more things for younger kids (i.e. a park with a play structure, a children's golf course)

downtown soledad urban design plan
what we heard in the community meeting

have poem

I am glad Downtown...

- has the railroad
- has a clean street feel, paved sidewalks
- has nice and friendly merchants
- is a walkable community
- has this layout (an easy layout)
- is small / compact
- has a pharmacy
- has pedestrian lighting
- has visibility from highway
- has a bowling alley
- has an updated Front Street
- has access to rapid transit
- has nowhere to go but up
- has a variety of different types of buildings
- has the OSBA (Office of Small Business Assistance)
- has Mexican restaurants
- has good infrastructure
- has a strong streetscape character
- has great crosswalks
- has available parking
- has landscaping; urban furniture (established seating / furnishings)
- has people out and about and walking around
- has stop signs to slow traffic
- has multicultural stores
- has nicely paved streets
- has scenic vistas
- has a variety of stores, retail businesses (i.e. a good size grocery store, a post office, a bank, a government center, an auto parts store)
- has lights on roofs; during holiday lighting
- has a Farmer's Market
- has adequate parking
- has beautiful buildings that reflect the local history
- has a cohesive theme; ability to expand
- has no heavy auto traffic; character
- has night light; easy access; growing trees for proficient shadings;

6.6. Wish poem and have poem findings summarized for the Downtown Soledad, California, Urban Design Plan project

6.2.3. PARK Analysis

PARK analysis provides a more systematic approach to the goal-setting process. PARK is an acronym for "Preserve, Add, Remove, Keep out." In this method, participants are encouraged to think about existing conditions and consider what they would like to

- preserve that exists now in the project area and is positive,
- add to the project area that is lacking in the existing conditions,
- remove from the project area that exists now and is negative, and
- keep out of the project area that would be negative for the future of the project area.

Participants in goal-setting activities can use PARK as a framework for evaluating the existing conditions and proposing future directions for the project area (Sanoff 2000). As with the likes and dislikes analysis and wish poems, this method works well if individual participants first develop their own ideas and then share them with members of a small group in a workshop setting. The community designer collects the agreed-upon outcomes from each group and notes them on large-format sheets of paper.

Another acronym-labeled method that has been frequently used in community design processes is SWOT analysis, where SWOT stands for "Strengths, Weaknesses, Opportunities, Threats" and is borrowed from the strategic planning field (Sanoff 2000).

Instruments for PARK Analyses. The common PARK instrument is a single sheet of paper with a simple graph. The left column of the graph bears the letters PARK vertically, and participants write responses in the right column opposite each letter (Figure 6.7). A large-format print is recommended to record the findings from participants as the community designer facilitates the discussion.

Example: During the Downtown Morro Bay, California, Enhancement Plan development process, Cal Poly graduate students conducted a PARK analysis in a community workshop setting under their studio instructors' supervision. Participants were asked to write down their ideas on letter-sized PARK sheets first, and then to read aloud their ideas to a small group of five to eight participants. Once each group of participants agreed on a list of ideas, their spokesperson read the group's results to the entire group of participants. Findings from this exercise were analyzed and used in future steps of the process.

Downtown Morro Bay Enhancement Project (Phase I)
Community Meeting I

Please think of Downtown Morro Bay today.
What do you think about the future of Downtown?

P **preserve** what we have now that is positive	
A **add** what we do not have that is positive	
R **remove** what we have that we would like to remove	
K **keep out** what we do not have that we would like to keep out	

6.7. Sample PARK instrument

6.2.4. Interviews

Interviews afford less formal, more in-depth goal-setting opportunities. They can be conducted either in the field (e.g., street interviews, resident interviews, business owner interviews) or in an activity setting (e.g., a community workshop environment). Interviews oriented toward identifying project goals need to address similar issues as are covered by the likes and dislikes analyses, wish poems, and PARK analyses. Interview questions should therefore focus on identifying those features of the project area that are (1) positive for the residents, that is, those features that are liked, used, attached to, and so forth, and (2) negative for the residents, that is, those features that need improvement, replacement, or change. As in the likes and dislikes analysis, asking participants to specify the top three to five things they would do to better their environment helps identify goals and prioritize them.

The next issue to consider when using interviews for goal setting is whether to use field interviews or activity setting interviews.

Field Interviews. With field interviews, community designers can take the goal-setting process out into the project area and beyond. The advantage of field interviews is that they can be conducted at the participants' convenience. For example, residents and business owners can be visited at a time that works for their schedule. The community designer is also able to spend more time with the respondents and cover issues and opportunities in detail. Street interviews, on the other hand, may be more time-limited since they are conducted spontaneously. The advantage of street interviews is that they give the community designer an opportunity to interview a good cross section of the community. For example, if the first few interviews have been conducted mostly with elderly community members, the community designer may elect to interview younger individuals in the following steps in an effort to get wider coverage of issues.

Activity Setting Interviews. Interviews can also be conducted in the activity setting, that is, the workshop or meeting environment. The advantage of conducting interviews in an activity setting is that distractions can be minimized and in-depth interviews can be conducted. Such interviews, however, are limited to those individuals who can attend the activity, ordinarily individuals who do not have time or distance constraints.

Depending on project objectives and the availability of staff, activity setting interviews can be conducted in focus group format or individually. Focus group interviews typically involve key stakeholders related to the project or its particular aspects. The questions are raised openly with a group of individuals and answers are developed through discussion. Individual interviews, on the other hand, are conducted on a one-to-one basis. While conducting individual interviews with a group of participants can turn out to be more time-consuming, in some cases this format may be advantageous, particularly if controversial issues are involved, since people tend to be more comfortable speaking individually. Focus group interviews, on the other hand, may help identify common goals earlier in the process through cross-pollination of ideas during discussions.

Telephone Interviews. Conducting interviews by phone is another option for the community designer. Phone interviews reduce the need to travel and hence are good for keeping time and budget costs down. On the other hand, phone interviews lack the breadth of a face-to-face interview, during which facial expressions and gestures might give clues to the community designer as to which questions to follow up.

Interview Instruments. Interview instruments are manual or mechanical/digital means of recording. They can be simple question-and-answer sheets on which the interviewer takes notes about the answers received. Mechanical/digital means of recording may involve sound and video recording instruments. While these instruments can record answers with high precision, concerns of privacy and anonymity need to be addressed. Interviewees may be less comfortable being recorded while answering questions. In such cases the community designer must get consent from the interviewees, and may have to guarantee the anonymity of their answers.

Example: During the Downtown Delano, California, Concept Plan development process, the community design team conducted focus group interviews with the participants as a follow-up to the awareness walk. Participants initially formed two groups and discussed their observations from the awareness walk. The issues identified by each group were noted by the community design team facilitators and then shared with the rest of the participants. The activity ended with the entire group of participants discussing and identifying main issues to be covered in the following community workshop. For more information on the Downtown Delano, California, Concept Plan development process, see Chapter 8.

6.2.5. Goal Prioritization Methods in Community Design

A crucial step in the community design process is the prioritization of goals once they are identified. Community members, especially those who have not been through a similar process, need to understand from the beginning that (1) prioritization of goals yields better implementation by narrowing the focus to the most important issues first and (2) it is usually not possible to achieve every single goal, depending on the priorities and resources of the community. To minimize or avoid future frustration on the part of the community members, the community designer should encourage prioritization and provide the direction and the means to achieve it. Two common means of goal prioritization involve numerical and visual methods (discussed below).

Once project goals have been identified, the community designer must facilitate a discussion about their prioritization. The objective of this discussion is to understand the rationale behind community members' prioritization preferences. By hearing the rationale for others' preferences, all community members can make better informed decisions, and it is much more likely they will reach agreement on a list of priorities.

Goal Prioritization Using Numerical Means. In this method, the community members are first asked to prioritize the goals individually. For this, they are given a sheet of paper listing goals and are asked to assign a number reflecting priority (i.e., 1 = first priority, 2 = second priority, etc.). Once the individual participants have finished prioritizing the goals, the sheets are collected and the goals are ranked according to the assigned points. An individual respondent's top-rated goal is assigned the maximum number of points. For example, a goal that has received the first priority from an individual among 10 goals receives 10 points. The second priority receives 9 points, the third priority receives 8 points. The community designer assigns the points and adds them for each goal. As a result, the goal that gets the highest points receives the first priority (Figure 6.8).

GOALS	PRIORITY	POINTS ASSIGNED
GOAL A	5	3
GOAL B	2	6
GOAL C	6	2
GOAL D	1	7
GOAL E	7	1
GOAL F	4	4
GOAL G	3	5

6.8. Sample prioritization sheet for an individual participant. In this example, there are seven goals: the top-rated priority goal is assigned seven points by the community designer, the second priority goal is assigned six points, and so on.

Example: During the Traver, California, Concept Planning process, the community design team asked participants in a workshop setting to prioritize the goals that had been identified by the community members. Participants prioritized the goals individually and then discussed their priorities with the rest of the participants in small groups of five to six. Each small group then agreed on one prioritization of all the goals. These results were communicated to the community design team members, who marked the results on large poster format sheets. Through the point assignment system a single list of goals with priority points was developed. The participants had a final discussion about the list to ensure it paralleled their concerns. The workshop was completed with a single list of goals prioritized by the participants.

Goal Prioritization Using Visual Means. In this method, community members are asked to visually assign priorities to goals. A common way of implementing this method is to provide community members with a number of dot stickers and ask them to assign dots to goals based on their priority for themselves. Project goals identified by the community members are posted on a large-format sheet, and community members are asked to place dot stickers next to goals that are high priority for them.

The number of dot stickers provided varies depending on the extent to which community members need to prioritize the goals. For example, if the community has particularly limited resources, it may be necessary to pick the absolutely crucial goals and focus on them. In such cases community members may be provided with fewer dot stickers than there are goals, and then choose the goals that matter the most.

Another way of encouraging thinking about prioritization is to allow community members to place more than one dot sticker next to the goals they want to prioritize (Figure 6.9).

Whether prioritization is done using numerical or visual means, it is crucial that the process and findings of prioritization activities be thoroughly discussed by the participants so that the outcomes are widely agreed on. Doing so not only builds confidence in the process, it also strengthens the likelihood of success by minimizing potential disagreements that could undermine future steps in the process.

6.9. During the Downtown Soledad, California, Urban Design Plan process participants prioritized project goals using dot stickers.

6.3. METHODS AND INSTRUMENTS FOR STRATEGY IDENTIFICATION

Thinking about strategies to achieve the goals that have been identified and prioritized carries the process one step further and prepares community members for the reality that progression toward goals occurs step by step. The question at this point in the process is, "What paths can we follow to achieve our goals?" Community members are asked what strategies could be followed in the context of their community (given the physical environment, role players, and availability of economic and human resources) to achieve the goals identified. The community designer may follow individual or group methods in asking community members to identify strategies.

6.3.1. Strategy Identification as a Group: Methods and Instruments

As in goal-setting methods, community members are asked to think about strategies individually first, with the floor then opened to a discussion of how likely it is that the identified strategies can achieve the desired goals. Once strategies are identified by individual participants, the community designer asks the participants to read aloud the strategies identified for each goal. The strategies identified are noted on large-format sheets, and the community designer initiates a discussion about the efficacy of each strategy for achieving the intended goals. Based on this discussion, strategies are assigned to goals.

A simple set of instruments to use in the group identification of strategies consists of letter-sized sheets of paper for individual idea generation and large-format sheets or a whiteboard for recording all the group's responses. For each goal identified, letter-sized sheets are provided, with the goal noted at the top and blank spaces for community members to note down identified strategies (Figure 6.10). Large-format sheets are scaled-up versions of the letter-sized sheets for recording the agreed-upon strategies for each goal. For clarity, it is advisable to have one sheet per goal. If the goals can be grouped into themes, color coding the themes will make the steps in the process visually identifiable.

6.3.2. Strategy Identification through Individual Discussion: Methods and Instruments

The community designer may also conduct interviews individually with community members to identify strategies for each goal. Question-and-answer sheets or some other recording instruments are commonly used in individual interviews. The main advantage of conducting personal interviews for strategy identification is that some community members may be more comfortable discussing strategies individually. Furthermore, the interviews can be scheduled at a time convenient for the individual interviewee. Nevertheless, conducting individual interviews is generally more time-consuming than a group-based effort, and the advantages of group discussion and idea generation will not be part of the process unless the community designer conducts an additional round of meetings with individuals to identify commonalities in strategy identification.

6.4. METHODS AND INSTRUMENTS FOR ACTION PLANNING

Action planning is an important step in community design. During action planning, community members and the community designer are forced to think about the real-world implications of the project goals and strategies.

In the action planning process, the community designer asks community members to identify specific action steps that can be taken to realize each strategy and achieve project goals. Depending on the project goals and timeline, details can be added to the action planning process. For example, community members may be asked who or what entity in the community could take the first step for each action. Another detail that can be added to the action planning process is identifying sources of funding. In many cases, funding determines whether or not the project will go forward. Community members may be asked to identify potential funding sources and encouraged to think about possible individuals or entities that could help fund certain actions. Such thinking may yield pleasant surprises. Project participants commanding resources—labor, equipment, or PR knowledge, as well as financial

project name
strategy identification

individual strategy identification

INSTRUCTIONS: PLEASE DEVISE AT LEAST ONE, AT MOST THREE POTENTIAL STRATEGIES FOR ACHIEVING THE GOAL BELOW.

GOAL:
STRATEGIES:
1.
2.
3.

project name
strategy identification

group strategy identification

INSTRUCTIONS FOR THE FACILITATOR: PLEASE DISCUSS THE POTENTIAL STRATEGIES FOR ACHIEVING THE GOAL BELOW, AND SEEK AGREEMENT ON THE TOP THREE STRATEGIES. ONCE FINISHED, LIST THESE STRATEGIES IN THE SPACES PROVIDED.

GOAL:
STRATEGIES:
1.
2.
3.

6.10. Sample strategy identification instrument. Top: instrument for individual idea generation; bottom: instrument for the facilitator

resources—may realize they are in position to take certain actions. Although the discussion is about funding, in the process the community may realize it has resources that could alleviate some of the funding pressures to get certain actions done. Overall, action planning is the process in which the community places a "filter of reality" over the ideas generated in goal setting and strategy identification. This is a healthy discussion that helps community members double-check the viability of their ideas and find solutions to work toward their goals, even if there are limitations.

Instruments for Action Planning. Letter-sized charts for community members to fill in can be used for developing action planning ideas individually.

One action planning sheet is prepared for each project goal, with the goal listed at the top and the strategies listed down the left side. Opposite each strategy are cells allocated to specific actions: the first steps to take, who would take them, and potential funding sources. Depending on the project goals and community context, further action details can be added to this chart (Figure 6.11).

Since action planning encourages community members to identify or even nominate individuals and entities to take concrete steps, this activity should be undertaken as a group. This way the community designer can avoid disagreements that have the potential to escalate because concrete actions are being proposed for specific individuals or entities. Action planning as a group helps community members think thoroughly before identifying individuals or entities that might take action steps. Furthermore, group action planning enhances a feeling of solidarity among community members since at this point, individuals are working on the question, "What specific steps can we take to make these changes in our community?" Such experiences may even encourage individuals or entities with certain resources to step forward and propose allocating these resources to the community's identified goals.

CAL POLY community design

Downtown Delano Concept Plan

a participatory process

ACTION PLANNING FORM GROUP NO:___

GOAL 2: Preserve and enhance activity and walkable character

**** THIS FORM TO BE COMPLETED INDIVIDUALLY****

STRATEGIES	FIRST STEP TOWARD IMPLEMENTATION WHAT WOULD BE AN APPROPRIATE FIRST STEP TO IMPLEMENT THIS STRATEGY?	PERSON[S] TO INITIATE ACTION WHO SHOULD TAKE THE FIRST STEP TO IMPLEMENT THIS STRATEGY?	FUNDING SOURCE[S] WHICH SOURCE[S]WOULD BE BEST TO SUPPORT THE IMPLEMENTATION OF THIS STRATEGY?
Downtown housing			
Making High Street more people friendly			
Preserve Main Street amenities			
Preserve eateries and bank locations			
Street landscaping (medians, street furniture, etc.)			
Diversity of eateries and shopping (preserve and enhance)			
Replace current ways of parking			

6.11. Sample action planning instrument

Example: During the Traver, California, Concept Planning process, an action planning exercise was held following strategy identification in a community workshop setting. Participants were provided with action planning worksheets, each of which identified one project goal and affiliated strategies. The participants were asked to identify action steps to follow each strategy. Specifically, they were asked to identify what steps to take first, potential individuals or institutions to take the first step, and potential funding sources. Once participants identified action steps individually, the results were discussed in small groups of five to six, and group-identified action steps were shared with the rest of the participants. Following the discussion on results from all groups, participants identified the best possible action steps to follow.

6.5. METHODS AND INSTRUMENTS FOR PHYSICAL PLANNING AND DESIGN DECISION MAKING

Translating relatively abstract goals and strategies into physical planning and design decisions helps community members apply a second reality check to their ideas. This process is therefore parallel to action planning in the sense that it encourages community members to consider the limitations and resources of their physical environment regarding the project area. In some cases, action planning may follow the physical planning or design decisions. In the following paragraphs we examine the methods and instruments available to community designers for use in physical planning and design decisions. We start with methods that allow conceptual thinking and move toward methods that encourage more concrete decision making.

6.5.1. Images-of-Life Method

The images-of-life method allows community members to identify planning and design concepts that follow their previous decisions as well as suit the future they are imagining for the project area. In this method, the community designer provides base maps of the project area. Community members sort into small groups of five to eight individuals. (The groups may be larger, though hands-on exercises do not work well in crowded groups.) The groups are then provided with old magazines with many images. Community members are asked to go through these magazines, find images that represent what they have in mind for various parts of the project area, cut out the images, and paste them on the areas of the base map where they think the planning and design concepts illustrated in the images are appropriate. This method triggers conceptual thinking and helps community members think beyond what they already have in mind.

As a result of this exercise each group develops a collage on the base map it was provided. The groups then present their collages to the rest of the community members attending the activity. The community designer initiates a discussion of the collages, during which community members develop awareness about one anothers' ideas. The objective of the method is not to make final decisions but to exchange ideas and expand community members' horizons about the project area's future. The collage discussions are often lively and fun, and they trigger new ideas. Throughout the discussion the community designer notes the ideas, then collects the collages. The design concepts are integrated into a conceptual diagram—a single set of design concepts—for the project area's future, to be discussed in a following meeting.

Instruments for the Images-of-Life Method. The images-of-life method has a simple set of instruments: the base map, old magazines, child-safe scissors (young children may be brought to the activity by their parents), glue, and pens or markers (Figure 6.12). The base map should have sufficient labeling that community members can identify key locations on the project area for purposes of orientation. The images need not be about planning and design specifically. It is, however, important that the exercise connect with community members' day-to-day experiences, so common weekly magazines about quotidian experience—housekeeping, health, travel, lifestyle—are well suited.

6.5.2. Planning Games

Planning games are commonly used in community design processes. Depending on the scale of the project, such games may be prepared with varying levels of specificity. In the case of planning processes, community members are often provided with base maps of the project area; a legend specifying color codes and symbols for land uses, activities, design features, and circulation types; and a drawing-and-coloring kit containing pens and markers. Community members are asked to form small groups of five to eight people. Collaboratively, each group develops an ideal plan scheme, which is then shared with the rest of the community members attending the activity (Figure 6.13).

The community designer asks each group to identify spokespersons (on a voluntary basis) to present the group's ideal plan to the rest of the community members. During the presentation process, idea exchanges are highly encouraged. These discussions are often engaging and fun, and help community members understand each other's concerns and ideas. As in the images-of-life method, the objective of planning games is not to finalize

6.12. The instruments and a typical outcome of the images-of-life method

decisions but to generate and exchange ideas. At the end of the activity the community designer takes the ideal plan schemes and integrates the ideas into a conceptual diagram or a single set of planning concepts.

Instruments for Planning Games. The instruments for planning games include base maps, a legend, and nontoxic (for children) colored pens and markers for drawing, writing, and coloring. The base maps feature should have sufficient labeling to help community members identify key locations on the project area for purposes of orientation. Based on the level of detail reached in previous meetings, the community designer may prepare a legend of land uses, activities, design features, and circulation types that reflect the decisions made to that point. Additionally, it is good practice to provide blank spaces for items that may have been forgotten or that may be proposed by community members during the activity.

6.5.3. Design Games

In the case of smaller scale urban design problems, site-design problems, and architectural design problems, the community designer may introduce more specific ways of making decisions. Design games are often used for this purpose. Design games are similar to planning games but have more variables, such as space limitations. In site-specific design problems and at the scale of architectural design, space limitations may come into the picture (e.g., limited square footage on a site, as opposed to the high square footage developed

Example: During the Downtown Morro Bay, California, Enhancement Plan development process, graduate Cal Poly students conducted a planning game with community members under their studio instructors' supervision. In a community workshop setting, participants were asked to form small groups of five to eight. Each group was provided with a base map of the project area and a legend specifying land uses and circulation options. Each group developed an ideal downtown scheme and presented its agreed-upon scheme to the rest of the participants. Three major schemes were identified. Students developed conceptual diagrams based on the three schemes, to be discussed in the following stages.

6.13. The planning game kit and community members playing the game

by the community members in previous meetings). In such cases the discussion needs to go beyond the locations and interrelationships of land uses and spaces and take space limitations and sizes into consideration. At this point the community designer needs to develop the space or land-use icons proportional to the relative area they would occupy in the available amount of land. Icons must reflect the uses or spaces discussed in the earlier stages of the community design process. Additionally, to help community members visualize the scale and size of spaces they are working on, a grid with cells of known dimensions may need to be superimposed on the base map (e.g., one square on the grid = 100 square feet, etc.) (Figure 6.14).

As in planning games, the community designer asks community members to form small groups of five to eight people. Each group is provided with icons that reflect space uses and activities and a base map. Community members then work collaboratively to develop an ideal design proposal for the project site. In doing so, community members place icons on the base map, making decisions about the interrelationships of and connections between spaces and activities. Since the icons are prepared proportionally, community members need to consider the area allocated for activities, as well as trade-offs in cases of limited space availability on the project site. At the end of this process the community designer asks each group to identify a volunteer spokesperson to present the group's ideal design proposal to the rest of the community members. As in the planning game, proposals usually generate ideas during the discussion. The object of the design game is not to finalize any decisions but to generate and exchange ideas about the future of the project site. At the end of this process, the community designer takes the design proposals and integrates the ideas into a single set of design concepts or a single conceptual diagram.

Instruments for Design Games. The instruments for design games include base maps, icons representing spaces and activities, and scissors and glue. To avoid cutting and pasting, it is advisable to prepare the icons as stickers. In addition, having colored markers and pens available and providing some blank stickers allow the participants to add spaces or activities that may not be addressed by the icons. This precaution also communicates the message that the process is still open to new ideas and that community members are not limited by the instrument.

Example: During the Sandhills, North Carolina, Family Heritage Association Community Center design process, the community design team conducted a design game in a community workshop setting. Based on previously conducted focus group interviews, the community design team prepared a design game kit. The kit included a base map of the project site with a grid superimposed to provide a sense of scale, and icons that represented spaces and their relative sizes (e.g., a library space icon the size of one square, a classroom icon the size of four squares). During the workshop, participants worked in small groups of five to eight, each provided with a design game kit. Each group developed ideal floor plan schemes and shared their scheme with the rest of the participants at the end of the workshop. After the workshop the community design team integrated the schemes into one scheme and conducted a mail survey of the community members to receive feedback. Based on this feedback the plan layout of the community center was clarified.

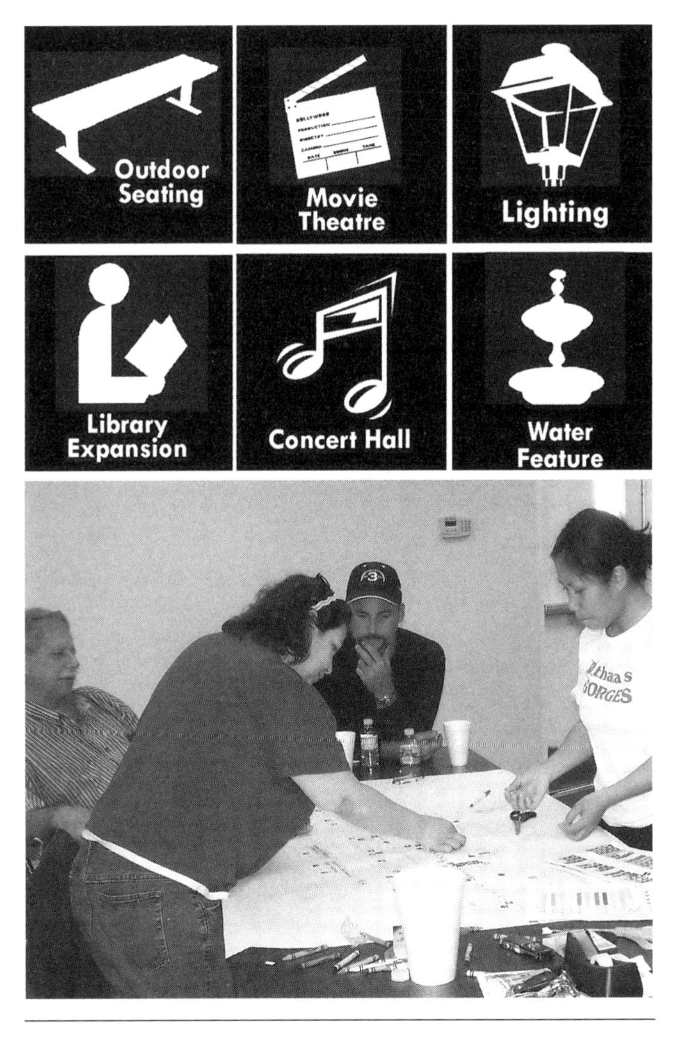

6.14. Top: sample design game kit icons; bottom: community members playing the game

6.5.4. Methods Based on Selecting from among Alternatives

The community designer may also provide alternatives to the community members and ask them to select from among the alternatives. This approach relies heavily on visual stimuli but may also include providing additional written information about the alternatives. For example, a preference survey that asks the participants to identify street lighting types for their community may also provide information about the sizes of lighting types, their uses, and their power consumption levels.

The selection among alternatives method may be limiting when a customized solution is needed for a community. The objective thus should not be to make final decisions about the alternatives provided but to identify tendencies and educate community members about project features that may come up in future meetings. It is important not to make final decisions using a selection among alternatives method. The method may yield "winners and losers" and polarize the community if it is not integrated into a larger discussion. To avoid such outcomes, such methods should always be accompanied by follow-up discussions on the rationale of participants' selections and suggestions for other methods participants can use to expand their contributions. Methods based on selecting from among alternatives may use a survey, poster, or game format.

Survey Format. In the survey format, alternatives are presented to community members on standard sheets of paper with information provided in visuals aids and text. Text should be used only to describe the properties of the alternatives and their advantages and disadvantages for the given problem. While the participants may be asked to select a certain number of alternatives (sometimes only one), prioritizing alternatives based on their properties, advantages, and disadvantages is better handled in the follow-up discussion (Figure 6.15).

Visual Preference Survey. A visual preference survey may be used in conjunction with other techniques to acquire community input about the aesthetic attributes of alternatives (e.g., a residential architecture style). Community members are prompted to rank alternatives with regard to certain attributes on a scale such as the Likert scale. The Likert scale presents options on a topic, and respondents specify to what extent they agree or disagree about each option (Zeisel 2006). For example, the survey may ask how appropriate a certain amount of urban density is for a particular context on a scale of 1 to 5, where 1 is the least appropriate and 5 is the most appropriate (Figure 6.16).

Visual preference surveys should be used with caution because the images provided for evaluation may lead to significant bias in the rating. Since the method is oriented toward ranking visual qualities, little to no textual information is provided. Consequently, community members rely heavily on the visual information communicated through the images. Certain properties of the images presented, therefore, can introduce significant bias in

MADERA RANCHOS AVENUE 12 STREET LIGHTING OPTIONS

Please put a check mark next to the light types that you think are most appropriate for Avenue 12

HEIGHT: around 12ft.

Pedestrian oriented, located on the sidewalk. The purpose is to illuminate the sidewalk. Is not affected by street trees.

HEIGHT: around 16 ft.

Pedestrian oriented, located on the sidewalk. The purpose is to illuminate the sidewalk and the road to a certain extent.

HEIGHT: around 20 ft.

Road oriented, located on the sidewalk. The purpose is to illuminate the road and the sidewalk. Street trees can block its light from illuminating the sidewalk.

HEIGHT: around 26 ft.

Road oriented, located on the sidewalk. The purpose is to illuminate the road. Street trees can block its light from illuminating the sidewalk.

HEIGHT: 30 ft. and higher

Road oriented, located on the median. The purpose is to illuminate the road. Street trees can block its light from illuminating the sidewalk.

6.15. A survey used for street lighting selections in Madera County, California

the ranking of alternatives. For example, the color scheme, the weather, or the presence of greenery or people in the images may influence community members' responses. Various techniques are available to minimize or eliminate such bias. For example, the use of color may be minimized, and images with similar backgrounds may be selected. Nevertheless, the visual preference survey should not be used for decision-making purposes but to understand general visual preferences, to initiate and sustain a discussion, and to expand community members' horizons regarding the available options.

Poster Format. The poster format presents the same information as the survey format but allows the alternative selection or prioritization process to be more interactive. In this method, posters covering the target information are posted in a community activity setting. They are designed so that there is sufficient space on them for the community members to mark their selections. To ensure that participants have equal input, they are provided with a number of dot stickers, the exact number depending on the number of alternatives available (Figure 6.17). Usually participants are given fewer dot stickers than the number of available alternatives and are allowed to allocate as many of those stickers to the alternatives they pick as they wish. For example, if one alternative is very important for one community member, that person might dedicate all her stickers to that alternative.

Much as in the goal prioritization process discussed earlier, during the selection process the activity becomes very interactive. Community members reviewing the alternatives selected start discussing the properties and advantages and disadvantages of each as they wait to provide their input. Consequently, this method communicates to the community members that their participation is not limited to voting or finalizing decisions.

Game Format. The game format provides a fun and visually appealing option for selecting among alternatives. A relatively uncommon method in this format is the "best fit slide rule" (Sanoff 2000). This method comes with a unique instrument, which provides the community members with an elevation view of the existing conditions of a streetscape. The object is to

6.16. A visual preference survey question to be ranked on a scale of 1 to 5

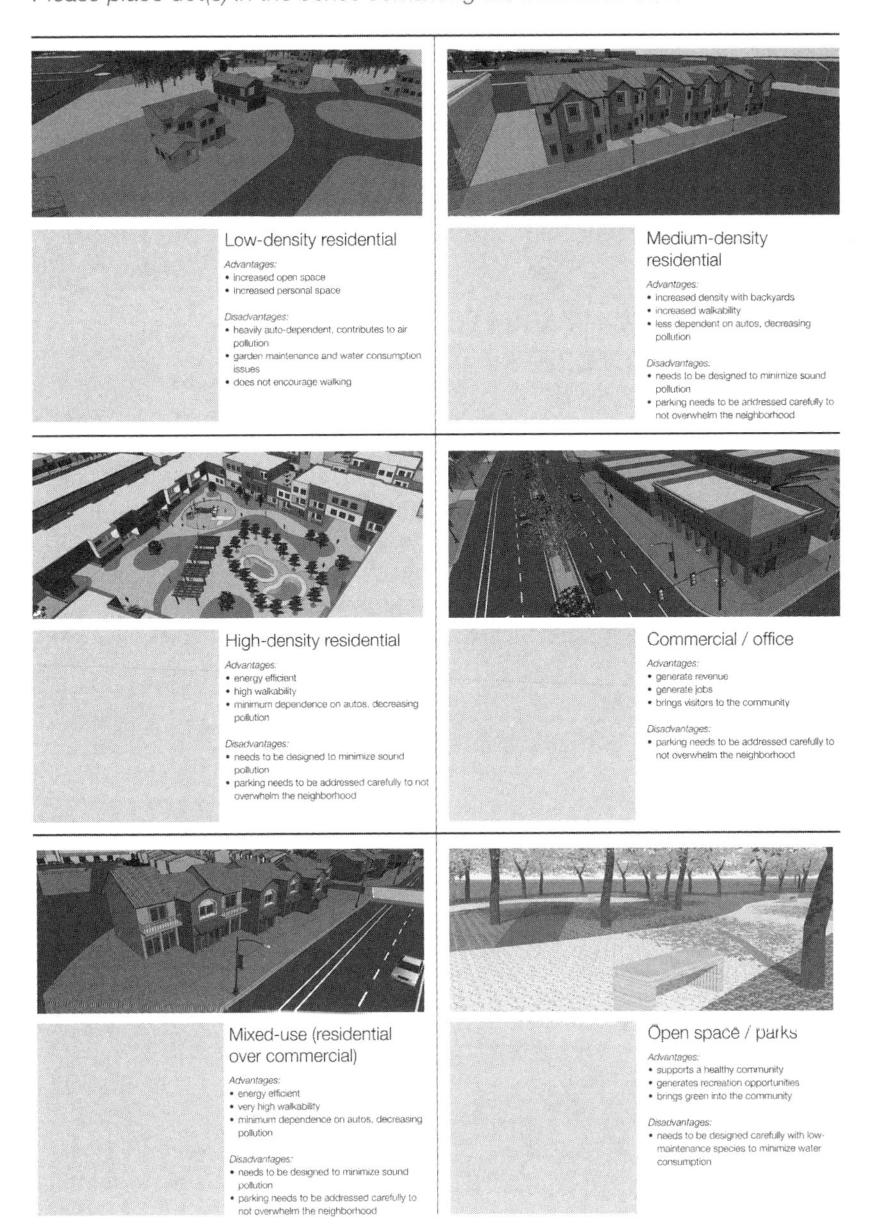

Madera Avenue 12 Concept Plan | Land Use Options
Please place dot(s) in the boxes containing the best Land Uses for Avenue 12
Low-density residential
Advantages:
• increased open space
• increased personal space
Disadvantages:
• heavily auto-dependent, contributes to air pollution
• garden maintenance and water consumption issues
• does not encourage walking
Medium-density residential
Advantages:
• increased density with backyards
• increased walkability
• less dependent on autos, decreasing pollution
Disadvantages:
• needs to be designed to minimize sound pollution
• parking needs to be addressed carefully to not overwhelm the neighborhood
High-density residential
Advantages:
• energy efficient
• high walkability
• minimum dependence on autos, decreasing pollution
Disadvantages:
• needs to be designed to minimize sound pollution
• parking needs to be addressed carefully to not overwhelm the neighborhood
Commercial / office
Advantages:
• generate revenue
• generate jobs
• brings visitors to the community
Disadvantages:
• parking needs to be addressed carefully to not overwhelm the neighborhood
Mixed-use (residential over commercial)
Advantages:
• energy efficient
• very high walkability
• minimum dependence on autos, decreasing pollution
Disadvantages:
• needs to be designed to minimize sound pollution
• parking needs to be addressed carefully to not overwhelm the neighborhood
Open space / parks
Advantages:
• supports a healthy community
• generates recreation opportunities
• brings green into the community
Disadvantages:
• needs to be designed carefully with low-maintenance species to minimize water consumption

6.17. A poster used for alternative selections in Madera County, California

have the community members think about the alternatives that could infill a vacant parcel on the streetscape or replace an existing building. In either case, the parcel considered for an alternative treatment is cut out of the existing streetscape. On a separate worksheet, the alternatives considered for the parcel are provided. Community members can use these two sheets to consider and compare alternatives for the parcel by putting the alternatives sheet behind the existing streetscape sheet and moving the alternatives (Figure 6.18).

Table 6.1 provides a comparative analysis of these community design stages, methods, and instruments.

6.6. EMERGING VISUALIZATION TECHNIQUES FOR COMMUNITY DESIGNERS

The sophisticated image editing and three-dimensional modeling software that has come onto the market over the past two decades has made rendering design and plan decisions fast and easy. The improved quality and features are especially noticeable when one compares plan proposals and documents from the 1980s and 1990s with those made using today's software. Contemporary plan proposals and documents not only are visually more appealing, they are more communicative than their predecessors. Advances in computer-based techniques for diagramming and plan drawing

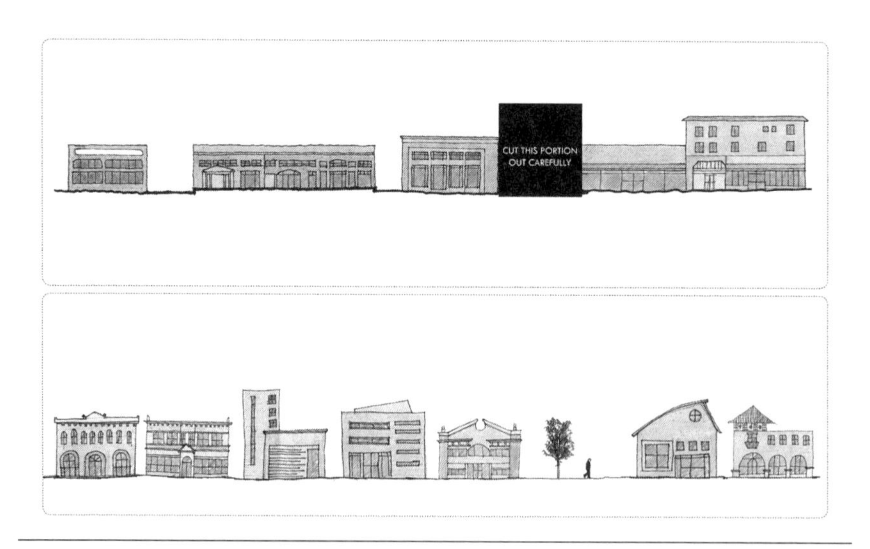

6.18. A "best-fit slide rule" instrument prepared for San Luis Obispo, California (based on Sanoff 1979). Once the black area is cut out, the options on the lower strip can be placed under the upper strip to review the possibilities.

COMMUNITY DESIGN: STAGES, METHODS, INSTRUMENTS

STAGES	METHODS	INSTRUMENTS
PRELIMINARY EXPLORATION	Awareness walk Awareness camera Awareness walk on community members' own time	Route maps Note taking instruments Cameras
GOAL SETTING	Likes / dislikes analysis Wish / have poems "PARK" analysis Interviews Goal prioritization	Note taking instruments Wish / have poem worksheets / posters PARK worksheets / posters Interview instruments Wish / have poem/ PARK Posters / sticker dots
STRATEGY IDENTIFICATION	Group strategy identification Individual strategy identification	Note taking instruments Group strategy identification worksheet Individual strategy identification worksheet Note taking posters
ACTION PLANNING	Action planning exercise	Note taking instruments Action planning worksheet Note taking posters
PHYSICAL PLANNING / DESIGN DECISION MAKING	Images of life Planning games Design games Selecting from alternatives	Old magazines, Scissors, glue Markers / crayons Planning / Design game icon stickers Planning / Design game base maps Alternative posters, Sticker dots Alternative surveys

Table 6.1. Comparative analysis of community design stages, methods, and instruments

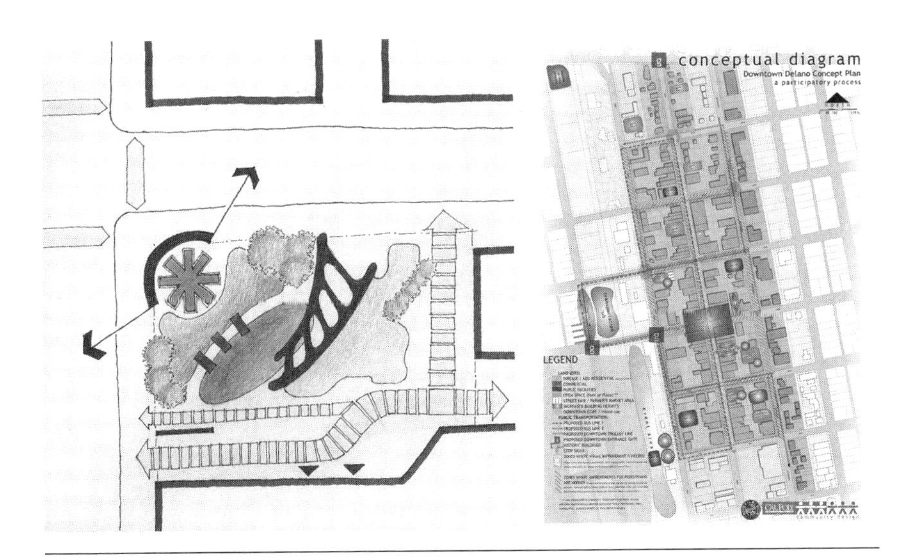

6.19. Conceptual diagrams can be formatted differently for different projects. Left: hand-rendered conceptual diagram developed for a small site; right: computer-rendered conceptual diagram summarizing options for downtown Delano, California

especially have made two-dimensional means of communication much more effective than earlier versions. Diagrams and plans in contemporary plan documents are, in many cases, a lot more understandable and intuitive, thanks to the wide variety of colors, patterns, and other options available.

The implications of new visualization techniques for community design processes must be carefully evaluated, however. The very precision afforded by these new techniques during the community design process can be a pitfall. A hand-drawn conceptual diagram easily communicates that the decision-making process is in an early stage and the situation is still fluid. A computer-generated conceptual diagram based on the exact same ideas, however, may give the impression that decisions have been made and the changes proposed are inevitable (Figure 6.19). If community members get such an impression, it may be very challenging to continue the process.

This risk may be amplified when image editing and computer-based three-dimensional modeling enter the picture. The conventional artist's rendering created through freehand sketching is familiar to people without any planning or design expertise. It communicates an imagined future, and people have a certain level of comfort with it. The same imagery can also be created with high levels of precision and realism using contemporary three-dimensional modeling and image editing software (Figure 6.20). Computer-based three-dimensional modeling may have similar implications. Using such software, one can easily recreate the existing conditions of a physical environment and alter it according to plan or design proposals (Figure 6.21).

Such computer-based visualization techniques also bring unique advantages previously unavailable to planners and designers. First, local governments can review design proposals with precision, and their physical implications can be clarified prior to construction. Second, plan and design scenarios may be rendered for different points of future development, allowing community

6.20. Left: rendering generated through freehand sketching; right: rendering developed using three-dimensional modeling and image editing software.

6.21. The existing conditions and altered version of an urban context to communicate proposed changes

Example: A three-dimensional computer model was developed for downtown San Luis Obispo, California, by the author. The object was to develop a highly precise model, one the city of San Luis Obispo could use to test various design proposals received. Using high-resolution aerial photography, GIS data, and computer-aided design software, a highly precise model was developed. The model (Figure 6.22) is now being used by the city in review processes.

6.22. Computer-based three-dimensional model of downtown San Luis Obispo, California

members to clearly understand the phases and the speed of the proposed changes. Finally, by easily making multiple views and walk-through animations of plan and design proposals, the community designer can communicate the ideas proposed by community members and their implications efficiently.

Ultimately, the community designer needs to follow the rapid developments in visualization techniques closely and identify potential risks for the community design process. The key point is that such new techniques must be used to support the participatory decision-making process. If used without such considerations, these techniques have the potential to undermine the community design process rather than facilitate it.

6.7. FINALIZING THE PLAN OR DESIGN PROPOSAL AND DEVELOPING THE PROPOSAL DOCUMENT

After the participatory decision-making process the community designer puts together the design or plan proposal. In the proposal, the ideas, recommendations, and comments provided by the community members are integrated into a single plan. A three-step process is recommended for finalizing the design proposal: proposal development, community review, and document development.

The plan or design proposal must cover a certain amount of information to demonstrate how it has been developed. Therefore, the community designer must ensure that the proposal clearly documents the existing conditions in the project area, as well as the methods and results of the participatory decision-making process. After a description of the participatory process and the methods used, the proposal presents the input received from the community members, including project goals, accompanying strategies, proposed action steps, and design concepts. This presentation gives the proposal credibility in the eyes of the community and provides community members with an invaluable record of their participation in the decision-making process. The proposal statement also notes how the input received from the community members has been integrated into the proposal. Finally, the plan or design proposal must incorporate the rationale for the proposed changes, providing the underlying reasons and community connections for each proposed idea. It is also advisable to include community design activity outputs (e.g., conceptual diagrams developed through design games, activity photographs, etc.) as appendixes to the proposal document.

Once the proposal is ready, a review by the community members is usually requested by the leading group. This review is educational for the community designer and allows community members to voice their concerns if any part of the proposal needs additional review. After the community review, the plan or design proposal document is finalized and presented to the community.

Despite all outreach efforts, it is usual for some community members to comment on the plan or design proposal after it is finalized. Moreover, it is not unusual for these comments to be negative or for community members to request modifications. At this point, it is up to the leading group to request an extension of the project to address these comments. In many cases the members of the leading group do not receive such requests positively because of limited time, limited resources, or the extensive effort already invested in the project. This is one of the reasons why the proposal document must clearly describe the participatory decision-making process, the input provided by the community members, and how the input was incorporated into the final document. The better this documentation is, the stronger the case of the proposal will be. A sample proposal document outline is provided in Table 6.2.

Sample Proposal Document Outline
1. Introduction
2. Existing conditions
3. The participatory decision-making process
4. Input provided by the community (project goals, strategies, actions, design concepts)
5. Implications of community input for proposal development
6. Plan or design proposal and rationale
7. Appendixes: Community design activity output

Table 6.2. Sample proposal document outline

Example: During its Community 2050 visioning process, the San Luis Obispo Council of Governments (SLOCOG) asked the author to develop computer-based three-dimensional models of two local communities. One major urban corridor was modeled for each of the two communities to demonstrate existing conditions. In addition, for each community, three other models were developed to demonstrate how these corridors would look in 2020, 2035, and 2050 if smart growth principles were followed (Figure 6.23). From each model still shots and walk-through animations were generated by the author. SLOCOG used these still shots and walk-through animations to inform participants and receive feedback in a variety of community workshops throughout the Community 2050 planning process.

6.23. Samples of still shots of a local community in 2008 and 2050, as developed for SLOCOG by the author

7 Community Design Activity Formats

The community designer needs to make decisions about the formats of planned participatory decision-making activities when starting a project. Like community design methods, the activity formats available to the community designer have strengths and weaknesses depending on the project area, context, the community, and the resources available. In this chapter we look at community design activity formats and the appropriateness of the community design methods described earlier for one or another activity format.

Overall, community design activity formats are of two types: workshop- or meeting-type formats and informal formats. Workshop- or meeting-type formats include interactive workshops, booth-based workshops, informative/reactive meetings, and charrettes. Informal formats include the planned street presence, the on-the-spot street presence, and the plan van gathering.

7.1. WORKSHOP AND MEETING FORMATS

Workshops and meetings provide an organized, formal environment for community design activities. Their main advantage is that community members can focus exclusively on the community design issues discussed. However, workshops and meetings must be organized at optimal times to maximize attendance. One of the challenges associated with these formats is that there will always be community members who will not be able to attend.

7.1.1. Interactive Workshop

The interactive workshop format is commonly used in community design. The workshop starts with a description of the process and the introduction of the leading group, the community designer, and the participants. After the introductions, the activities planned for the day begin. The interactive workshop format tends to promote an informal, comfortable environment. Therefore, the format is useful in almost all phases of the "V" process: goal setting, strategy identification, action planning, and physical planning and design decision making.

Workshop Organization and Spatial Arrangement. Interactive workshops work well with participants organized into small groups of five to eight persons. The small-group format affords greater opportunity for all participants to express their opinions. All communities have individuals who are outspoken, comfortable with expressing their opinions, or relatively quiet. By splitting the participants into smaller groups, the community designer can ensure that participants get higher chances of voicing their opinions than that of an organization where a large group of people needs to wait for each other to talk. The small-group format also has some logistical advantages. For example, when design games are anticipated, a larger group would need a physically larger base map, a larger table to work at, and so on.

In interactive workshops the community designer will have to have a team of facilitators to help manage each group of participants and facilitate the discussion. This is very important, for if participants are forced to select their own facilitator, those unwilling to facilitate or those who tend to dominate the discussion may end up as facilitators.

Organizing small groups around tables works well. To ensure a comfortable, more interactive environment, a hierarchical physical layout, such as one using a stage or a podium, should be avoided. As facilitators work with participant groups, the community designer walks among tables and ensures that questions are answered.

Interactive community workshops should not take more than two hours. In workshops longer than two hours participants start to lose focus or leave. Interactive community workshops work well with a variety of methods and instruments: likes and dislikes analyses, wish poems, PARK analyses, interviews, goal prioritization activities, group strategy identification activities, action planning activities, images-of-life activities, and planning and design games.

Example: During the Madera County, California, Avenue 12 Concept Plan development process, interactive community workshops were held. The workshops were organized in the large local high school cafeteria space. Participants sat at round tables in small groups, and the community design team facilitated the discussion at each table throughout the exercises. Overall, an informal atmosphere was encouraged and formal presentations were avoided.

7.1.2. Booth-Based Workshop Format

Booth-based workshops tend to be used for projects in which large amounts of project-specific, technical information need to be conveyed to participants. Examples of such data are traffic and transportation engineering–related information or scientific information related to the natural environment and climate. Therefore, the interaction is mostly one-way. These workshops are organized so that participants first receive technical information about a number of topics on the project, then respond to questions or select from among alternatives. The workshop starts with an introduction of the process, the leading group, the community designer, and the participants. Following the introductions the planned activities are undertaken. Typically, participant groups visit different stations or booths to learn different kinds of information about the project and to provide input on a variety of issues. At the end of this process a recap or summary session concludes the workshop.

The booth-based workshop format may be useful in the earlier stages of the "V" process, when the project participants need to learn technical information so that they can respond to questions in early stages of the process, as well as participate in decision making in future phases. Thus, booth-based workshops work well in preliminary exploration, goal setting, and strategy identification.

Workshop Organization and Spatial Arrangement. In booth-based workshops the information that needs to be communicated in many cases will need to be organized into topics. Therefore, facilitators should be available at each booth to interact with participants, and the participants will need to divide up into smaller groups, with multiple booths visited simultaneously. The size of participant groups depends on the total number of participants, the nature of the technical information, and the number of booths. Generally, however, it is safe to say that as participant numbers exceed 10, the time needed to communicate all the information and answer and discuss questions will increase.

The information booths should be adequately dispersed in the available space so that participant groups can move from booth to booth comfortably. Another consideration in spacing information booths is the noise generated at each booth. Individuals at one booth should not be distracted by noise or conversation at other booths. The displays, interaction tools, and input instruments should be designed so that participants can easily understand and respond to them. As participants visit booths, the community designer walks around the booths and makes sure all questions are answered.

Like interactive workshops, booth-based community workshops should not take longer than approximately two hours. Participants may start to lose focus or may have to leave when workshops take longer than two hours. Booth-based community workshops work well with a variety of methods and instruments: preliminary exploration activities (e.g., the presentation of technical information), likes and dislikes analyses, goal prioritization activities, and group strategy identification activities.

Example: During the Climate Action Planning Process for the City of San Luis Obispo, California, students organized booth-based community workshops under the supervision of their studio instructor. The subject matter of the planning process required the communication of technical information in certain instances. The booth-based workshop format helped the students provide participants with information while receiving feedback about their proposed climate action plan concepts.

7.1.3. Informative/Reactive Meeting Format

The informative/reactive meeting format is commonly utilized by local government bodies around the United States. The familiar public hearings employ this format. The meeting features two types of information flow: first, a one-way, formal presentation from presenters to the audience; and second, a two-way interaction, as individuals in the audience respond to the presenters, who provide additional remarks. Through this process the presenters hear what the audience members like or dislike about the content of the presentation. Decision making, however, in most cases remains limited to the presenters' side. Beyond local governments, this format is sometimes used in community design processes to present the work accomplished to date and elicit feedback from the audience. The format is not designed for participatory decision making, though it does allow interested parties to receive information and provide feedback about the topic under consideration. As a result, the format can be useful closer to the presentation phases, such as to present and review a plan or design proposal already prepared.

Meeting Organization and Spatial Arrangement. Informative/reactive meetings have a formal organization, both socially and spatially. The presenters, either local government representatives, public sector planners, or designer(s) who are proposing the project, are assigned one side of the meeting space, typically an area equipped with a stage, a microphone, and a projection screen. The audience occupies the other side of the space in rows of chairs facing the presenters. In between the two areas it is common to see a second microphone and an area for individuals to stand up and address the presenters.

After the presentation of project ideas the audience is invited to provide feedback. Typically the audience members are allowed to provide input individually, introducing themselves and using the microphone to comment or ask questions.

The informative/reactive meeting format does not lend itself well to most community design methods because of the limited interaction possibilities. It is most commonly used by local government bodies for public hearings. Although it is not advisable, this format has been employed in certain community design processes. The community designer or team presents for about one hour, and input is solicited after the presentation. For community design purposes this format lacks genuine participatory decision making and promotes an "us versus them" dynamic.

7.1.4. Charrette Format

The charrette format has become increasingly popular in the past two decades. The term refers to a collaborative decision-making activity compressed into two or three days. The community design team arrives at the project location and is assigned space to conduct interactive meetings, make presentations, and develop planning and design proposals. The space assigned to the community design team should be large enough to accommodate these activities.

The charrette may begin with a preliminary exploration activity such as an awareness walk. The main emphasis at the beginning of the charrette, however, is on community members' knowledge and opinions about the existing conditions of the project area. During the first day of the charrette the community design team to a large extent hears from the community members. Toward the end of the day community members leave, and the community design team launches into an intense process of preparing plan and design proposals for the project area. The team includes specialists in planning, urban design, architecture, landscape architecture, and computer-based and hand rendering of planning and design concepts. Through this intense process the community design team crafts a series of proposals that offer solutions for problems, design ideas, and planning ideas. The following day the community members return to discuss the proposals and provide feedback. The community design team integrates this feedback into the plan or design proposal at the end of the charrette.

The charrette format can therefore be employed for goal-setting, strategy identification, and design concept development. Because of the compressed schedule, however, it is challenging to explore action planning and conduct planning and design games. For decision making related to the physical environment, the process is conceptual, and planning and design concepts tend to be created by the community design team rather than by the community members. In this sense, the charrette format has a reactive character in relation to design or plan concept development.

Charrette Organization and Spatial Arrangement. The charrette format is heavily dependent on the community design team's ongoing work and community members' feedback. The charrette environment therefore needs to accommodate professionals working together, professionals discussing ideas with community members, and community members reviewing professionals' work. Spatially, these different activities translate into a work area, a meeting area, and a presentation area. Spaces that offer flexible arrangements are especially useful for the charrette format. During the charrette, various presentations and discussions are undertaken. Therefore, the community design team may choose to reorganize the community members several times throughout the process according to the task at hand.

As a result of the limited time and compressed decision-making processes, charrettes are likely to employ community design methods that can yield results in relatively short periods of time. Likes and dislikes analyses, PARK analyses, goal prioritization, and group strategy identification are among the methods that may be used in charrettes. Additionally, toward the end of the charrette, to receive timely feedback from the participants, poster format methods that allow participants to select from among alternatives may be preferred.

A principal disadvantage of the charrette format is that it requires the community designer to become familiar with the project context within a brief time frame. This is augmented by the fact that decision making is limited to a highly compressed process of community involvement and alternatives development. Therefore, charrettes should ideally be supported by other activities. The lack of additional activities may lead to oversimplified problem definitions and generic solutions that do not respond to community members' input.

Example: The author visited a charrette while it was being held for downtown Salinas, California, on the project site. The firm hired for the process had a presence of about 15 staff members conducting the charrette. The community design team arrived on the site and met with community members. Following discussions with the community members, staff generated plan ideas for the project site and asked for feedback from the community members. A large-scale physical massing model of the project area was also constructed in the charrette space for community members to provide better informed feedback.

7.2. INFORMAL FORMATS

Despite intense outreach and scheduling efforts, it may not be possible for some community members to attend community design activities. Informal community activity formats allow the process to reach those who cannot attend the formal activities. By setting up booths at community events or interviewing community members on the street or in their homes, the community designer can reach those who cannot make it to formal community design activities.

7.2.1. Planned Street Presence

Many communities have organized outdoor events and street events such as farmers markets, festivals, and street fairs. Such events provide the community designer with excellent opportunities to conduct outreach and receive input from community members about the project.

Planned Street Presence Organization and Spatial Arrangement. In this format, working with the local organizers, the community design team organizes a booth or a stand. Using the methods appropriate for the community design process phase, the community design team gathers input from community members or informs the community about upcoming community design activities. A planned street presence works best when it is organized in conjunction with a workshop or a meeting in the larger scheme of a community design project.

A planned street presence works very well in all phases of the community design process: goal setting, strategy identification, action planning, and physical planning and design decision making. The informal and fun environment also supports many community design methods and instruments, such as likes and dislikes analyses, wish poems, PARK analyses, interviews, goal prioritization activities, individual strategy identification activities, action planning activities, images-of-life activities, and planning and design games.

The booth or stand prepared for a planned street presence must feature a visually distinct presentation to attract community members' attention. Posters, displays, and flyers that inform community members about the process are highly recommended. Finally, the booth or stand must have a sufficient number of community design team members to engage all community members interested.

Example: During the Downtown Morro Bay, California, Enhancement Plan development process, Cal Poly graduate students set up a booth at the local farmers market under their studio instructors' supervision. The objective of the booth was to inform community members of the upcoming community design process and receive initial feedback. The students conducted wish poem/have poem exercises with individuals and groups that visited their booth. Each visitor was also invited to upcoming community workshops. Throughout the process the atmosphere was informal and friendly. Valuable information was gathered from the visitors, and the booth's help with outreach was demonstrated by the strong turnout in following community workshops.

7.2.2. On-the-spot Street Presence

Distinct from a planned street presence, an on-the-spot street presence entails the community design team going to the project area to gather input on a busy day. The design team members can use a number of instruments to gather input from community members.

On-the-Spot Street Presence Organization and Spatial Arrangement. The community designer picks a day and time of the day that is very busy with community members pursuing their day-to-day activities, such as a grocery store on a weekend. The community design team gets permission from local business owners and sets up a small table, booth, or stand. Using the methods appropriate for the community design process phase, the community design team gathers input from community members and informs visitors about upcoming community design activities. Like a planned street presence, an on-the-spot street presence works best when organized in conjunction with a workshop or meeting in the larger scheme of a community design project.

The on-the-spot street presence works well in all phases of the community design process: goal setting, strategy identification, action planning, and physical planning and design decision making. The informal atmosphere supports many community design methods and instruments, such as likes and dislikes analyses, wish poems, PARK analyses, interviews, goal prioritization activities, individual strategy identification activities, action planning activities, images-of-life activities, and planning and design games. One advantage of this format is that community design team members can also walk around the area, conducting interviews and inviting community members to visit the community design table.

The community design table (stand, booth) used for an on-the-spot street presence must be visually distinct to attract community members' attention. Posters, displays, and handouts that inform about the process are highly recommended. As in a planned street presence, the table should be staffed by a sufficient number of community design team members to interact with all community members interested.

Example: During the Downtown Soledad, California, Urban Design Plan Development process, Cal Poly undergraduate students set up an on-the-spot desk in the project area under their studio instructor's supervision. The location selected for the booth was in front of a busy supermarket, and the time chosen was a Saturday afternoon. The desk featured inviting posters on both sides. The students conducted wish poem/have poem exercises with their visitors and invited them to the upcoming community workshops. The students received valuable information from their visitors, which was instrumental in the following community workshops.

7.2.3. Plan Vans

A relatively less known format is the plan van. Coined by Daniel Iacofano in 2001, the term "plan van" refers to the community design team visiting several locations in and around the project area to gather on-the-spot input from community members. In this sense the format is not very different from that of the on-the-spot street presence except that a van decorated to reflect the process is used for transportation. There are two distinct advantages of this format. First, with the decorated vehicle, the community design team can attract extra attention: it is unusual for planners and designers to approach community members this way, and it makes the activity fun and friendly. Second, in a vehicle, the community design team can visit several locations in one day, increasing the opportunities to receive input.

Plan Van Organization and Spatial Arrangement. Using a plan van requires extra time and economic resources. The community design team needs to arrange for the vehicle and its decoration in advance. When in action, the community design team should go to popular locations during busy periods. Tables, informative posters, and handouts should be available during activities. Plan van activities work best when used in conjunction with other community design activity formats throughout the project process.

Plan vans work very well in all phases of the community design process: goal setting, strategy identification, action planning, and physical planning and design decision making. Their informal atmosphere supports many community design methods and instruments, such as likes and dislikes analyses, wish poems, PARK analyses, interviews, goal prioritization activities, individual strategy identification activities, action planning activities, images-of-life activities, and planning and design games.

Table 7.1 provides a comparative analysis of these community design activity formats in terms of their organization, timing, and spatial arrangement.

	ACTIVITY FORMAT	ORGANIZATION
WORKSHOP / MEETING FORMATS	INTERACTIVE WORKSHOP FORMAT	Small groups of participants (5-8 people) complete community design activities for idea generation and decisin making.
	BOOTH-BASED WORKSHOP FORMAT	Small groups of participants (5-8 people) visit information booths to receive technical information and provide input about decisions.
	INFORMATIVE/REACTIVE MEETING FORMAT	Presenters relay information to participants through presentations. Participants then provide feedback formally through microphone.
	CHARRETTE FORMAT	Professionals work on plan / design proposals in a venue open to public. Public provides feedback through interactive meetings.
INFORMAL FORMATS	PLANNED STREET PRESENCE	Community design team has a booth at a planned community event such as a farmers' market. Through a variety of methods they seek input about people's wishes, etc.
	ON-THE-SPOT STREET PRESENCE	Community design team forms a booth in front of a busy location in the community. Through a variety of methods they seek input about people's wishes, etc.
	PLAN VAN	Community design team parks a decorated van in front of a busy location in the community. Through a variety of methods they seek input about people's wishes, etc.

Table 7.1. Comparative analysis of community design activity formats in respect to organization, timing, and spatial arrangement

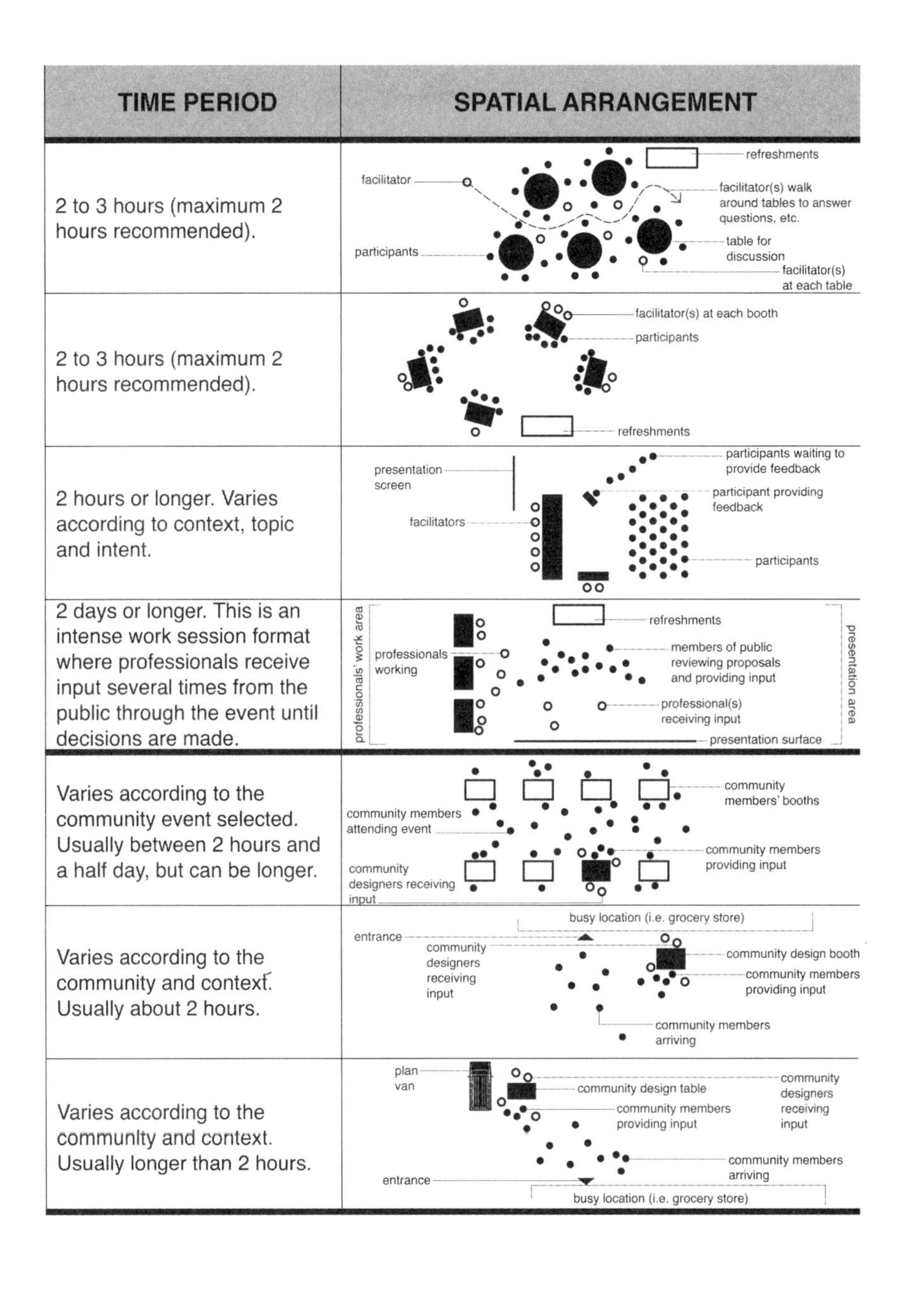

TIME PERIOD	SPATIAL ARRANGEMENT
2 to 3 hours (maximum 2 hours recommended).	refreshments facilitator facilitator(s) walk around tables to answer questions, etc. participants table for discussion facilitator(s) at each table
2 to 3 hours (maximum 2 hours recommended).	facilitator(s) at each booth participants refreshments
2 hours or longer. Varies according to context, topic and intent.	presentation screen participants waiting to provide feedback participant providing feedback facilitators participants
2 days or longer. This is an intense work session format where professionals receive input several times from the public through the event until decisions are made.	professionals' work area refreshments presentation area professionals working members of public reviewing proposals and providing input professional(s) receiving input presentation surface
Varies according to the community event selected. Usually between 2 hours and a half day, but can be longer.	community members' booths community members attending event community members providing input community designers receiving input
Varies according to the community and context. Usually about 2 hours.	busy location (i.e. grocery store) entrance community designers receiving input community design booth community members providing input community members arriving
Varies according to the community and context. Usually longer than 2 hours.	plan van community design table community designers receiving input community members providing input community members arriving entrance busy location (i.e. grocery store)

Example: During the City of Delano, California, Strategic Plan development process, Cal Poly undergraduate students conducted a plan van activity under the supervision of their studio instructors. A Saturday afternoon was selected for the activity. The plan van, decorated with posters advertising the project, was parked in front of one of the busiest supermarkets in the city. The students' presence was announced in the supermarket and residents were invited to visit the plan van. Tables with planning game kits were set up around the van (Figure 7.1). The students conducted planning games and interviewed their visitors throughout the process. Valuable information as well as resident positions on land uses and their locations was obtained from the activity.

7.1. The plan van used during the activity conducted by Cal Poly undergraduate students in Delano, California

PART 4
COMMUNITY DESIGN SCALES

The previous parts of this book presented the social and historical background of community design and introduced activity formats, methods, and instruments useful in different phases of the community design process. In Part 4 these methods and activities are applied to planning projects of different scales, moving outward from the scale of urban design and planning to the larger scale of community planning, encompassing an entire town or city, to regional planning. Then we turn the optics around and look at the smallest scale discussed in the book, site-specific or architectural design. Each chapter in this part discusses one project scale and presents examples of community design processes for projects at that scale.

We start this discussion at the scale of urban design in Chapter 8. Urban design provides a canvas on which relationships between methods, activities, and formats and their outcomes can be demonstrated easily and clearly. We expand to the community planning scale in Chapter 9 and discuss the use of community design methods, activities, and formats in the development of plans for entire neighborhoods, towns, and cities. At this scale the numbers and kinds of role players tend to be different from what is seen at the urban design scale, and the geographic area covered by the plan is larger. In Chapter 10 we expand the scale to regional-level processes. As the geographic area covered in these processes broadens and the number of individuals affected by their outcomes grows, the community design methods, activities, and formats employed may change.

In Chapter 11 we shrink the project scale to the site-specific or architectural design scale. Initiators of projects tend to be conscious of the fact that people who stand to be affected by the process should be involved, and therefore they are open to the idea of community design. Site-specific or architectural design scale projects, however, tend to have smaller numbers of project initiators, such as the owner institution of a project site. Consequently, even if the project were likely to affect a larger number of individuals, such initiators may prefer decision making with no or minimal involvement of the people plausibly most affected.

The chapters in Part 4 examine the implications of project scale for community design processes. Each chapter discusses these implications and presents case studies to demonstrate the use of community design methods, activities, and formats for the project scale under consideration.

8 Participatory Decision Making at the Urban Design Scale

To discuss the application of community design methods, activities, and formats to urban design processes, we need to understand urban design scale. *Urban design scale* is the basic scale at which to explore the relationships among the elements of the physical urban environment: how a building relates to neighboring buildings, to the street, to the sidewalk; how a bench relates to moving pedestrian and vehicular traffic and to people's interactions patterns; how a street light relates to the safety and security of an area, to the pedestrian, and so on. *Urban design* is the process of shaping the built environment by molding public space, private space, or both:

> Urban design focuses on the public realm, the quantity and workability of the public spaces that connect and engage buildings and other activities (some may occur on private property), at all scales. Urban design addresses the whole of these places, how they look and how they work as the continuum of experience for the citizens who depend on them to connect with each other and with the activities that make up daily life. (Dobbins 2009, 2)

The object of the urban design process, therefore, is to help shape the development of public urban space within a set of guidelines and codes. The guidelines and codes may affect the very surfaces of and objects in public spaces, such as the shape of, and materials composing, sidewalks, benches, streetlights, and pavement. Or they may affect the shape of objects and buildings on private property so that these objects connect to the rest of the physical environment. The guidelines and codes are written so that when individual buildings are designed, placed, and used accordingly, a particular urban atmosphere—social, visual, and economic—results.

Since urban design processes shape public space, it is critical that those who will be affected by them are involved in decision making. Community participation in urban design, therefore, is particularly important for the definition of the desired atmosphere. This chapter discusses how the concept of community design, its methods, activities, and formats, can be instrumental in urban design.

8.1. PROJECT DESCRIPTION AND PROJECT AREA IDENTIFICATION

The level of detail targeted in urban design processes varies. Depending on the project objectives and the social, historical, and economic background of the area, urban design plans can provide guidance on one or more of the following topics: land use, circulation, open space structure, and design guidelines or form-based codes. Beyond these topics, urban design plans can also provide guidance on public and private signage, landscaping, vegetation, street lighting, and the placement of street furniture such as benches, trash receptacles, and planters. Which of these or other details need to be covered in an urban design plan? This is one of the two initial questions the community designer faces when tackling an urban design problem: project description.

The level of detail targeted in an urban design process may also influence the project area identification. The leading group that requests the project may not have a clear idea of the boundaries of the project area. For example, the boundaries of a "neighborhood" may be defined differently by people who live in the neighborhood and by people who have only heard about it. In such cases the project area needs to be identified with community members. It may need to be construed further according to time and budget limitations, as well as the level of detail targeted.

The process begins with the leading group. Once it requests the project, the community designer works with the leading group to develop a list of individuals or organizations that should be contacted to start the outreach process. While the initial outreach effort is being conducted, the people on the list may also be asked to provide additional contacts who they think should be involved in the process. By this means a wider group is reached.

An early awareness walk (section 6.1.1) of the general project vicinity by the initial set of contacts and the leading group, followed by individual or focus group interviews, is highly advisable for project description and identification of the project area. The leading group members have project area boundaries in mind, but an awareness walk will better define them. Seeing the project area in person and as part of a group (especially one comprising individuals who joined the process as a result of outreach efforts) can help clarify ideas and lead to modifications of the initially envisioned project area.

The project description can similarly be clarified by this first set of activities. The awareness walk, while helping identify the project area boundaries, also functions as a reminder of existing conditions and issues in the project area. Therefore, after the awareness walk, individual or focus group interviews help refine the project objectives and clarify the expectations of parties for the upcoming process. During individual or focus group interviews, methods such as a likes and dislikes analysis (section 6.2.1), wish and have poems (section 6.2.2), or a PARK analysis (section 6.2.3) can be used to help individuals engage in systematic thinking.

The first set of activities does not need to be limited to the leading group and those community members who responded to the first round of outreach efforts. A project area can also be defined by distributing a brief survey to people living or working in and around the envisioned project area. Respondents may be asked to draw boundaries around the area they think should be worked on, or they may simply be asked to write down the boundaries they have in mind for the project area. The survey may also include questions about respondents' expectations of the process, in this way helping to support project definition.

After the project area is clarified, a project timeline needs to be established. This is the point at which the community designer identifies the number and formats of activities, with consideration for time and budget constraints. Project area boundaries and budget and time limitations all contribute to decisions on how many activities to conduct and in what format. Once the project timeline is established, it is time to devise individual community design activities and start the process.

8.2. FORMATS AND METHODS FOR IDENTIFYING GOALS, STRATEGIES, AND ACTIONS

Project area definitions for urban design projects often cover areas that can be toured within a reasonable period of time, either on foot or in a vehicle. Even if the leading group conducts a tour of the project area beforehand, it is always advisable to initiate the first activity with a tour for all participants. Depending on the time of the day and year, awareness walks or awareness camera activities can help organize fun, informal kick-off events. If climate or timing issues do not allow a group tour of the project site, community members may be asked to tour the project area on their own time before the follow-up activity. Nevertheless, touring the project area together as the first community event has advantages. First, participants see and discuss the site together, which helps initiate idea generation. Second, the experience supports community building: as participants tour the project area together, they start understanding each other's concerns and wishes.

After the project area tour, the goals of the project should be identified. Goal identification (section 6.2) at this point helps community members set targets and identify expectations. Regardless of the methods selected, it is a good idea to conduct one round of goal-setting exercises immediately after the project area tours, when observations are fresh in participants' minds. Complementing the project area tour with a likes and dislikes analysis, wish poem, or PARK analysis, therefore, is recommended. Through these activities not only are project goals identified in a time-efficient manner, participants also go through a productive analysis and idea generation session. In the case of smaller projects, group interviews may also be used to identify project goals.

After goal identification, it is recommended that strategy identification be left to a later event. Starting strategy identification (section 6.3) with a prioritization of project goals helps community members not only revisit previously identified goals but also mentally prepare for strategy identification. Both group and individual strategy identification methods can be used at the urban design scale. Based on the length and intensity of the strategy identification event, an action planning exercise (section 6.4) can be undertaken during the same event, or it may be left to a following event. If project resources allow, it is a good idea to separate the strategy identification and action planning events so that the participants are not overwhelmed by project issues and multiple tasks in one event.

The methods discussed in this section can be utilized in a variety of activity formats (section 6.8). For goal setting, strategy identification, and action planning, workshop and meeting formats are helpful, especially interactive workshops and charrettes. Online data-gathering methods, such as using a project website to recruit ideas, can also be used for goal identification, strategy identification, and action planning. Because some community members may not have access to computers or may prefer not to use an electronic response medium, it is strongly recommended that online methods be supplemented by face-to-face formats.

8.3. DIGITAL APPLICATIONS IN MUNICIPAL URBAN DESIGN DECISION MAKING

Over the past two decades, communication in community design processes has been greatly enhanced by the expanding availability and richness of digital applications. Computer software that makes audio-visualization of potential decisions possible offers increasingly sophisticated means of scenario planning to community designers and community members alike. The availability of such digital applications has significantly increased information flow among community designers and community members, potentially removing roadblocks to communication.

A variety of digital applications can be utilized to help make better-informed decisions, especially in goal identification. During strategy identification, three-dimensional modeling can be used to display the implications of each strategy. By viewing the implications of each strategy, community members can more fully grasp the possible advantages and disadvantages of each strategy.

A good example of the use of digital media in urban design decision making is the concept planning process undertaken by the Tenants and Owners Development Corporation (TODCO) for San Francisco's South of Market (SOMA) district (section 8.7). In this process, TODCO asked the author to develop visualizations of plan decisions and the design implications of these decisions as project meetings continued. Before project finalization, a series of three-dimensional computer models was generated for a sample block in the project area by the author. Still shots of these models were then integrated with photographs of existing conditions using the photomontage technique. In this way, before and after visualizations of plan decision implications were made available to participants. TODCO is continuing its effort to reflect its constituents' wishes in ongoing formal planning processes for this area, and the visualizations serve as tools to connect these ideas to decision-making mechanisms (Figure 8.1).

8.1. Top: existing conditions of a selected block in San Francisco's SOMA district; bottom: implications of plan goals and strategies visualized in the same image for effective communication

8.4. TRANSLATING PROCESS OUTCOMES INTO URBAN DESIGN DECISIONS

Once the goals and strategies for the project area are identified and subjected to a reality check through action planning, the uses and activities proposed for the project area become clearer. At this point, planning games or design games (sections 6.5.2 and 6.5.3) are advisable to help community members translate their decisions into visual terms. Intermediary or supportive community design methods at this stage are images-of-life exercises (section 6.5.1), which provide participants with ideas or design concepts, and methods that allow participants to select from alternatives (section 6.5.4), which help clarify the advantages and challenges associated with each decision. Based on how the process has developed from the beginning, the community designer can mix and match methods at this translation stage to ensure that urban design decisions emerge.

Once a set of urban design decisions is made, but before the urban design proposal or plan is finalized, a community review of the draft version is highly advisable to mitigate future disagreements. Since urban design proposals are often lengthy documents, with sections on site analysis, land use, circulation, and design guidelines (or form-based codes), a summary of the proposal may be prepared for community members' ease of review. Nevertheless, the original proposal should also always be available for the public to review.

Commonly, the plan or proposal is opened to public review through the informative/reactive format. In a conventional public hearing, the plan or proposal is presented to the community and a review period is set for community members to respond. This format, however, is not an ideal ending to a participatory process for the reasons discussed in Chapter 6.

As a better alternative, interactive workshops and meetings or charrettes would provide a much more open and flexible response environment. In a community workshop setting, for example, interactive discussions can provide the community designer with candid feedback from community members. While it may be challenging to integrate such comments into the proposal on the spot, the format still enables the community designer to hear feedback and integrate it into the proposal after the workshop or meeting.

The charrette format could overcome this challenge. A one-day charrette organized for community feedback could easily function as an environment in which the community designer acquires feedback, integrates the feedback into the proposal, and presents the revised proposal to the community members in one day. This would require that the proposal be presented to the community members in the morning, followed by a feedback session. The community designer would then work on integrating the feedback into the proposal without community members present. Later in the day, the community members would be presented with the revised proposal incorporating the additional feedback. The advantage of a charrette format, therefore, is that community members can observe how their feedback has been heard and integrated into the plan or proposal.

During the review process, visualization has an important role in communicating design ideas to community members. Three-dimensional views of proposed changes help community members better understand the proposed land use, circulation decisions, and design guidelines. At this point, digital applications once again prove helpful to the community designer. Visualizations are not limited to electronic media, however. Hand renderings, photomontages, and fly-through animations are all useful tools for communicating the proposal to community members. Since these formats may require a greater investment of labor and time, the charrette format could be helpful in accommodating the integration process.

8.5. CASE: DOWNTOWN DELANO, CALIFORNIA, CONCEPT PLAN

Leading group: City of Delano Community Development Department

Project team: Umut Toker; Jennifer Venema, Brian Barnacle, Orchid Monroy, Jimmy Ochoa (Cal Poly City and Regional Planning students); Keith Woodcock (City of Delano Community Development Department)

Project Duration: Approximately 4 months

Project Timeline:

Activity formats used: Awareness camera exercise, focus group interviews, interactive community workshops

Methods used: Focus group interviews, likes and dislikes analysis, strategy identification, action planning, design game

Instruments used: Interview instruments, likes and dislikes analysis instruments, strategy identification instruments, action planning instruments, design game board, legend, markers or pens, icons

The Community Development Department of the City of Delano, California, initiated this community design project. The objective of the project was to develop a concept plan for downtown Delano that would lead to a specific plan. Downtown Delano, an approximately 18-block area, is home to a variety of businesses. It is a pedestrian-friendly, human-scale environment with some historical buildings, as well as buildings from the 1960s, 1970s, and 1980s (Figure 8.2).

Delano has a population of approximately 40,000 people and is located in California's Central Valley. Its economy is mostly agriculture-oriented. The main challenge for downtown Delano as for other cities of similar scale in the Central Valley is that it cannot attract enough visitors to maintain a vibrant, active atmosphere. Over the second half of the 20th century the city expanded horizontally, creating mostly neighborhoods of single-family homes. Consequently, the population is motor vehicle dependent, and people are likely to drive to strip malls for their day-to-day shopping. Further, the city is within easy driving distance of the larger city of Bakersfield, which provides a lot of shopping and entertainment options, luring people away from downtown Delano. Over the years these conditions have affected downtown Delano. Declining economic activity has had negative

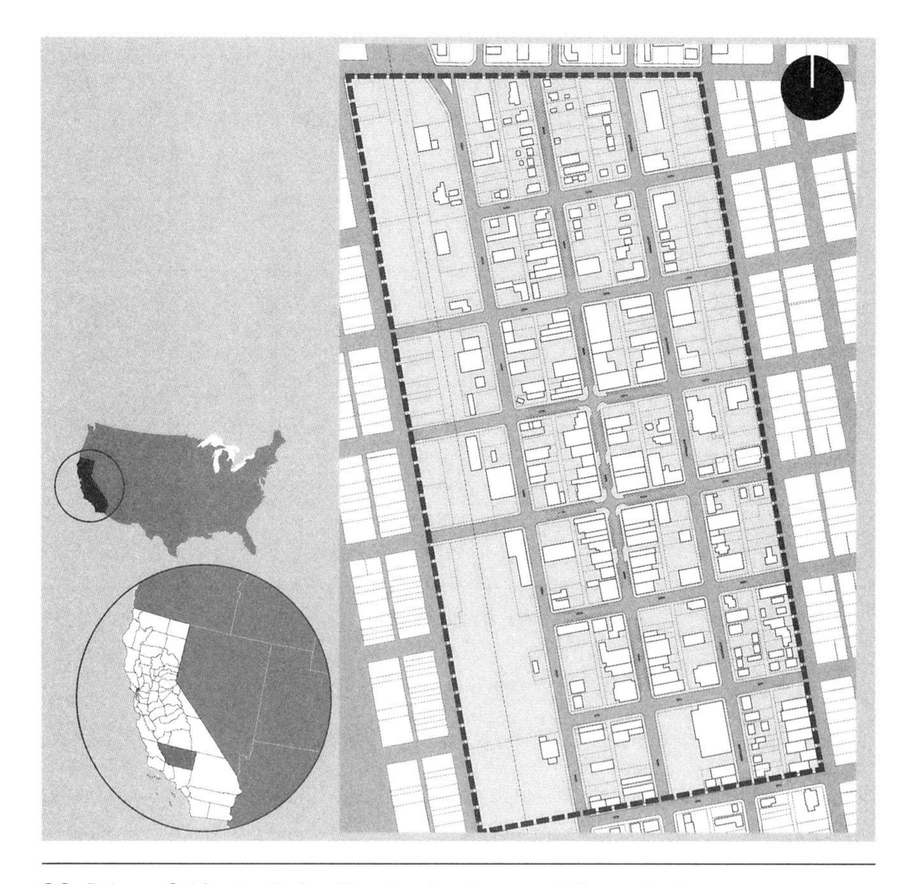

8.2. Delano, California: its location, its downtown, and the project area

effects not only for the vitality of businesses but also for the maintenance of downtown buildings.

The main request of the leading group was to involve the people of Delano in the development of a target for the future of the downtown area. The concept plan would be circulated in the community to develop a common understanding of wishes for the future of downtown and to build support for a downtown-specific plan. Visual definitions of goals and design concepts for the downtown area, as well as a conceptual diagram displaying various land-use options, were among the anticipated outcomes, in addition to a plan document.

In consultation with the leading group, the community designer developed a four-activity timeline. The community design process started with Delano's Community Development Department initiating outreach. A key participant in this process was the Chamber of Commerce administration, which helped with inviting downtown business and property owners to participate. Other outreach efforts conducted by the Community Development Department included contacting the local newspaper, businesses, and community colleges and circulating flyers designed by the community design team. These flyers were designed with messages and images that invited the residents of Delano to participate in the process. As recommended in Chapter 4, a common visual language for the flyers was used for consistency (see Figure 4.4).

Activity 1: Awareness Camera Exercise and Focus Group Interviews. The community design team and participants, including members of the Chamber of Commerce, downtown business owners, and Delano residents, met at the local community center. The community design team introduced the process and the project timeline (Figure 8.3) and then began an awareness camera exercise. The team provided each participant with two disposable cameras, one with a green label, "Photos of what I like about Downtown Delano," and one with a red label, "Photos of what could be improved about Downtown Delano." The community design team and participants visited the project area, and participants stopped from time to time to discuss issues (Figure 8.4). Throughout the tour the participants took many pictures with both cameras. Extra cameras were made available to participants who wanted to take additional photographs.

After this exercise the participants gathered back at the community center and formed focus groups. During the focus group interviews they were asked to identify aspects of the downtown area that should be preserved and aspects that needed improvement. Participants were first asked to individually note their ideas on the interview instrument provided, which was a letter-sized sheet of paper with the two questions and adequate blank space to write ideas. Once individual ideas were noted down, each participant was asked to read her or his ideas, and then the group had an open discussion. Eventually the focus groups came together and main

Downtown Delano Concept Plan

a participatory process

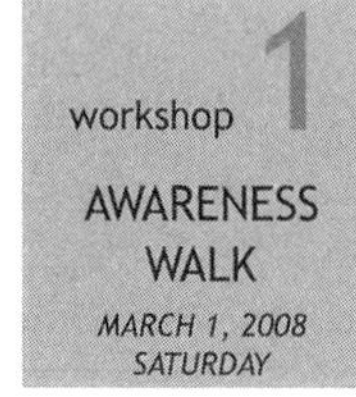

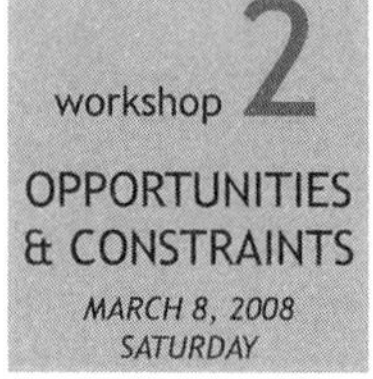

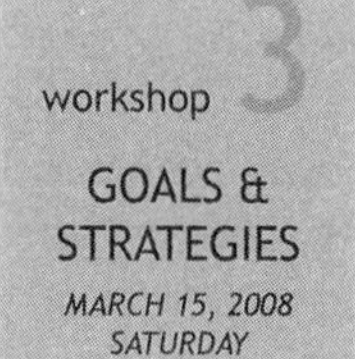

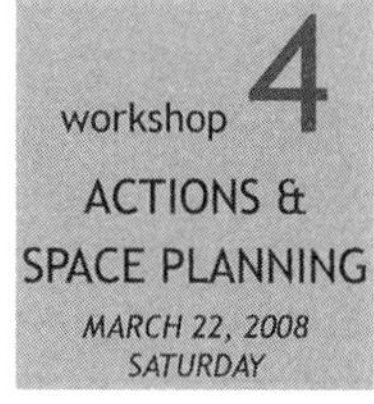

workshop 4
ACTIONS & SPACE PLANNING
MARCH 22, 2008
SATURDAY

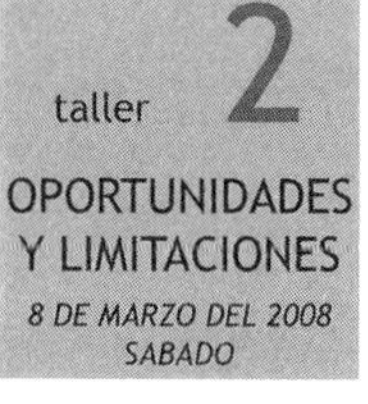

taller 2
OPORTUNIDADES Y LIMITACIONES
8 DE MARZO DEL 2008
SABADO

taller 3
METAS Y ESTRATEGIAS
15 DE MARZO DEL 2008
SABADO

taller 4
PLAN DE ACCION
22 DE MARZO DEL 2008
SABADO

LET'S WORK ALL TOGETHER TO MAKE OUR DOWNTOWN BETTER. TRABAJEMOS JUNTOS PARA MEJORAR EL CENTRO DE DELANO.

8.3. The project timeline introduced to the participants

8.4. Participants touring the project area during the awareness camera exercise

ideas were identified and noted by the community design team. Conducting focus group interviews immediately after the awareness camera exercise proved very effective in idea generation since participants engaged in the discussion having just refreshed their perceptions of downtown.

Activity 2. Interactive Community Workshop 1—Goals and Strategies. An interactive community workshop was held the following week, during which community members identified goals for the future of downtown and strategies that would help them achieve those goals. Participants split into small groups of five to six, and each person identified goals and strategies individually. Then participants shared their goals and strategies with the rest of the group, and the group had a discussion. Each group was asked to develop an agreed-upon list of goals and strategies. Once this exercise was completed, group spokespersons read their goals and strategies to the rest of the participants, and a list of goals and strategies was formed.

Activity 3. Interactive Community Workshop 2—Action Planning. The next interactive community workshop started with introducing the goals and strategies identified in the previous workshop. For this, the community design team developed a handout including the goals and strategies (Figure 8.5) and shared it with the participants. At this point participants were asked to double-check the goals and strategies they had identified and to make any necessary additions or modifications. There was agreement on the goals and strategies identified. After this discussion an action planning exercise was held. Participants were provided with action planning forms, each identifying one goal and its accompanying strategies. For each strategy, participants were asked to think about and generate ideas for the first step toward implementation, potential persons to initiate action, and potential funding sources (see Figure 6.11). Participants generated ideas individually first, and then discussed these ideas in small groups. As groups read out the ideas they generated, the community design team recorded them. The action planning exercise proved effective in helping participants think about the real-world implications of the goals and strategies they had identified.

Activity 4. Interactive Community Workshop 3—Design Game. In the final community workshop, participants were asked to develop their "ideal downtown" ideas using a design game developed by the community design team. The game included a base map of the project area with parcels and streets, as well as icons based on the findings from previous activities. The icons represented land uses (e.g., commercial) and specific activities and business types (e.g., a restaurant). Using the base map, icons, and colored markers, community members developed ideal downtown schemes in small groups. Groups then presented their schemes to the rest of the workshop participants (Figure 8.6).

This community design process yielded a concept plan for downtown Delano. The plan document identified recommendations based on community wishes concerning land use, economics, urban form, visual quality, circulation, transportation, public amenities, recreation, and implementation.

CAL POLY community design **Downtown Delano Concept Plan**

a participatory process

GOALS & STRATEGIES IDENTIFIED BY THE COMMUNITY

goal 1: ENHANCE COMMUNITY CONNECTIONS AND COMMUNICATIONS

strategies
- Form a downtown business association
- Daily newspapers
- Community center
- Better communication between downtown, city, and community

goal 2: PRESERVE AND ENHANCE ACTIVITY AND WALKABILITY CHARACTER

strategies
- Downtown Housing
- Make High Street more people friendly
- Preserve Main Street Amenities
- Preserve eateries and bank locations
- Street landscaping (medians, street furniture, etc.)
- Preserve and enhance diversity of eateries and shopping
- Replace current ways of parking

goal 3: CREATE MORE DOWNTOWN OPPORTUNITIES FOR YOUTH

strategies
- College expansion
- Rec center
- Bring more jobs for youth

goal 4: MAKE DOWNTOWN VISUALLY MORE PRESENTABLE

strategies
- Maintenance of facacde displays
- Store signage
- Activate a facade program
- Code enforcement and implementation
- Clean Alleys
- Clean streets and sidewalks

goal 5: BRING MORE RECREATIONAL OPPORTUNITIES TO DOWNTOWN

strategies
- Enhance night activity
- Downtown park
- Library expansion
- Community center
- Weekend entertainment
- Downtown dancing activities
- Open space

goal 6: BRING NEW DEVELOPMENT TO DOWNTOWN

strategies
- Increase building heights
- Infill for vacant lots
- Downtown housing

goal 7: MAKE DOWNTOWN A DESTINATION WITH CHARACTER

strategies
- Preserve historic buildings
- Gateway on 11th Street and Main Street
- Public art
- Landmark and placeholders

LET'S WORK ALL TOGETHER TO MAKE OUR DOWNTOWN BETTER. TRABAJOMOS JUNTOS PARA MEJORAR EL CENTRO DE DELANO.

8.5. Goals and strategies for the future of downtown Delano as identified by participants

8.6. A participant presenting one of the "ideal downtown" schemes

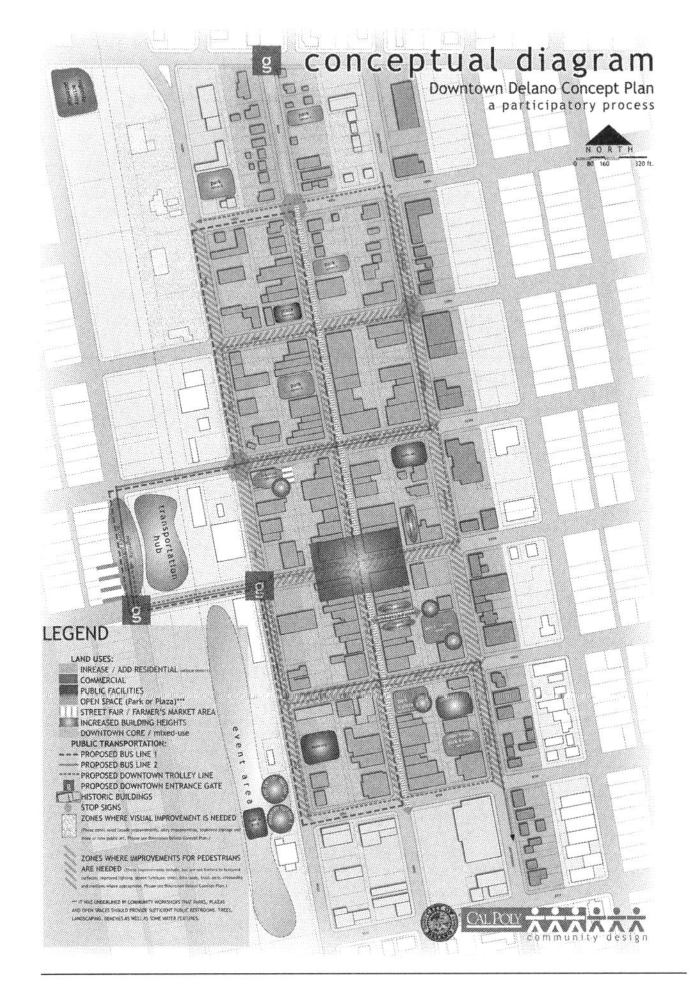

8.7. Conceptual diagram for downtown Delano

The plan also provided a conceptual diagram that integrated and visually summarized the findings from the design game and other community design activities (Figure 8.7). The conceptual diagram was accompanied by before-and-after three-dimensional visualizations to inform the community about the design implications of the recommendations (Figure 8.8). The plan was presented to the city council and wider Delano community. The plan has proved instrumental in planning and design processes undertaken by the city in the following years. The plan also served as a record of community wishes about their downtown during the City of Delano Strategic Plan development process (see section 9.4).

8.8. One of the before-and-after three-dimensional visualizations developed to inform the community about the design implications of recommendations

8.6. CASE: DOWNTOWN MORRO BAY, CALIFORNIA, ENHANCEMENT PROJECT, PHASE I

Leading group: Two planning commission members and one city council member from the City of Morro Bay, California

Project team: Umut Toker, Chris Clark (Cal Poly City and Regional Planning faculty); graduate students in city and regional planning (Cal Poly)

Project duration: Approximately 3 months

Project timeline:

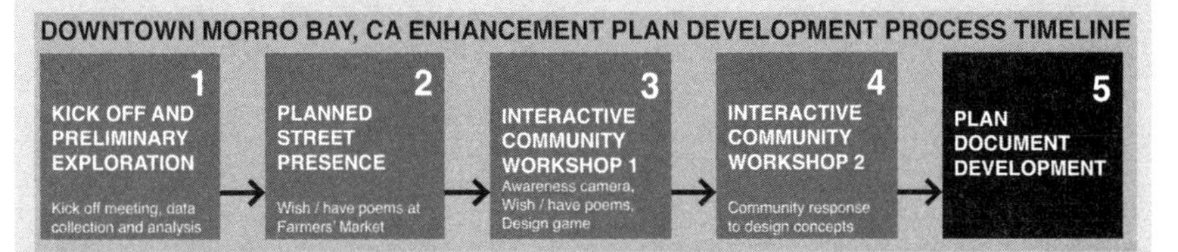

Activity formats used: Planned street presence, interactive community workshops

Methods used: Awareness camera, wish poems, PARK analysis, design games

Instruments used: Wish poem instruments, PARK analysis instruments, design game board, legend and markers / pens

Morro Bay is located on the Central Coast of California. Home to approximately 10,000 residents, Morro Bay is also rich in natural beauty. The Central Coast as well as the famous Morro Rock make Morro Bay a popular destination for tourists from the vicinity as well as from around the world (Figure 8.9). Morro Bay has two significant activity centers. The first is the waterfront, or the Embarcadero, which houses a high number of tourist-oriented businesses and local fishing facilities. The harbor on the waterfront is busy with fishing boats and tourist boats. The second is downtown Morro Bay, stretching on both sides of the main spine of the town, Morro Bay Boulevard. Unlike the Embarcadero, the downtown area is more oriented toward local residents in terms of the businesses it accommodates. Additionally, downtown Morro Bay features a number of hotels. Morro Bay Boulevard runs perpendicular to the Embarcadero, and ends with stairs leading to it.

The leading group that requested the project consisted of two planning commission members and one city council member from the city of

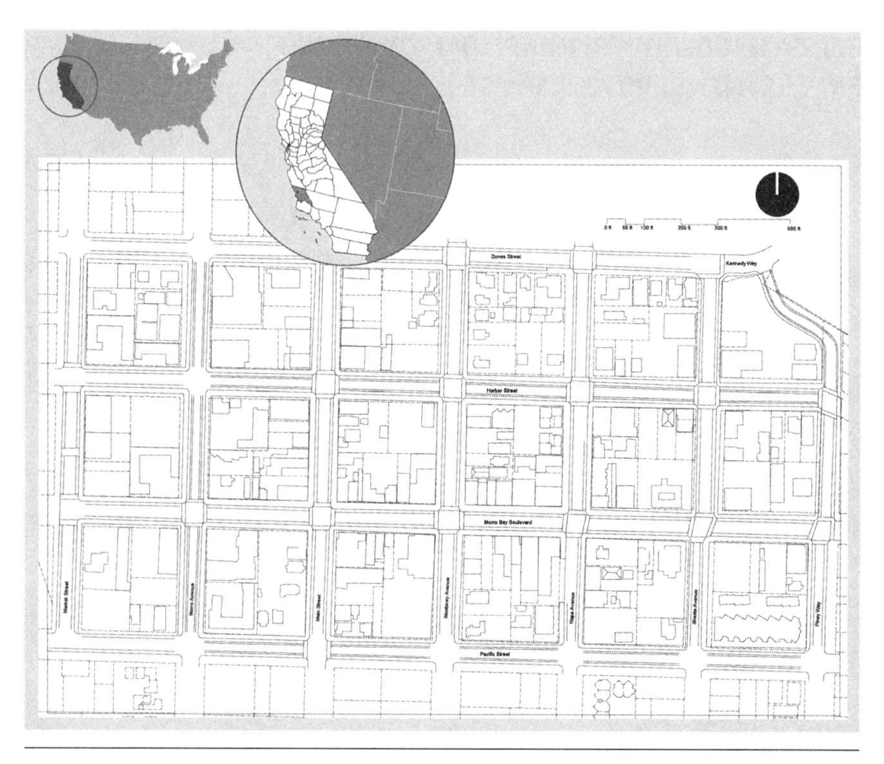

8.9. Morro Bay, California: its location, its downtown, and the project area

Morro Bay. The main concerns of the leading group were related to the atmosphere and vitality of this central spine. With the eventual objective of moving toward a Downtown Morro Bay Specific Plan, the leading group approached Cal Poly's first-year graduate specific planning studio. The goal of the process was to develop alternative plan proposals based on the community's needs and wishes. These proposals would then be presented to the community members, and the city would work with consultants in the development of the Downtown Morro Bay Specific Plan.

The community design team that responded to this request consisted of 12 graduate students in Cal Poly's first-year graduate planning studio under the supervision of the author and Chris Clark. A five-step community involvement strategy was developed for the process: a kick-off meeting, a site analysis visit, two community workshops, and a final presentation to the community. As the process moved forward, it was customized to the needs of the community.

The kick-off meeting with the community members and the leading group was held at a coffee shop in the project area. The venue provided a relaxed, comfortable atmosphere. During the meeting, project goals and the timeline were introduced. Then the students walked around the project area and distributed flyers to businesses, residents, and visitors. Next, in a site analysis visit the students took a parcel-by-parcel inventory of the project site. Environmental conditions and circulation were also analyzed.

The project team made an appearance at the local farmers market the following Saturday afternoon, which gave the team an excellent opportunity to collect information from community members as well as to invite them to the upcoming community design activities. The students set up a booth and conducted wish poem and have poem exercises in a planned street presence format. Meanwhile, others toured the project area, talking to visitors at the farmers market and distributing flyers to them and to local businesses. Efforts to make the booth visually appealing and interesting also paid off. The project team had a temporary shelter structure that drew attention to the booth's presence. The team placed two invitational posters on the two sides of the booth, one in English and one in Spanish. Overall, the farmers market activity turned out to be a good information collection and outreach activity for the project (Figure 8.10).

One week later the community design team held its first interactive community workshop. The activity started with an awareness camera exercise. Since the venue selected for the activity, the local community center,

8.10. Booth set up for the project at the Morro Bay downtown farmers market

was within easy walking distance of the project site, it was practical for the team to organize a one-hour awareness camera exercise right before a goal-setting exercise. After being introduced to the process, participants walked out to the site, with two cameras assigned to every two to three participants. As in the Downtown Delano Concept Plan case, the cameras were labeled in green for taking photographs of positive aspects of the project area and in red for taking photographs of those aspects of the project area that need improvement. After one hour of touring the project area participants returned to the community center.

At the community center, participants were asked to form small groups of six to eight at the round tables provided. First the findings of the wish and have poems from the farmers market were introduced. Then participant groups were provided with PARK (Preserve, Add, Remove, Keep out) analysis instruments. Participants were asked to first respond to the exercise individually and then discuss their individual responses with others in their group. Each group then developed an agreed-upon list of items in the PARK categories (Figure 8.11).

After the PARK analysis, participants engaged in a design game. Blank base maps of the project area were provided to the participant groups, along with a legend of land uses and circulation. Each group was also provided with a set of colored markers. Each group developed an "ideal downtown" scheme with the instruments provided and presented it to the rest of the participants (Figure 8.12).

The results of the wish and have poems, the PARK analysis, and the ideal downtown exercise were analyzed by the team. Findings from the wish and have poems and PARK analysis were summarized on 18 x 24-inch posters. Meanwhile, photographs taken during the awareness camera exercise were developed, digitized, and summarized on two 18 x 24-inch posters, one on the positive aspects of the project area and one on aspects of the project area that needed improvement (Figure 8.13).

Finally, findings from the ideal downtown designs were analyzed and three alternative conceptual diagrams with accompanying design concepts were developed by student teams. These diagrams were compiled on three posters that represented the three alternatives developed in the first community workshop (Figure 8.14).

The analysis and summary posters developed based on the first community workshop were taken to a second workshop in the same venue two weeks later and posted on the walls. Participants were first asked to prioritize the findings from the wish and have poems, the awareness camera exercise, and the PARK analysis. Using dot stickers, participants identified which items on each poster they agreed with. The number of stickers on items helped identify the most important issues. Participants were then asked to form small groups of six to eight and give feedback on the conceptual diagrams that summarized findings from the ideal downtown

DOWNTOWN MORRO BAY ENHANCEMENT PROJECT (PHASE 1)

Community Meeting II

Please place a dot next to the ideas generated from Community Meeting I that you agree with

P

Preserve

What We Have Now That Is Positive

- Historical Buildings
- Trees
- Bushes, Planters, Flower Boxes
- Bay Theater
- Parks
- Walkability
- Small Town Atmosphere
- Eclectic Architecture Character
- Local Businesses
- Street Furniture
- Local Art, Murals, Public Art
- Farmer's Market
- Tree Lights
- Cafes and Restaurants
- Colorful Trashcans
- Views
- Well-Maintained Facades
- Banks
- Post Office and Civic Center Near Town Center
- Variety
- Lampposts
- Urban Agriculture/Garden/ Farms
- Fishing Industry
- Police Department
- Directional Signage
- Music Festivals
- Roundabout
- Festive Signage
- Streetscape
- Flags
- Ornaments
- Bike Parking
- Local History
- Local Nurseries
- City Events
- Small Buildings
- Colorful Paint
- Beach Town Feel
- Wide Sidewalks
- Local Materials
- Quality of Life
- Kid-Friendly Events
- Courtyards/Gardens Behind Buildings

A

Add

What We Do Not Have That Is Positive

- Improve Sidewalks and Streets
- Trees
- More Colors
- Banners
- Public Restrooms
- Outdoor Dining
- Mixed-Use
- Visitor Center
- Decorative Art/Murals
- Water Features
- Better Street Lighting
- Planters
- Signage
- Historic Markers
- Family/Kid-Friendly Activities
- Outdoor Seating
- Bike Racks
- Bike Paths
- Mosaic Trashcans
- Tree/Bush Lighting
- Landscaping
- Decorated Tree Wells
- Pedestrian-Only Streets
- Low-Impact Trees
- Curb Appeal for the Park
- Nightlife
- Parking
- Storefront Maintenance
- Landscape Maintenance
- Architectural Standards
- Plaza
- Speed Bumps
- Unifying Design
- Bike Store
- More Lighting with A Theme
- Museum
- Variety Of Retail Shops
- Bike Lanes
- Art Gallery
- Plaques
- Restaurants
- Bulb-outs
- Sidewalk Aesthetics
- Identity
- Dog Bags on Streets
- Statues
- Courtyards
- Updated Businesses
- Stormwater Gardens
- Map of Assets
- Improve Cohesion of Homes
- Recycling
- Wind Barriers
- Fences Around Trash Receptacles
- Larger Farmer's Market
- Community Garden
- Parades
- Carousel
- Totem Pole
- Code Enforcement
- People Living Downtown
- Better Connectivity
- Sense of Place
- Walking Path
- Tax Generating Businesses
- Fishing Ind. as Living History
- Streetscape Standards
- Link to Embarcadero
- Parks
- Theater with a Stage
- Parking Meters
- Drinking Fountain
- Volunteers
- Round-Abouts
- One-Way Traffic
- Streets that Rise to Sidewalk
- Mechanical Bollards

R

Remove

What We Have That We Would Like To Remove

- Utility Lines
- Blighted Facades
- Vacant Lots and Buildings
- Sidewalk Cracks and Potholes
- Weeds/Dead Plants and Trees
- Excess Similar Businesses
- Parking Lots in Front of Buildings
- Newspaper/Magazine Boxes
- Sidewalk Sandwich Boards
- Dilapidated Buildings
- Unnecessary Poles/Posts
- Cigarette Smoking
- Liquor Signs
- Impervious Surfaces
- Bad Dumpster Locations
- Loud Building Colors
- Banner Flags
- Tree lights only on Tree Trunks
- Eucalyptus Trees
- Astroturf/Artificial Plants
- Obsolete/Dilapidated Signage
- Large Storage/Shipping/Cargo Containers
- Light bollards
- 'Parking in Lieu' Fees
- Diseased and Damaged Trees
- Monotonous Building facades
- Rusty Storefronts
- Boring Paving
- Regulations that Stifle Small Businesses/Startups
- Tree Lights
- Chain Link Fences
- Cars
- Neon Signs
- Civic/Gov't. Buildings Centrally Located
- Bad Bike Racks
- Generic Sidewalk Trashcans
- Gutters to Stormdrains
- Light Pollution
- Narrow Sidewalks
- Excessive Lawns
- Shabby Fences
- Trees that Crack Sidewalks
- Trees that Drop Seed Pods
- Blank Walls/Boring Facades
- Cobra Head Street Lights
- Concrete Street Furniture
- Life-size Statues
- Large Setbacks
- Sprawling Street Front Parking Lots
- Power Boxes Near Street Trees
- Bars on Doors and Windows
- Bollard Sculptures
- Brick Facades
- Nails in Trees

K

Keep Out

What We Do not Have That We Would Like To Keep Out

- Chain Stores
- Fast Food Restaurants
- Big Box Stores
- Adult Stores
- Neon Signs
- Large Out of Scale Projects
- Marijuana Dispensaries
- Excess Similar Businesses
- Non-Retail
- Parking Meters
- Tattoo Parlors
- Large Signs
- Contemporary Design
- Boxy Two-Story Buildings
- Vacant Storefronts
- Cookie Cutter Design
- Cheesy Stuff
- Unattractive Storefronts
- Bars on Windows
- Stucco
- Chain Link Fences
- Brothels
- Businesses that Alarm Tourists
- More Liquor Stores
- More Real Estate Offices
- More Motels
- Heavy Industry
- Absentee Business Owners
- Dead Plants/Trees
- Light Bollards
- Light Pollution
- More Parking
- Impervious Surfaces
- Driveway Cuts
- Seagulls
- Smoking
- Crime

8.11. Summary of findings from the PARK exercise conducted in the first interactive community workshop in Morro Bay

8.12. Participants presenting their "ideal downtown" scheme

8.13. Summary of photographs taken during the awareness camera exercise showing positive aspects of the project area on one poster and aspects in need of improvement on the other

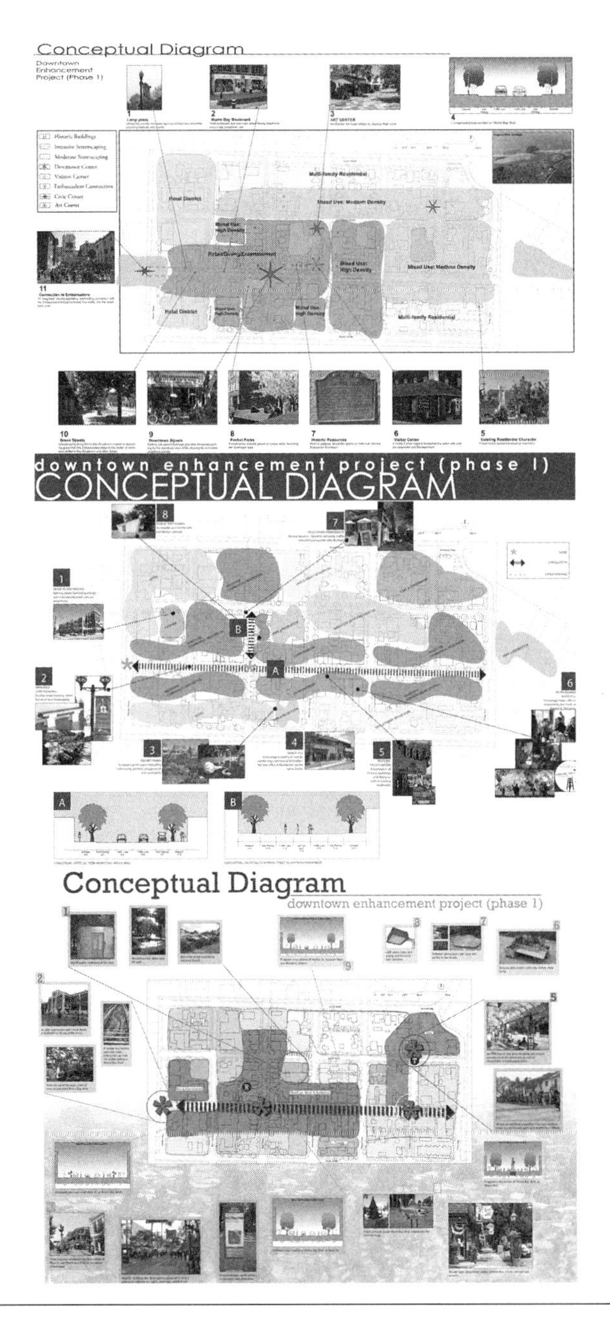

8.14. Conceptual diagrams with accompanying design concepts compiled on three posters representing the three alternatives developed in the first community workshop of the Downtown Morro Bay Enhancement Plan Project. Posters and the information they provide were developed by the students.

exercise. The workshop then switched to a booth-based format. The three student teams gathered around the conceptual diagrams they had developed. Participant teams were asked to visit the stations, talk to the students, and provide feedback.

The findings from the second community workshop were analyzed, and the process of developing three alternative specific plan proposals was initiated. Over about six weeks, student teams developed their specific plan proposals with chapters on land uses, circulation, design guidelines, capital improvement costs, and implementation and phasing strategies. These documents also provided a large variety of visualizations, from two-dimensional diagrams to still shots from three-dimensional models and before and after views.

The specific plan proposals were presented to the community and the Morro Bay Planning Commission. The Planning Commission as well as the community members received the proposals very positively. The Planning Commission recommended that the city move forward with the development of a Downtown Morro Bay Specific Plan based on the students' work. The Downtown Morro Bay Enhancement Project development experience indicated that the "V" process could be executed in a fairly compressed schedule (10 weeks) if the timeline was carefully managed and existing venues were used to the advantage of the process. The students' presence at the farmers market and their visits to the local businesses proved invaluable in generating community input for the process. By carefully allocating labor resources, student teams were able to develop sophisticated specific plan proposals within the given time constraints.

8.7. CASE: SAN FRANCISCO, CALIFORNIA, 4TH/5TH STREETS SOMA STUDY

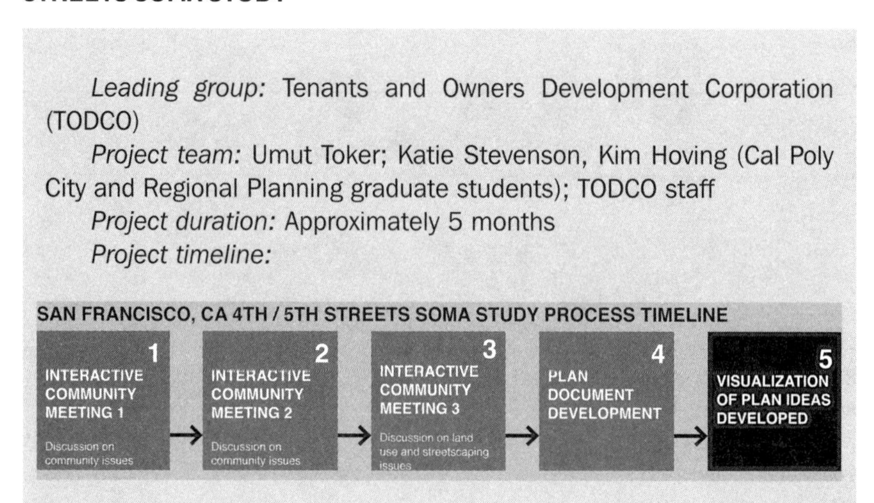

Leading group: Tenants and Owners Development Corporation (TODCO)
Project team: Umut Toker; Katie Stevenson, Kim Hoving (Cal Poly City and Regional Planning graduate students); TODCO staff
Project duration: Approximately 5 months
Project timeline:
SAN FRANCISCO, CA 4TH / 5TH STREETS SOMA STUDY PROCESS TIMELINE
1
INTERACTIVE COMMUNITY MEETING 1
Discussion on community issues
2
INTERACTIVE COMMUNITY MEETING 2
Discussion on community issues
3
INTERACTIVE COMMUNITY MEETING 3
Discussion on land use and streetscaping issues
4
PLAN DOCUMENT DEVELOPMENT
5
VISUALIZATION OF PLAN IDEAS DEVELOPED

Activity formats used: Interactive community meetings
Methods used: Visualizations
Instruments used: Three-dimensional modeling and image editing software

The TODCO 4th/5th Streets SOMA (South of Market) Study, conducted in San Francisco, California, introduces another model in which the community designer becomes instrumental in translating the community design process into a visual language. The Tenants and Owners Development Corporation (TODCO), a nonprofit organization that focuses on affordable housing, initiated the project. TODCO has been developing affordable housing alternatives in the SOMA area for four decades (Figure 8.15). The city of San Francisco was gearing up for a planning process that would result in decisions for an area that also included SOMA. TODCO wanted to develop a plan document that reflected the needs and wishes of its clientele and would be presented to the city during the upcoming planning process. In essence, TODCO's objective was to conduct a community design process and summarize its clientele's viewpoint about the future of the neighborhood in a plan document.

Having worked on affordable housing for four decades, the staff and directors of TODCO had knowledge and experience of community design processes and participatory decision making. TODCO did not, however, have any members on the project team with experience in visualization. Therefore, the leading group approached the Cal Poly community design team, requesting its attendance during the decision-making process and its assistance in translating findings into visuals. They also asked the team to find examples of planning and design interventions in similar urban areas.

TODCO organized three interactive community meetings, to which key role players in the SOMA area were invited. Participants included residents, developers, and city staff. The meetings focused on the goals of the group, as well as the physical development of the project area. The Cal Poly team developed a visual language that TODCO staff and participants were comfortable with. Instead of a conventional plan language, the visuals developed throughout the process employed a mixture of icons and colored symbols and an aerial photograph of the project area. At the end of the plan development process, plan ideas were integrated into one visual display that used the same language (Figure 8.16).

At the end of the planning process, some of the key ideas in the plan were visualized for one block of the project area. Three-dimensional visualizations of increased densities, adaptive reuse, and midblock alleyways with landscaping were presented using three-dimensional modeling and photomontage techniques (Figure 8.17). The final plan document text was

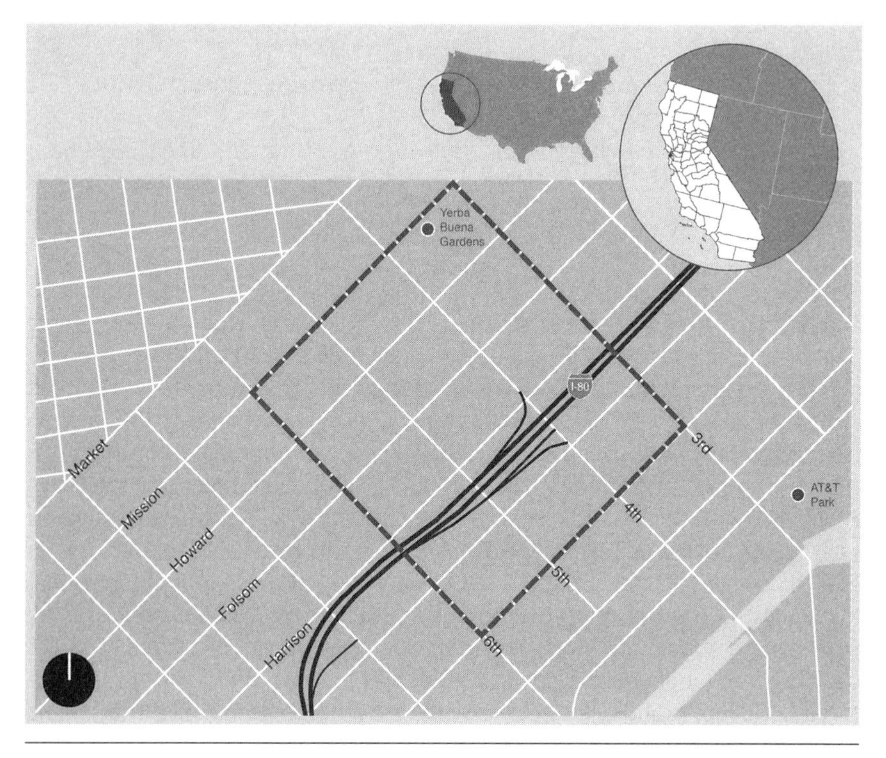

8.15. San Francisco, California, 4th/5th Streets SOMA Study project area

developed by TODCO staff and incorporated visualizations developed by the Cal Poly community design team. Both were presented to the city and to local residents.

The collaboration between the Cal Poly community design team and TODCO staff is another model of the community designer helping in the development of participatory decision making. In this case, two teams with community design knowledge and expertise worked together in translating the community's ideas into a plan document, accompanied by visual materials. This model can especially inform the business practice of community design professionals with a strong background in visualization methods.

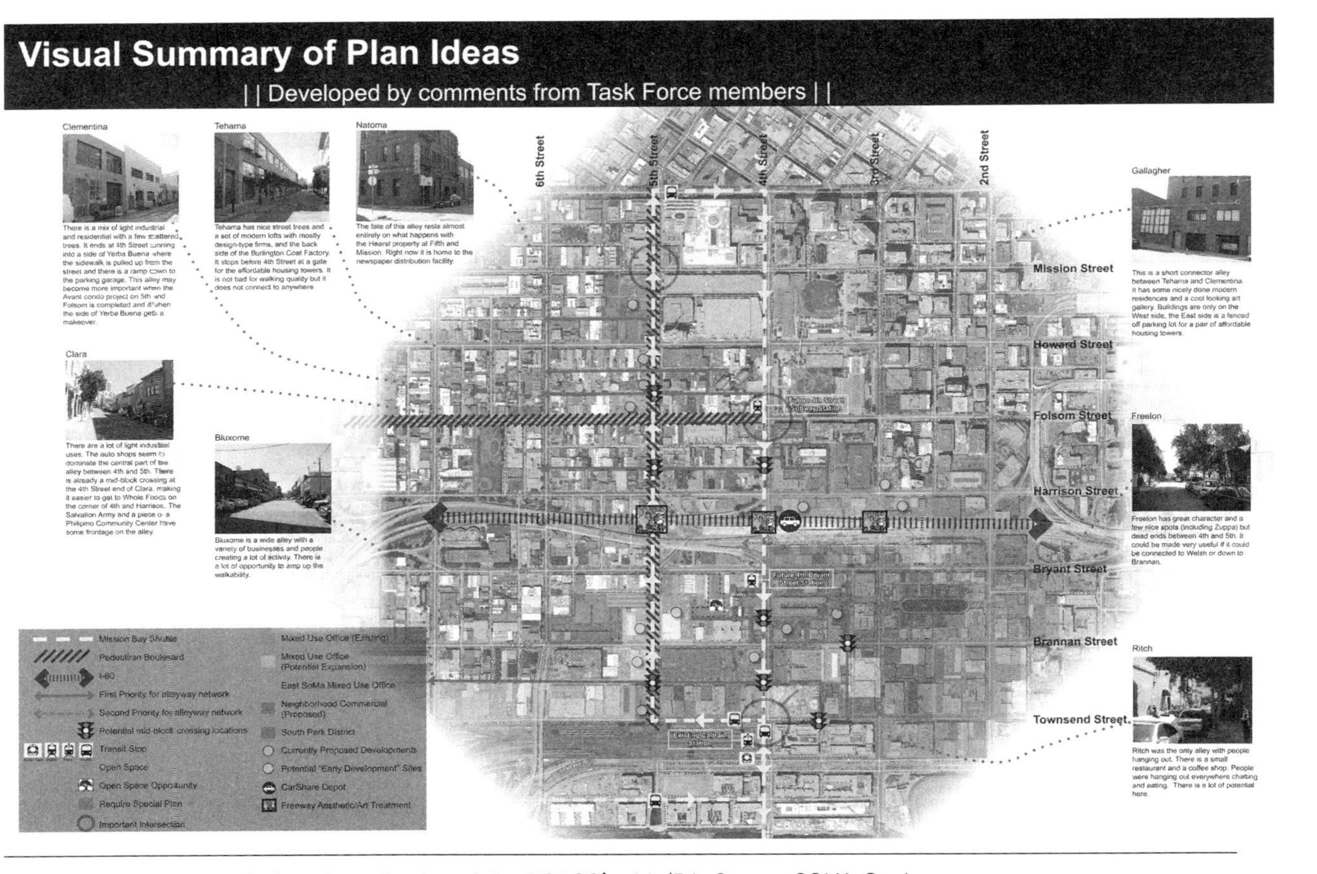

8.16. Visual summary of plan ideas developed for TODCO's 4th/5th Streets SOMA Study

8.17. Plan ideas visualized for TODCO: increased densities, adaptive reuse, and midblock alleyways with landscaping

9 Participatory Decision Making at the Community Planning Scale

Moving beyond the scale of urban design, we enter the realm of planning for areas of wider scope and larger geography. The term *community planning* as used in this book refers to either communitywide planning, applicable to whole towns or cities, or areawide planning, applicable to smaller units such as neighborhoods and districts. Plan decisions made at this scale go beyond physical or design issues and enter the realm of policy development.

The objective of larger scale community planning processes is to help guide the social, economic, and physical development of neighborhoods, towns, and cities by providing a series of policies and planning recommendations. These plans tend to take a longer view than urban design plans and provide guidance on both physical and nonphysical planning. According to Berke and Godschalk (2006), community-wide planning addresses the spatial organization of land uses in terms of location, type, mix, and density, while area planning addresses urban areas within communities (e.g., neighborhoods) or open spaces within communities (e.g., farmlands).

The policies and recommendations are developed to provide public and private entities with guidance when making decisions that will affect the future of the community. Since such large-scale decisions will have significant impacts on the day-to-day lives of residents, participatory decision making is imperative. Participatory decision-making methods in community planning help residents develop a common vision and incorporate their input into the regulations and guidelines pertaining to the future of their community.

9.1. PROJECT DESCRIPTION, IDENTIFICATION OF PARTICIPANTS, AND OUTREACH

Once the leading group contacts the community designer for the project, the next step is to develop a project description. Owing to their scale and scope, community planning processes need to be clearly described in terms of geographic impact as well as policy area influence. Since community plans include spatial and nonspatial issues, the community designer must understand the boundaries of the issues that need to be covered by the project.

To reach a commonly agreed-upon project description, it is a good idea to conduct either a preliminary study or a series of meetings with the leading group. The objective of this effort is to have a concentrated discussion and analysis of community issues to help develop a project definition. Reaching a commonly agreed-upon project definition is important because community planning processes tend to consume longer periods of time and more resources because of their scale. A definition helps participants keep the larger target in mind and minimizes frustrations with the process along the way.

The preliminary study will require analysis of existing information about the community, as well as discussions about the analysis to help define the project objectives. The interactive meeting format, which can accommodate either individual or focus group meetings, can yield good material for the preliminary study. In such meetings, findings from analyses of existing technical information are shared and discussed with participants, and nontechnical input from participants is acquired. Open-ended questions in focus group or individual interviews (section 6.2.4), as well as open-ended methods such as likes and dislikes analyses (section 6.2.1) and wish/have poems (section 6.2.2), are efficient means of acquiring content for the preliminary study.

Once the project description is developed, the project timeline and tasks are defined. An important task at this juncture is identifying participant groups and key contacts for outreach. Because large-scale plans need extensive outreach efforts to ensure genuine participation, sufficient time and effort must be spent to (1) inform all community members of the upcoming effort, (2) get feedback about the preferred timing and location of community design activities, and (3) get feedback about community design activity formats (e.g., the plan van being advantageous in one community, community workshops in another).

Community planning efforts in many cases take long periods of time. Therefore, continuing outreach throughout the duration of the project is very important. It is then possible for community members who cannot attend certain community design activities to provide input through other activities. Using the "snowballing" approach, in which each participant in community design activities is reminded to invite family, friends, and neighbors to the next one, throughout the project, the community designer can continue to expand the numbers of community members providing input to the project.

9.2. FORMATS AND METHODS FOR IDENTIFYING GOALS, STRATEGIES, AND ACTIONS

After the preliminary study is completed, several community design activities are needed to identify goals, strategies, and action steps. As a result of the scale, scope, and contents of the planning process, various formats and multiple activities are likely to be needed for each stage. Since larger scale goal identification is a starting point in community planning processes, many of the goal-setting methods can be efficiently used: likes and dislikes analyses (section 6.2.1), wish poems (section 6.2.2), PARK analyses (section 6.2.3), and individual and focus group interviews (section 6.2.4).

During the goal identification process, these methods are often used in multiple activity settings and multiple formats. Since the objective is to maximize outreach, it is common, for example, to see individual or focus group interviews conducted before a community design activity for which a likes and dislikes analysis is planned. Similarly, there are many methods and opportunities for participants to rank order the identified goals. Ultimately, the leading group, community members, and the community designer need to evaluate whether the community input that has been received is sufficient. This evaluation will vary from person to person and from community to community. In some cases the leading group will want to stop the input process at a certain point, or community members may ask that a specific group be invited. The community designer's task is to maximize the community input without compromising the monetary or time budget available to the community.

Strategy identification and action planning processes in community planning are similar to goal identification in the sense that multiple rounds of activities in various formats may be needed to expand the decision-making basis. Group and individual strategy identification methods and action planning methods will often need to be used in multiple community design activities and through multiple formats. Multiple activities and multiple formats not only maximize community input, they also help expand the breadth of decisions covering physical planning as well as policies on social, economic, and environmental issues.

The two methods that are very helpful in connecting plan goals, strategies, and actions to physical planning decisions are planning games (section 6.2.5) and identification of alternatives (section 6.5.4). Planning games are useful in figuring out land-use allocations, circulation issues, and possible growth directions. Methods of identifying alternatives are helpful for evaluating scenarios as some elements are changed and others held constant. Particularly with the fast scenario modeling available with current software, identifying alternatives has become easier for community designers. We discuss the use of scenario modeling in community planning in the next section.

The length and complexity of the community planning process make it conducive to the use of a variety of community design activity formats. Both workshop and meeting formats (section 6.8.1) and informal formats (section 6.8.2) can be effectively used for goal identification, strategy identification, and action planning activities. To maximize participation, it is advisable to use both formal community workshops and meetings and informal street presences, either planned (section 6.8.2.1) or on the spot (section 6.8.2.2). Plan vans (section 6.2.8.3), because of their flexibility and appeal, are effective. All these formats can also accommodate planning games and alternative identification methods when it is time to convert goals, strategies, and actions into physical planning decisions, such as land-use allocations, circulation issues, and possible growth directions.

9.3. DIGITAL APPLICATIONS IN COMMUNITY PLAN DECISION MAKING

The community planning process includes decisions that have long-term implications for members of the community and their environment. During the planning process it is important that community members understand or at least consider the consequences of their proposed ideas. Scenario planning allows community members to review the implications of their proposed decisions (Peterson, Cumming, and Carpenter 2003). With GIS software, land-use allocations and circulation options can be entered and the implications of these decisions can be visualized in three ways: (1) two-dimensionally, on a plan view; (2) three-dimensionally, by developing aerial overviews of the community based on different assumptions; and (3) numerically, in terms of the impact of these decisions on other variables, such as the impact of population growth assumptions on the community's future energy and water needs.

Beyond large-scale scenarios, specific project sites can also be visualized at the scale of community planning to address the implications of certain decisions and their visual outcomes. For example, proposed density changes on an urban corridor can be visualized through three-dimensional modeling (Figure 9.1), or a variety of traffic-calming strategies for an intersection can be visualized through computer-based renderings to demonstrate alternative outcomes to community members. The more options and their implications are visualized by means of scenario modeling or computer-based three-dimensional modeling, the better informed decisions will be.

9.1. Proposed density changes on an urban corridor visualized through three-dimensional modeling. Top: a rendering of the existing conditions; bottom: a rendering of proposed density changes

9.4. CASE: CITY OF DELANO, CALIFORNIA, STRATEGIC PLAN

Leading group: City of Delano, California, Community Development Department

Project team: Umut Toker, Kelly Main (Cal Poly City and Regional Planning faculty); Keith Woodcock (City of Delano Community Development Department); Cal Poly city and regional planning students

Project duration: Approximately 10 months

Project timeline:

CITY OF DELANO, CA STRATEGIC PLAN DEVELOPMENT PROCESS TIMELINE

P1 PRELIMINARY STUDY
Three focus group interviews and one phone interview with City Staff

P2 PRELIMINARY STUDY DOCUMENT

1 STREET INTERVIEWS
Interviews with residents

2 INTERACTIVE COMMUNITY WORKSHOP 1
Goal and strategy identification

3 INTERACTIVE COMMUNITY WORKSHOP 2
Goal and strategy identification

4 PLANNED STREET PRESENCE
Strategy prioritization during holiday celebration parade

5 PLAN VAN
Planning game in front of local grocery store

6 PLAN DOCUMENT DEVELOPMENT

Activity formats used: Focus group interviews, street interviews, interactive community workshops, planned street presence, plan van

Methods used: Focus group interviews, interviews, wish poems, selecting from among alternatives, planning games

Instruments used: Interview instruments, wish poem instruments, posters, planning game board and icons

Following the Downtown Delano Concept Plan development process (section 8.5), the Delano Community Development Department requested additional work on the development of a strategic plan for the city. The City of Delano Strategic Plan was envisioned to inform the Delano General Plan Update process (Figure 9.2). The project timeline included two phases. In the first phase a preliminary study was conducted to design the subsequent strategic planning process. In the second phase the strategic planning process itself was undertaken.

The project started with the preliminary study. The scale of the upcoming strategic planning process indicated that the preliminary study would help (1) identify outreach methods, (2) establish the strategic planning process timeline, and (3) gather background information about the city and significant issues. To achieve these outcomes, three focus group interviews were held with the city staff and key role players in the city, and one phone interview was conducted with the community services director. Interviewees who attended the focus group meetings included city staff specializing in community development, economic development, transportation, and public works; the mayor pro tem; members of the city council; planning commissioners; members of the local Chamber of Commerce; members of local nonprofit organizations; and residents of Delano. Findings from the interviews were summarized in a preliminary study report.

Based on the findings of the interviews from the preliminary study, a five-activity community design process timeline was devised. This process was undertaken in two academic quarters as a studio project with Cal Poly–San Luis Obispo's senior undergraduate city and regional planning studio. The strategic planning process started with data collection about the city and initial outreach efforts. While data on demographics, land uses, and transportation were collected and analyzed, students started sending out flyers to residents and placing phone calls to local institutions such as schools and temples. On their first visit to the city, students conducted street interviews and distributed flyers to inform residents and businesses of the upcoming community design activities.

Two interactive community workshops were then conducted. In these two workshops, residents identified goals for the city. Since the strategic plan covered topics beyond physical planning issues, the two workshops were not sequential. The goals identified in the first workshop were brought to the second workshop for the residents to further discuss and edit as necessary. The outcomes of these workshops were disseminated through local media and Delano's Community Development Department.

Students studied the goals identified in the community workshops and proposed strategies for the city to achieve its goals, based on the information gathered to that point. These strategies were summarized in six areas: housing, education, youth, downtown, safety, and economic development. At this juncture it was important to check these strategies with the residents of Delano. To obtain the greatest community input, a planned street presence activity was selected. Because this phase of the planning process fell during the holiday season, the city's annual holiday parade and celebration was chosen as the venue for this activity. Students attended the parade and the celebration with six large posters that summarized the strategies. The posters were set up in front of the city hall, where part of the celebration was also taking place. Residents who dropped by the activity were each provided with dot stickers and asked to place them on strategies they thought were important. The residents welcomed the activity and provided the students with ample input. The

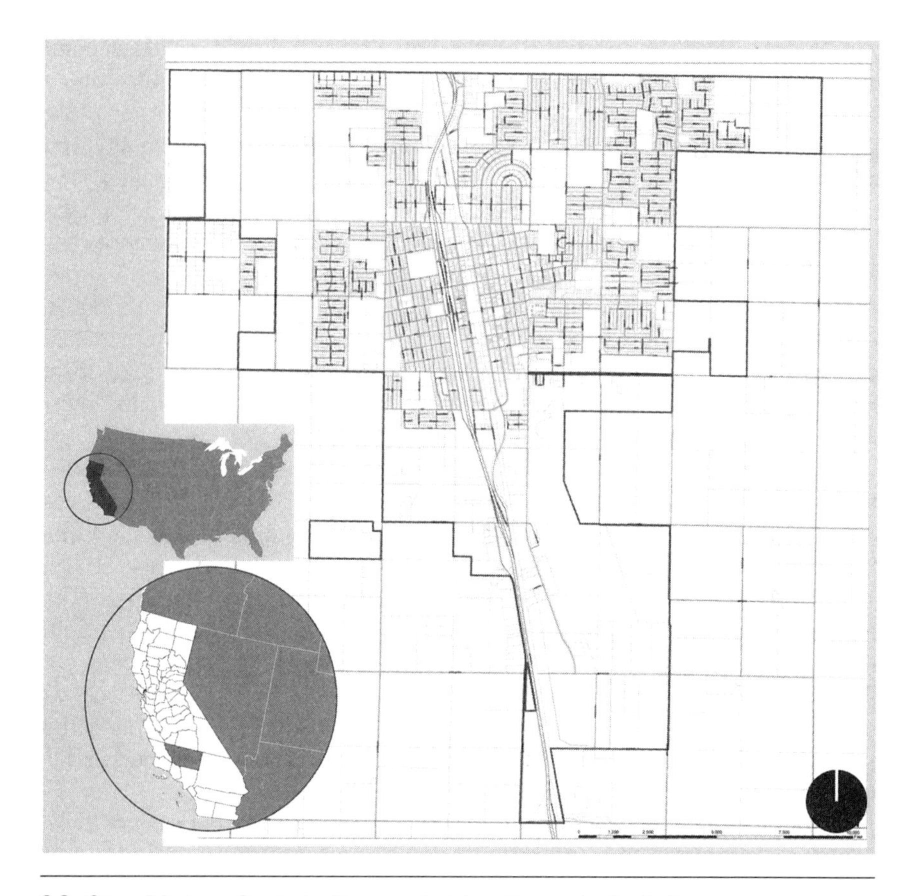

9.2. City of Delano Strategic Plan: project location and city limits

activity served not only as a double check of the strategies but also as a prioritization exercise. By the end of the activity, the students had a prioritized list of strategies that corresponded with the goals identified to that point in the planning process. The students then began expanding and detailing the strategies. In this process the students studied various cases and innovative solutions from around the United States, and in some cases from around the world.

As the strategies matured, students also started working on land-use and urban design issues. To gather input from community members about land use and urban design, a planning game was developed. The planning game consisted of a large base map of the city of Delano, a legend describing land uses, and icons representing land uses and other activities or facilities. All the land uses, activities, and facilities represented in the planning game kit had been developed based on the findings from previous interviews and community workshops.

To maximize the community input received in the planning game, the plan van format was selected. The plan van was organized on a Saturday afternoon. The parking lot of the most active storefront in the city at the time, a grocery store, was chosen as the location. The van was decorated with posters and balloons. Large tables and refreshments were set up next to the van, close to the entrance to the grocery store. The presence of the plan van was announced in the grocery store in English and Spanish. For more than two hours students received feedback from Delano residents of various ages, backgrounds, and incomes (Figure 9.3).

The findings from that exercise were analyzed and a land-use plan was developed that integrated the ideas collected. Students also developed urban design guidelines that accompanied the land-use plan. These guidelines were developed by incorporating the comments provided by the residents.

9.3. Top left: the plan van; right: a sample of the icons used in the planning game; bottom left: Delano residents playing the planning game with Cal Poly students

The City of Delano Strategic Plan was developed as an extension of the community design process. The plan included chapters on the community participation process, fundamental strategies for the future of Delano, land use, urban design guidelines, economic development, housing, community health and safety, and youth. The strategic plan was presented to the community and the city council and was well received. The strategic plan is now being used by Delano's Community Development Department as a guiding document as various elements of the general plan are updated.

9.5. CASE: MADERA RANCHOS, CALIFORNIA, AVENUE 12 CONCEPT PLAN

Leading group: Madera County Planning Department, Madera County Supervisor

Project team: Umut Toker; Adriana Neal (Cal Poly graduate student); Scott Kaiser (Madera County Planning Department); RBF Consulting

Project duration: Approximately 3 months

Project timeline:

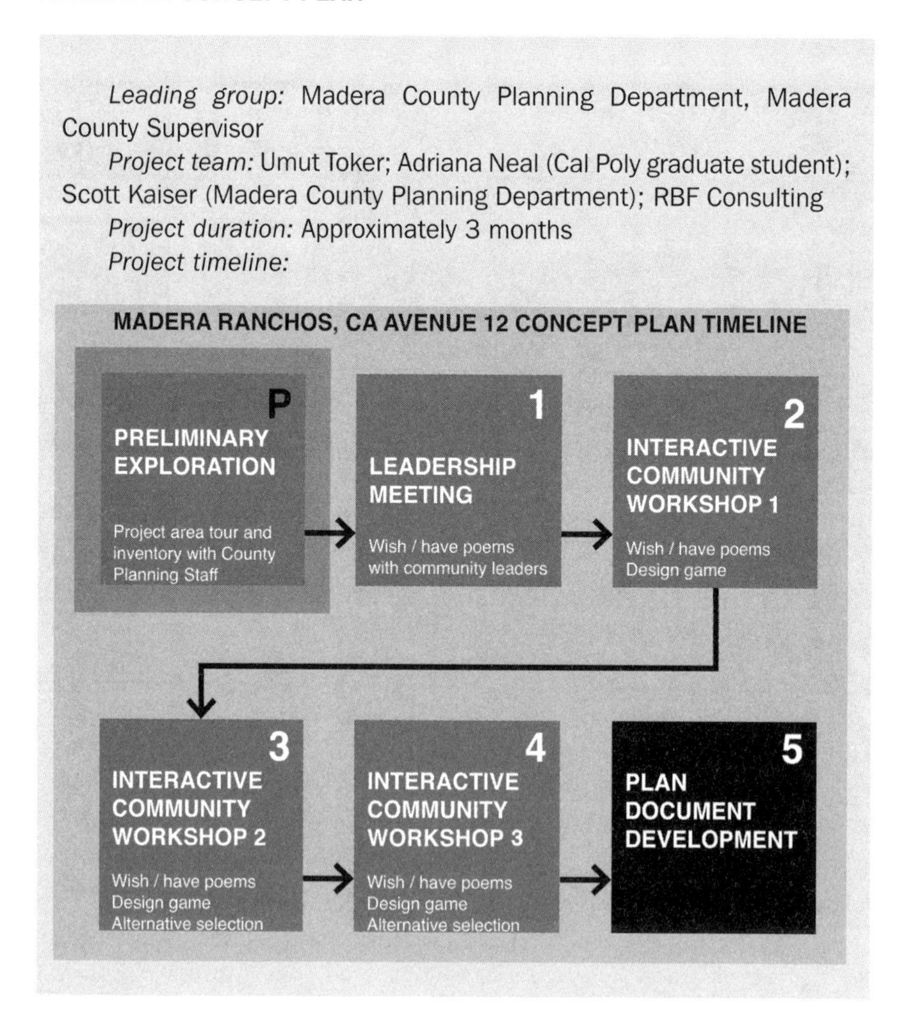

Activity formats used: Interactive community workshops
Methods used: Focus group interview, wish poems, surveys, design games
Instruments used: Interview instrument, design game board, legend, markers or pens

Madera Ranchos is an unincorporated community located north of Fresno and south of Madera, California. Including neighboring Bonadelle Ranchos to the north, the area is home to approximately 7,000 residents. Madera Ranchos was formed as a low-density community with single-family ranch homes. Originally oriented toward families living in Fresno, Madera Ranchos was planned to provide Fresno's residents with a lower density, ranch-style residential option. Over the past couple of decades the population density has increased, however, as Fresno, Madera, and other communities between the two cities have grown (Figure 9.4). The objective of this project was to develop a concept plan for Avenue 12, the main spine through Madera Ranchos, connecting State Highway 41 to the city of Madera.

Avenue 12 stretches for about 12 miles between State Highway 41 and State Highway 99. To the north and south of Avenue 12, commercial and residential buildings occupy a denser section of about two miles. The focus of this project was this more intensely used two-mile stretch. The leading group that initiated the project consisted of planners working for the Madera County Planning Department. The main concerns of the leading group were threefold. First, since Avenue 12 connected Highway 41 to Madera via Highway 99, traffic on this stretch had been steadily increasing in the years prior to the project. Second, residents of the area wanted a more pedestrian usable Avenue 12, which conflicted with the increasing traffic volume. Third, a bypass connection between State Highway 41 and State Highway 99 was in the works during the project duration. The anticipated use volume change due to the bypass project made a concept plan and a subsequent plan for Avenue 12 a necessity.

A three-phase strategy was offered to the leading group. In the first phase, a concept plan would be prepared through a participatory strategy. In the second phase, a transportation analysis of the anticipated traffic conditions would be conducted. In the third phase, an urban design plan for the area would be developed. This case study focuses on the first phase, concept plan development, since it formed the foundations of the process through integrating community input into a concept plan.

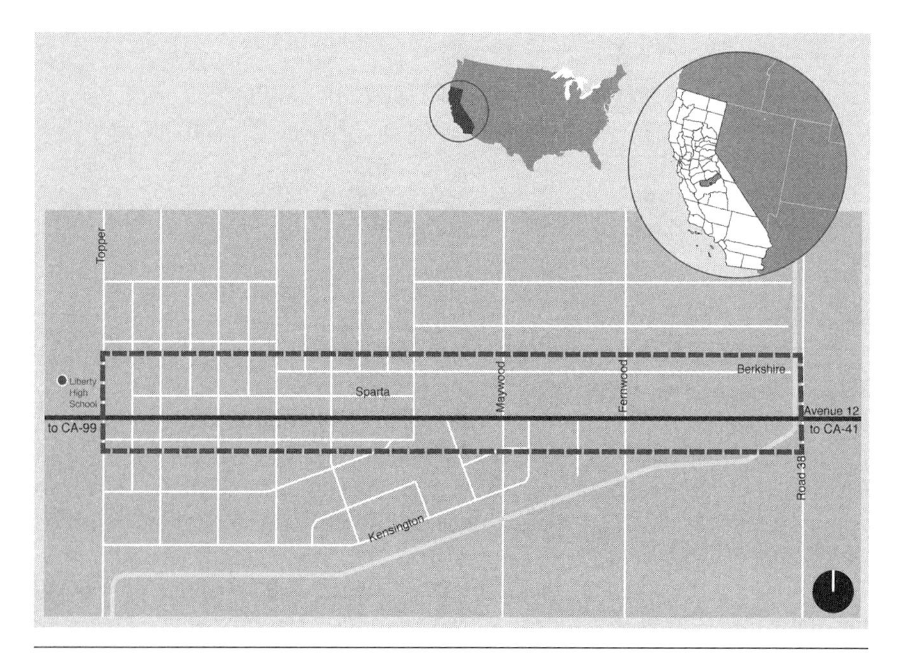

9.4. Madera Ranchos, California: its location and the project area

The concept plan development started with a preliminary exploration process. Members of the leading group and the community design team toured the project area and conducted a site inventory. Through this tour the leading group introduced key issues and site features to the community design team. The community design team followed up with collection and analysis of existing conditions as well as historical information about the community.

A "leadership meeting," so named by the leading group members, followed the preliminary exploration. The leading group preferred to kick off the process by discussing main issues with key stakeholders before any community workshops were held. This would enable the stakeholders to share the main issues identified with community members, increasing overall awareness in the community through a snowball effect. The key stakeholders attending the leadership meeting were mainly public service individuals, a local library representative, a local press representative, and local business owners.

The leadership meeting was organized as a small-scale interactive community workshop. Following the introduction of the parties the community design team used wish and have poems for idea generation. Participants were asked to identify their "wishes and haves" individually first, and then share them with the rest of the group; this exercise was followed by an open discussion. The meeting then developed into a group idea generation exercise. The community design team recorded the main issues identified and asked the participants to share these points with their friends, families, colleagues, and acquaintances in the community. In the meantime, the leading group initiated efforts for outreach, spreading the word throughout the community. Flyers, posters, and handouts were prepared and shared with community members after the leadership meeting.

The first interactive community workshop was held in the cafeteria of the local high school, which was located at the west end of the project site. The workshop started with an introduction to the key issues identified in the leadership meeting. Through this introduction observations and data about the site were discussed, as well as plans for the bypass in progress between Highways 41 and 99. Meanwhile, findings from the wish and have poem exercise conducted in the leadership meeting were displayed on posters. The posters summarized findings, and also provided additional available "I wish Avenue 12 . . ." and "I am glad Avenue 12 . . ." lines for participants to add their ideas. After the introduction there was a ten-minute break, during which participants were invited to visit the posters and add their input (Figure 9.5).

Following the break, a planning game geared toward designing the ideal Avenue 12 was played. Groups of five to eight community members were provided with large blank base maps of the project area and a legend with land-use and circulation symbols. Each group received a set of colored markers and pens. Through interactive discussion, groups developed ideal Avenue 12 schemes. Each group's scheme was shared with the rest of the participants through presentations at the end of the workshop. The workshop concluded with the presentations.

9.5. Participants were invited to add their input on posters featuring a wish poem and a have poem.

Three issues surfaced in the discussion of the groups' ideal Avenue 12 schemes. The first issue was which traffic-calming measures to focus on. While some participants advocated measures that would require modest interventions, such as bulbouts and paved intersections, others favored measures that would reorganize traffic flow, such as the installation of roundabouts. The second issue was the optimal types of vegetation for the area. Participants agreed that they wanted to add more vegetation to Avenue 12, in particular more shade trees to make walking more comfortable in the hot summer months. However, they were concerned about the water consumption of plants, since water is a scarce resource in this community. The third issue was the best kind of lighting for a public space. While the participants wanted to see increased street lighting to enhance safety on Avenue 12, they were not sure what would be most appropriate for this stretch.

Prior to the second interactive community workshop, the community design team focused on getting more information to community members on these three issues. For the traffic-calming measure, a large poster was created showing plan view diagrams of the different measures as they would appear and listing the advantages and ramifications of each (Figure 9.6). For the vegetation type issue, a survey was prepared that included photographs of tree and shrub types native to the area and information on the maintenance and water consumption requirements of each type. Similarly, for the lighting issue, a lighting survey was prepared with information on different types of illumination sources and their dimensions and use options (e.g., oriented toward pedestrians, parked vehicles, etc.). In addition to these instruments, to gather additional information and foster more informed decision making, the community design team developed a survey asking what kinds of businesses community members would like to see on Avenue 12 and a poster asking what density community members thought would be appropriate for the project area. The poster illustrating the various density options provided information on the advantages and implications of each density level.

The second community workshop started with a review and decision-making session on these issues. Throughout the review process community design team members provided information and answered questions. Participants were first asked to review the information on the traffic-calming measures poster and place dot stickers on the measures they thought would be appropriate for Avenue 12. Then participants were provided with the vegetation and lighting surveys and asked to review and mark vegetation and lighting options they considered appropriate for the project area. After this participants were asked to note down what kinds of businesses they would like to see on Avenue 12, using the businesses survey. Finally, participants were asked to review the information on land-use densities and place dot stickers on the densities they thought would be appropriate for Avenue 12.

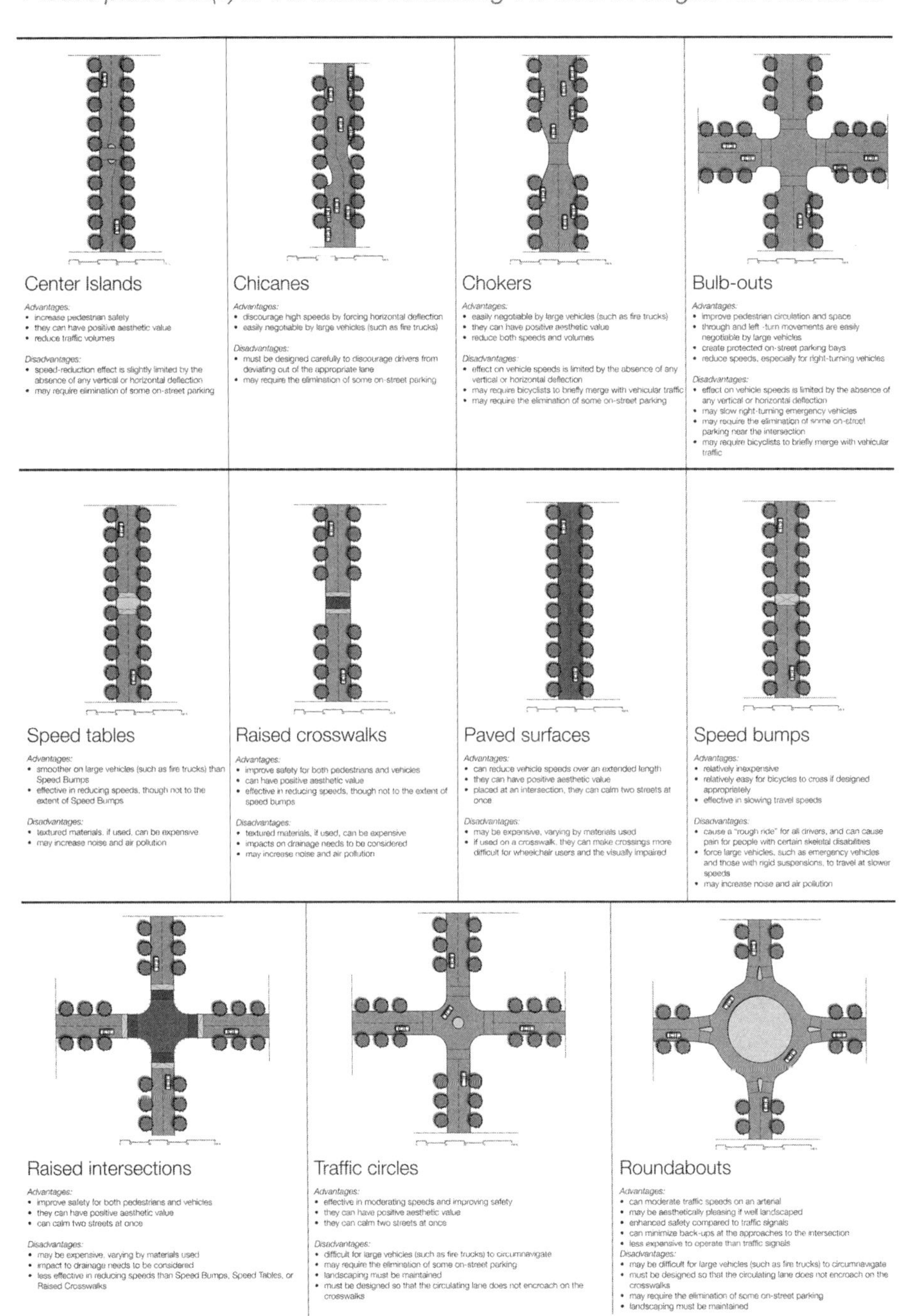

9.6. Left: Poster providing information on traffic-calming measures; right: survey providing information on vegetation options

In addition to these instruments, the community design team prepared large wish poem and have poem posters that displayed ideas garnered from both the leadership meeting and the first community workshop. In this workshop participants were asked to prioritize these ideas by placing dot stickers next to ideas they agreed with. Because the posters also had blank lines that started with "I wish Avenue 12 . . ." and I am glad Avenue 12 . . . ," participants were able to add new ideas that had not been introduced earlier.

After these activities participants met in small groups of five to eight and played the planning game conducted in the previous workshop to provide additional input. Those participants who had not attended the first workshop played the game with a blank base map. Those who attended the first workshop further refined the plan ideas developed there. At the end of this session participants shared the ideas generated and refined by each group.

For interested community members who could not attend either of the first two community workshops, a third community workshop was organized two weeks later. The structure of the third workshop was the same as the second. The same instruments were used, asking participants to provide input on the same issues. Community members were thus able to provide feedback and add any other ideas that had not been looked at earlier.

The community design team analyzed the information and ideas generated in the leadership meeting and the three community workshops. A draft plan document was developed and made available for review by the public and by members of the leading group. The plan document was then finalized by integrating the comments and recommendations. The plan document developed for Avenue 12 begins by describing the existing conditions of the site and giving some of the history of the Madera Ranchos community. The participatory process is described, and the outcomes of the community workshops and the leadership meeting are introduced. These outcomes are then interpreted and developed into plan decisions. The plan decisions developed for Avenue 12 focus on land uses, circulation, sustainability, and natural resources. The land-use section proposes a mix of uses and an expanded public space structure on Avenue 12. The circulation section considers traffic-calming and pedestrian-oriented features, including sidewalks and lighting. Finally, the plan introduces ideas for plantings on the two-mile stretch, a new topic of bicycle friendliness, and water consumption issues in the sustainability and natural resources section.

The Madera Ranchos Avenue 12 Concept Plan was introduced to the community as the starting point for the upcoming phases, which would take up transportation and urban design issues. The plan helped summarize the needs and wishes of the community regarding the future of Avenue 12. The process also introduced a variety of planning issues and concepts to the community, enabling it to proceed to the next two planning phases with better awareness and more knowledge.

10 Participatory Decision Making at the Regional Planning Scale

The next scalar step after community planning is a large one: regional planning. Regional planning provides guidance on long-term land-use and policy decisions that affect the future of towns and cities in the targeted region. The number of people who would be affected by regional plans in the long term is high, and therefore participatory decision making at the regional (or areawide) scale is particularly important. Because of the scope of regional planning projects, the large geographic area covered, and the number of role players involved, implementing community design methods in regional planning is a lengthy and challenging process. There is good reason, however, to practice community design methods and engage in participatory decision making at the scale of regional planning.

The plan types we will cover in this discussion are commonly referred to as regional plans or areawide plans. Regional or areawide plans provide guidance on long-term land-use and policy decisions that influence the future of towns and cities in the targeted region. Consequently the number of people that would be affected by regional plans in long term is high, and participatory decision making at this scale is particularly important. Since regional planning provides long-term land-use and policy guidance, towns' and cities' decisions on how to manage their urban versus rural areas, as well as their decisions on conservation efforts, are affected by these plans:

> The areawide land policy plan offers general guidance to future land use and development decisions. The plan is based on an analysis of land suitability and an analysis of demand for land for urbanization and open spaces. A key element of this plan is a map of three general land use policy districts: conservation, rural and urban. (Berke and Godschalk 2006, 61)

Also affected are rivers and ports, transportation corridors, and the expected future labor market. Virtually anything associated with large aggregations of humans is on the table in regional planning.

Recent trends toward urbanization around the world place regional plans in the spotlight as a means of influencing the future. As of 2006, more than half the world's population lived in cities, and this figure will only increase. Meanwhile, the number of metropolitan areas around the world has also been increasing, along with an accompanying increase in infrastructure and in the consumption of natural resources and agricultural land. Consequently, metropolitan areas are experiencing greater uncertainty about their ability to respond to resource shortages or natural disasters. The question facing metropolitan areas around the world today, therefore, is how to develop the resilience to absorb such changes while maintaining stability for their residents (Steiner 2006). Regional planning efforts aim at helping with these joint tasks through long-term decision making.

Because large populations are involved in long-term plans for metropolitan areas, the need for participatory decision making is self-evident. The issues at this level of decision making are complex and demand multifaceted expertise. On one side, the planning process must provide expert information on technical issues to the residents who will be participating in the decision-making process so that they can be better informed when communicating their needs and wishes. On the other side, the residents of metropolitan areas must provide the planning process with expert information on the complexity of their day-to-day lives, so that the planning process can respond to their needs. The planning profession has responded to this phenomenon by incorporating methods from various disciplines as well as developing new ones. In this chapter we review the application of these methods, from outreach to project completion.

10.1. PROJECT DESCRIPTION AND DEVELOPING AN OUTREACH STRATEGY

Regional planning efforts are often undertaken as joint ventures. In an effort to ensure the participation of large and complex resident groups, it is not uncommon for private, nonprofit organizations (PNPOs) to form. Such organizations may not be part of local government but are often funded by local government. By recruiting technical expertise and communicating local communities' day-to-day experience of a region, PNPOs provide the two-way information flow needed in such complex projects.

Another model for providing regional-scale organization and planning efforts entails the formation of a joint powers authority (JPA) by local governments in a region. In this model, several local governments voluntarily form a JPA to organize and provide regional planning efforts that are to the mutual benefit of their local communities. Councils of governments (COGs) are examples of JPAs.

To maximize community participation in regional planning, planners typically start by working with key groups. Key groups include regional decision makers, community leaders, and interested members of the general public. Since projects of this scale have long-term implications, it is also important to incorporate multigenerational concerns early in the process.

PNPOs and JPAs are instrumental in getting the project description off the ground. The two-way information flow they provide between communities and technical experts yields a project description that would be difficult to achieve without their efforts. Cases of regional planning like the ones discussed in this chapter uphold the accepted wisdom that the project description tends to evolve as the project moves forward. As more role players are engaged in the process and as previously unconsidered issues come up for discussion, the project description becomes more precise and well posed.

Along with firming up the project description, there must be expanded outreach efforts. PNPOs and JPAs are also instrumental here. To expand outreach at the metropolitan or regional scale, they may use multiple methods, both indirect, such as placing advertisements in local newspapers, in local media, and on the Internet, and direct, such as contacting local businesses, community organizations, and individuals. Outreach for regional planning needs to be sustained over the course of the project because of the large scale and large number of role players.

Since the outreach efforts must be quite large and continued for a long period of time, it is especially helpful to create a visual language for PNPOs, JPAs, and the planning process. With a unique visual language and lexicon—shapes, images, colors—these organizations and other interested parties can uphold the process visually in community members' minds throughout the project's duration.

10.2. FORMATS AND METHODS FOR IDENTIFYING GOALS, STRATEGIES, AND ACTIONS

Identifying goals at the regional planning scale requires considerable two-way information flow between technical experts and local communities. PNPOs and JPAs will need to invest in the education of local communities on technical issues. They will also need to be educated themselves about issues in the daily lives of the local communities. Since at this stage the intent is to identify longer term goals, methods such as likes and dislikes analyses (section 6.2.1), wish poems (section 6.2.2), and PARK analyses (section 6.2.3) can be used. One-on-one and focus group interviews (section 6.2.4) can help expand the goal identification effort in various informal settings such as local businesses and schools.

In strategy identification and action planning at the regional scale, the complexity and technical background of issues under scrutiny will often require that community members be provided with extensive information when making decisions. Beyond the complexity of issues, at this scale the unpredictability of future conditions is a concern. A method that has come into use in the past decade to reduce overall uncertainty is scenario planning, which presents a variety of possible futures as one or another element in the scenario is changed. Through the systematic analysis of possible futures and their implications, scenario planning allows planners and communities to make better informed decisions (Peterson, Cumming, and Carpenter 2003).

GIS-based scenario modeling software is developing rapidly. The long-term implications of regional-scale decisions can be modeled and presented to community members using such software. Visual depictions such as three-dimensional models or graphics showing visual or numerical changes over the long term can be shared with community members through scenario modeling. Scenario modeling therefore allows community members to identify strategies and action steps, and to rank order preferred options.

The scale and complexity of the regional planning process mandate the use of multiple community activity formats in decision making (section 6.8). Both community workshops and charrettes are frequently organized because the format supports in-depth discussions. Informal activities such as planned street presences, on the other hand, are advantageous because staffers can add to the outreach effort while acquiring input from community members. Finally, projects at the regional scale commonly use the Internet to disseminate information and increase outreach, communication, and recruitment of community input.

Regional planning projects need to be envisioned as multiformat, multimethod efforts. From the perspective of participatory decision making, the ultimate objective is to integrate as many individuals and institutions as possible into the process. Therefore, the community design activity formats and methods must fit these individuals' and institutions' schedules. Format and method selection will need to be done based on the local context.

10.3. METHODS FOR INVOLVING LARGE-SCALE COMMUNITIES

Because of the number of individuals and institutions that need to be integrated into the planning process, interactive discussions need to be approached carefully in regional planning. While these discussions are very informative and yield rich data, they are also relatively more time-consuming than some other methods. Consequently, in larger scale regional planning efforts, methods that provide alternatives and encourage people to make informed decisions come to the fore.

Goal setting in participatory regional planning will require more extensive deliberation through face-to-face interactions, especially at the beginning of the process. For goal setting, relatively conventional methods such as wish poems and likes and dislikes analyses can be rewarding. As the goal-setting process moves forward, methods offering the selection of alternatives are increasingly utilized. The selection from alternatives method (section 6.5.4) is used more often in strategy identification and action planning at the regional scale. By these stages in the process, participants have been exposed to a certain amount of information about the project and are better equipped to make selections from alternatives than they were at earlier stages.

Selection from alternatives methods may be executed using conventional instruments, such as on-the-spot surveys or mail-in surveys. The surveys provide information on the advantages, challenges, and implications of each alternative and are administered in workshops or at meetings, through street presences, or through media such as newspapers and the Internet.

A relatively new approach to survey instrumentation is the use of "clickers." Clickers are essentially remote electronic voting devices that enable individuals to pick from among the various alternatives presented (typically the choices are projected on a large screen). A clicker is especially advantageous when coupled with scenario planning. Two- or three-dimensional visualizations of strategies, actions, and their implications in a variety of scenarios can be displayed to the community and the responses collected. Most clicker systems also provide an on-the-spot summary of community members' responses, so the results can be observed immediately.

Perhaps the biggest advantage of clicker systems is their ability to allow the participation of large groups of people at once, with all the responses electronically recorded. One of the most successful examples of this use was demonstrated in the decision-making process for rebuilding structures and the surround at Ground Zero in Lower Manhattan. Thousands of people were able to participate in the process and share their opinions on options at once (Faga 2006). The method can be used the same way by PNPOs and JPAs in large-scale regional planning efforts to integrate community input into the process. A couple of cautions need to be kept in mind when using alternative selection–based methods, however: first, these methods provide quantified results that essentially mimic voting, and second, they yield more productive results when complemented with additional community design methods that allow for explanation, interaction, and developing a mutual understanding of issues.

10.4. CASE: ENVISION CENTRAL TEXAS

Leading group: Local civic leaders; Envision Central Texas
Project team: Fregonese Calthorpe Associates
Project duration: 2001–present
Project timeline:

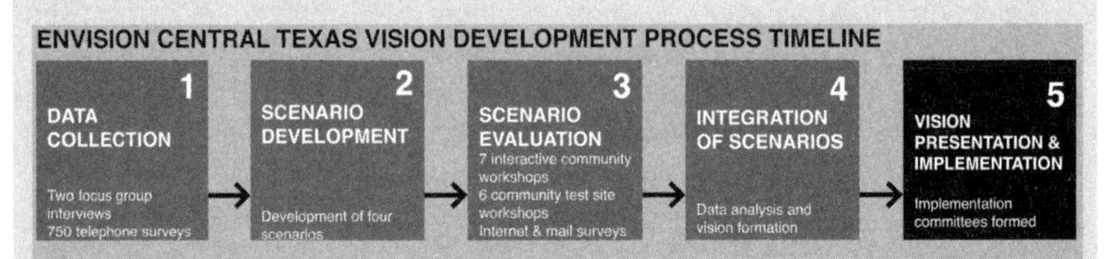

Activity formats used: Internet, mail and telephone surveys, interactive community workshops

Methods used: Planning games, Internet, mail and telephone surveys, focus group interviews, scenario planning

Instruments used: Planning game toolkits, survey instruments, interview instruments, GIS systems

The Envision Central Texas regional planning process is a rich example of community design at the regional scale, not only in terms of its size and the number of participants but also in terms of the variety of outreach and community involvement formats and methods. It is an example of local leaders organizing as the leading group to form a PNPO for action.

The Central Texas region covers the Austin metropolitan region and five surrounding counties: Bastrop, Caldwell, Hays, Travis, and Williamson (Figure 10.1). Throughout the 20th century, growth in the Central Texas region has been horizontal, in the form of low-density suburban environments. Until the Envision Central Texas effort, the Central Texas region did not have a comprehensive plan to manage its growth (Steiner 2008).

Local civic leaders founded Envision Central Texas in 2002 as a PNPO to help develop a vision for the future growth of the region. The organization's guiding principles were identified as follows:

> (i) The region's transportation system, environmental planning and preservation goals, social equity aspirations, and economic foundation should be coordinated to support a sustainable regional community. (ii) Regional policy choices should support choices of housing, transportation and employment. (iii) Central Texas values diversity in all policy choices. (iv) All decisions

should promote enhanced quality of life for the residents of Central Texas. (Envision Central Texas 2004)

In an effort to develop a vision for the region, Envision Central Texas hired Fregonese Calthorpe Associates, professionals nationally known for their work in participatory vision development at the regional scale. The initial community involvement process was launched in 2002 and continued for about two years, yielding a vision for the future in five phases.

In the first phase of the community involvement process, the leading group and the community design professionals conducted a series of interviews, interactive community workshops, and surveys. They gathered input from the region's residents about their ideas for the future of the region and their responses to possible growth scenarios. Early in this process, two focus group interviews were conducted to gather input for the development of the four scenarios. This was supplemented by 750 telephone surveys of randomly selected residents of the region.

In the second phase of the process, the community design team digitized this input in GIS format and integrated the ideas into four major scenarios. The four scenarios ranged from low-density, "business as usual"

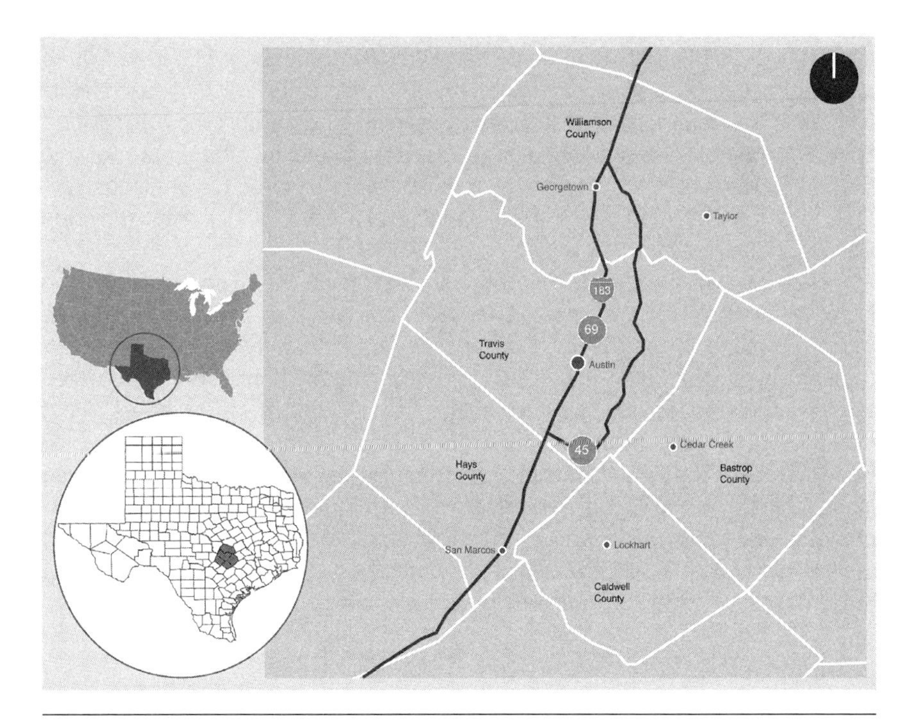

10.1. The Central Texas region: the Austin metropolitan region and Bastrop, Caldwell, Hays, Travis, and Williamson counties

suburban future growth to higher density vertical growth in the existing settlements of the region.

In the third phase, the region's residents were presented with the four growth scenarios. In addition, visualizations for individual sites were developed for the residents to see the implications of the emerging planning decisions. Through interviews, interactive community workshops, and surveys, community members evaluated and indicated their preferences for the four scenarios. A total of seven interactive community workshops were held to gather input about the scenarios developed. Meanwhile, six community test site workshops were conducted in which implications of planning decisions for specific sites were discussed using visualizations. Toward the end of this phase, a public feedback survey was conducted both through the Internet and by mail, and about 12,500 residents of the region answered it.

In the fourth phase, the four scenarios were compiled into one by the community design team. Finally, in the fifth phase, a "consensus vision" was presented to the community, and implementation task forces were formed to follow up with implementation. A total of seven implementation committees were formed, focusing on transportation and land-use integration, economic development coordination, housing and jobs balance, density and mixed uses, open space funding, social equity, and recognition of best practices (Steiner 2008). During the transition to the development of implementation committees, a "leadership workshop" with about 150 civic leaders was held to discuss implementation (Envision Central Texas 2004).

The vision document presented to the community in 2004 documents a total of six community input formats used in a large number of activities. Envision Central Texas continues to develop plans for the future of the Central Texas region. It is governed by a board of directors and has full-time staff for the management of planning processes and events (Envision Central Texas n.d.).

The Envision Central Texas case is an example of a community-based initiative to develop a community-based plan for the future of an entire region. Three key aspects of this process contributed to its success. First, through the utilization of multiple activity formats, methods, and instruments, the planning process successfully integrated thousands of residents' input into the vision and implementation efforts. Second, the timeline design provided feedback loops and multiple opportunities for area residents to provide input. Third, the formation and consistent attention of a PNPO helped the process move forward in an organized fashion. The ongoing involvement of the PNPO made the organization of a complex, large-scale decision-making process with an extensive number of participants manageable.

10.5. CASE: "HOW SHALL WE GROW?" CENTRAL FLORIDA'S VISIONING PROCESS

Leading group: Orlando Regional Chamber of Commerce; local civic leaders; Central Florida Partnership

Project team: Myregion.org, Renaissance Planning Group

Project Duration: 2006–present

Project Timeline:

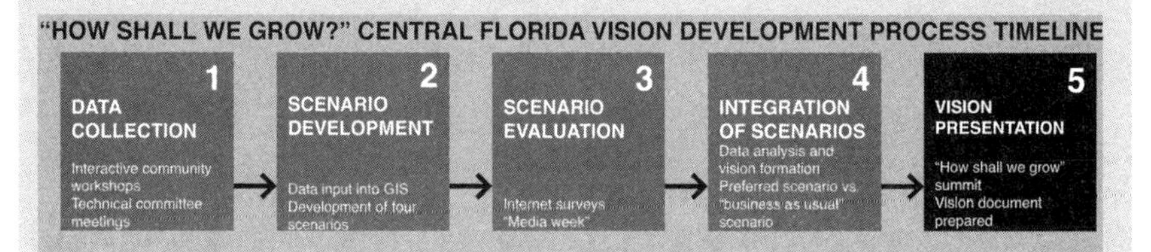

Activity formats used: Interactive community workshops, Internet-based surveys

Methods used: Planning games, surveys, scenario planning

Instruments used: Planning game kits, paper and Web-based survey instruments, GIS systems

Another regional planning process that exhibits a variety of community involvement formats, methods, and instruments applied at the regional scale is the "How Shall We Grow?" vision development process of Central Florida. The project encompasses seven counties in Central Florida: Brevard, Lake, Orange, Osceola, Polk, Seminole, and Volusia (Figure 10.2).

The roots of the "How Shall We Grow?" campaign reach back to the late 1990s, when the Orlando Regional Chamber of Commerce initiated Myregion.org, a PNPO that focuses on local regional development. Its main goals are (1) organizing and training regional leaders, (2) conducting regional research to guide regional efforts, (3) identifying key regional issues and opportunities, and (4) nurturing an understanding of regional collaboration (Myregion.org n.d.). Essentially, Myregion.org functions as a PNPO that gathers community members in the Central Florida region to help organize participatory decision making for the region's future. Myregion.org worked with Renaissance Planning Group in this process.

"How Shall We Grow?" was launched as a regional vision development process in 2006. Acknowledging the state of Florida's projection that the population of the region would double by 2050, Myregion.org staff conducted outreach. Input was sought from three sources: local governments,

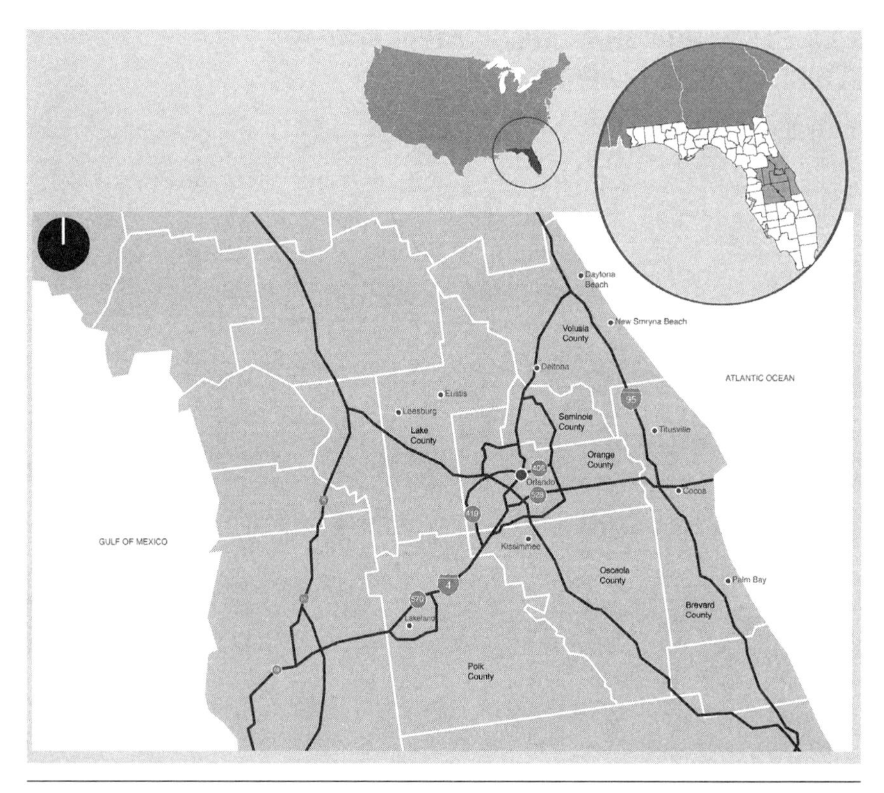

10.2. "How Shall We Grow?" encompasses Brevard, Lake, Orange, Osceola, Polk, Seminole, and Volusia counties in Central Florida.

key stakeholders such as community leaders, and Central Florida residents. During the first two years the process focused on developing possible scenarios for the future of the region. A combination of interactive community workshops and technical committee meetings was used in this process. The interactive community workshops were community input sessions in which methods such as planning games, mapping, and scenario evaluation were used. Between 100 and 300 community members participated in each community workshop. A total of approximately 20,000 community members attended various workshops throughout the process, which was dubbed "community conversation."

Technical committee meetings, on the other hand, focused on specific technical areas. Experts such as local government planners, elected officials, and civic leaders from the seven counties of the project area attended these meetings for idea generation and exchange. During this process, outreach to the community was also expanded. The website of the organization, the main information resource, was redesigned and a blog was created for updates. A regional event brought 450 community members together to discuss the future of the region.

The process yielded four scenarios that illustrated ways in which the population increase and growth of the region could be accommodated. One of the scenarios was dedicated to "business as usual," presenting how the region would look if it were to continue on its current path.

Through an online survey and a media week of activities, a common vision for the region was selected. More than 7,000 community members responded to the survey in the selection of the vision. The selected vision was presented at the "How Shall We Grow?" summit, which was a community event attended by 600 people. More than 86 percent of the participants had identified the "business as usual" scenario as the least desirable for the future. The respondents put particular emphasis on developing within existing urban centers instead of sprawl, preserving environmental and agricultural resources, and developing the transportation infrastructure that would efficiently connect people.

The vision, its background, and its rationale were summarized in a vision document titled "How Shall We Grow?" (Myregion.org 2007). The vision document presents the current state of the region and describes two scenarios for 2050, the first with the existing trends continuing and the second showing the region following the selected vision. The selected vision underlines that natural resources of the region should be preserved, the region's heritage of small villages and agriculture should be maintained, development should be accommodated in a variety of settlement sizes, and more transportation choices for people and freight should be developed. The document then presents key principles that need to be followed and actions that need to be taken to make this vision a reality (Myregion.org 2007).

The Envision Central Texas and Central Florida's visioning processes demonstrate that in community participation processes conducted at a regional scale, the leading group's formation of an organization to oversee the process is critical. In both cases, PNPOs were formed to help organize and facilitate the community involvement processes. These cases also illustrate that it is crucial to maximize community input despite the high numbers of community members that must be targeted through outreach methods.

Thus far we have considered participatory decision making concerning the built environment at increasingly larger scales, culminating in the regional scale, the largest we examine in this book. In Chapter 11 we turn the telescope around and look at projects of a much smaller scale and with many fewer users, those involving a single site.

11 Participatory Decision Making at the Site-Specific Design Scale

The rationale and objectives of community design methods at the site-specific scale and architectural form scale are not different from those associated with large-scale planning. The outcome, however, is a specific design proposal, not a plan proposal intended for use in overseeing various types of development, such as urban design plans, community plans, or regional plans. At the site-specific scale and architectural scale, the product may be a specific site design or a few alternative design proposals for a building. Such an outcome provides a specific guide for future steps and includes details that designs at larger planning scales do not try to provide. Consequently, while the methods are essentially the same, the instruments used to capture community wishes may need modifying. In this chapter we review methods and instruments for participatory decision making at the site-specific design scale and architectural form scale, and look at two examples.

11.1. UNDERSTANDING CLIENT NEEDS AND PROGRAM DEVELOPMENT

The leading group contacting the community designer for projects at the site-specific scale often will have close contact with either the end users of the project or individuals highly knowledgeable about project requirements. Consequently, the first step is to gather detailed information from the leading group about future users of the site or building.

Focus group meetings with the leading group are advisable to gather this information and develop a program. A program is a problem statement about how a site-specific or an architectural design should perform when built: it specifies the required activities to be accommodated, as well as their interrelationships, in terms of both space and use. William Peña and

Steven Parshall in *Problem Seeking* (2001) identify five steps for developing a program: establish *goals*, collect and analyze *facts*, uncover and test *concepts*, determine *needs*, and state the *problem*. The progression of these steps resembles that of the "V" process.

To understand end users' needs and develop a program for the site or the building, in-depth interviews and wish poems are advisable. Depending on the history and existing conditions of the site under consideration, a likes and dislikes analysis (section 6.2.1) and a PARK analysis (section 6.2.3) may be used to identify program needs in relation to the existing conditions. Once identified, program needs should be ranked by the community in order of priority. This helps the leading group think about potential shortages of time, space, or monetary resources and clarifies the direction the group would like to take.

11.2. CONCEPTUAL DESIGN, DESIGN DEVELOPMENT METHODS, AND ACQUIRING FEEDBACK

Once the program needs are identified and prioritized, a community or group activity should be undertaken to develop conceptual diagrams and design concepts. At this point the leading group and the community designer should expand the size of the participant group. Outreach can be conducted by the leading group as well as by the community designer, depending on the project context.

Planning games (section 6.5.2) or design games (section 6.5.3) are valuable activities during the conceptual design phase. The community designer first needs to develop the planning or design game according to the program needs. A base map of the site is prepared and, depending on the size of the project, a grid is overlaid to provide a sense of scale. At this point, various features of the site can be marked on the base map. For example, a key feature such as an old tree on the site can be marked as an asset on the base map. Other features surrounding the site, such as buildings, landmarks, and streets, can be marked to orient the participants. The intent is to provide participants with information to help facilitate creative thinking about the site, given existing conditions.

Once the base map is prepared, design game icons are fashioned to accord with program needs. The properties of design game icons depend on the level of detail achieved in the program development process. If the program provides area information about the activities, design game icons can be sized proportionally to the anticipated area of their spaces. The proportional sizing allows participants to take some key factors into consideration in the development of their ideal layout for the site or the building:

1. The size of spaces affects their locational interrelationships.
2. The location and size of spaces can affect the performance of other spaces.

3. Trade-offs may be necessary when available space is limited, and parts of the program may have to be accommodated on different floors.

The use of the design game in idea generation is similar to the use of planning or design games in decision making for larger scale projects. Members of the leading group and community participants divide into small groups to generate ideal layouts for the site, or schematic floor plans in the case of a building. Once each group finishes developing its ideal layout or schematic plans, it is asked to present its findings to the others. After this presentation, the community designer integrates the ideal site layouts or schematic floor plans into a single integrated schematic proposal that satisfies as many needs as possible. A community review of this integrated schematic proposal is then undertaken to be sure that all leading group members and participants are comfortable with it. Once feedback from the community review is received and integrated into the schematic proposal, the design development process can be initiated.

11.3. DESIGN DEVELOPMENT

Following program development and conceptual design development comes design development. At this point the community designer develops various aspects of the site or building and receives feedback from, in many cases, the leading group.

The design ideas developed in this phase are communicated through two-dimensional plan, section, and elevation drawings as well as three-dimensional views. Design development is a much more transparent process for the leading group and end users than it used to be, thanks to ongoing developments in digital design. Depending on the size of the project, the community designer can make the design development process open to the leading group and end users by (1) providing still images of how the design proposal is developing, (2) providing still images of how the design proposal would look on the existing site when built, or (3) providing fly-through animations of the design proposal and its various features.

Two and three-dimensional representations of design ideas are interconnected, and changes to the proposal will require updating of both. Recent developments in digital applications have made this process cheaper and faster than ever before, and this trend is expected to continue. At the site-specific scale, the equivalent of GIS, building information modeling (BIM) has made the process even faster and more efficient. By connecting two- and three-dimensional building attributes and other properties (e.g., material and area), BIM software now allows instant editing and updating of two- and three-dimensional representations as well as numerical data, such as costs.

Such new and developing digital applications make it easier to share information with the leading group and potential end users of the proposal, and to incorporate feedback. It is important to use the potential of digital applications to the advantage of the project, however. In this sense, digital applications need to be used as a means of providing the leading group and the end users with further access to the design development process. In doing so, it is crucial that the level of detail and presentation of ideas do not give the impression that design development is finalized. It is the community designer's responsibility to make digital applications an integral part of the open decision-making process.

11.4. CASE: SANDHILLS FAMILY HERITAGE ASSOCIATION COMMUNITY CENTER, SPRING LAKE, NORTH CAROLINA

Leading group: Sandhills Family Heritage Association (SFHA)

Project team: Henry Sanoff (North Carolina State University faculty), Umut Toker, Zeynep Toker (North Carolina State University graduate students)

Project duration: Approximately 3 months

Project timeline:

Activity formats used: Interactive community workshop

Methods used: Focus group interview, design game

Instruments used: Interview instrument, design game board and icons, mailed survey

Spring Lake is a town of approximately 8,000 in central North Carolina. It has a rich rural history, with many of the residents and families having known one another for decades (Figure 11.1). The town displays a good example of southern hospitality with its kind and friendly residents. The leading group approaching the community design team, the Sandhills Family Heritage Association (SFHA), wanted to help sustain this spirit with this project. The SFHA is a nonprofit organization that focuses on heritage preservation, land ownership, public education, and economic development. The project site was an existing community center that was not being used at the time the project started. The main objective of the project was to develop a design proposal for reuse and expansion of the existing building.

The leading group approached the community design team with a request to conduct a participatory design process to help develop this design proposal. The SFHA had hired a designer for the development of a design proposal prior to this project. However, the resulting proposal recommended demolishing the old building. The SFHA and community members felt this was not a desirable approach because the old building had sentimental value. Their family members and relatives had built the building in 1960s. Thereafter the building had been used for many community events, such as weddings, birthday parties, and dances. During the civil rights movement of the 1960s members of the community had many pro–civil rights meetings in this building.

The SFHA and community members therefore wanted to initiate a participatory design process, one through which community members' voices would be heard and their values reflected in the design proposal. The community design team proposed a four-phase design development timeline. The process would start with focus group interviews, which would serve as the basis for developing the program for the building. An interactive community workshop would then be held to develop the plan layout of the building. In the final phase, a design proposal would be developed, then finalized after community feedback.

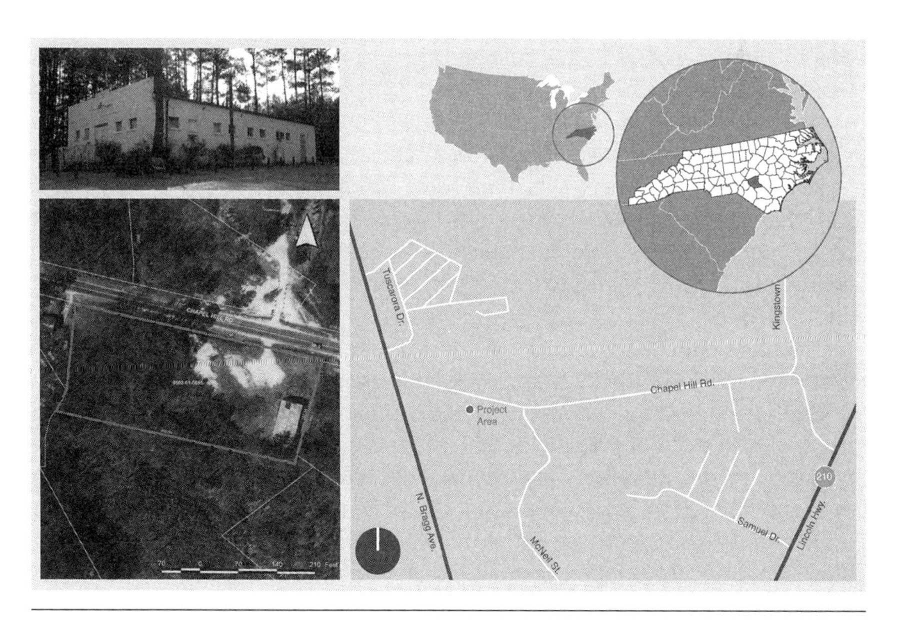

11.1. Spring Lake, North Carolina: its location, the project site, and the existing building

The SFHA directors accepted the proposed strategy, and the community design process was initiated. Initially, focus group interviews were conducted with about 10 members of the SFHA. Participants were asked to divide into two groups, and interviews were conducted with both groups. The participants were mostly elderly individuals, who introduced the community design team to the history of the community as well as the existing building. After this discussion the community design team asked the participants a series of questions about the activities that should be accommodated in the building.

The information gathered during the focus group interviews was analyzed, and the community design team developed a preliminary building program based on the findings. The preliminary program included spaces such as a soup kitchen, assembly space, exhibit space for historical items from the community's past, and classrooms for various training programs. For the community workshop that was to follow the focus group interviews, the team developed a design game. The game consisted of assigning icons representing the spaces in the program to a base map of the project site. The base map was prepared to show the existing building on the site, as well as site features such as a large level difference that existed on the site. A grid overlay on the base map gave participants a sense of scale. The icons for the use spaces were prepared in sizes that reflected the anticipated square footage of the spaces. Blank icons of various sizes were also prepared to give community members the option of creating additional spaces in case the focus group interviews did not yield complete coverage of activity ideas. By playing this game, not only would community members develop plan layouts for the building, they would do so keeping site constraints and space sizes in mind (Figure 11.2).

The community workshop for identifying building plan layout ideas was held in the meeting facilities of a local church. The workshop started with a discussion of the issues that had come up in the focus group interviews. After this discussion the design game was introduced. Working in small groups, participants developed their ideal plan layouts in approximately 90 minutes. Each group then presented its layout to the rest of the participants (Figure 11.3).

After the community workshop, the layout proposals developed by community members were analyzed and patterns of spatial relationships and activity locations were identified by the community design team. Based on this analysis, the community design team also prepared a proposal that integrated these ideas into one layout. This proposal was developed using the same base map and same icons as the ones used in the workshop so that the participants who attended the workshop could easily remember the visual language they had worked with and read the layout proposal. The layout proposal was reproduced on a feedback sheet that was mailed out to the community members along with pre-stamped, pre-addressed envelopes. By using the feedback sheet, community members could evaluate to what extent the proposal reflected the ideas generated in the workshop (Figure 11.4).

Once community members' responses were received, design proposal development started. The proposal was shaped around a central assembly space that was connected to the existing structure. Special emphasis was

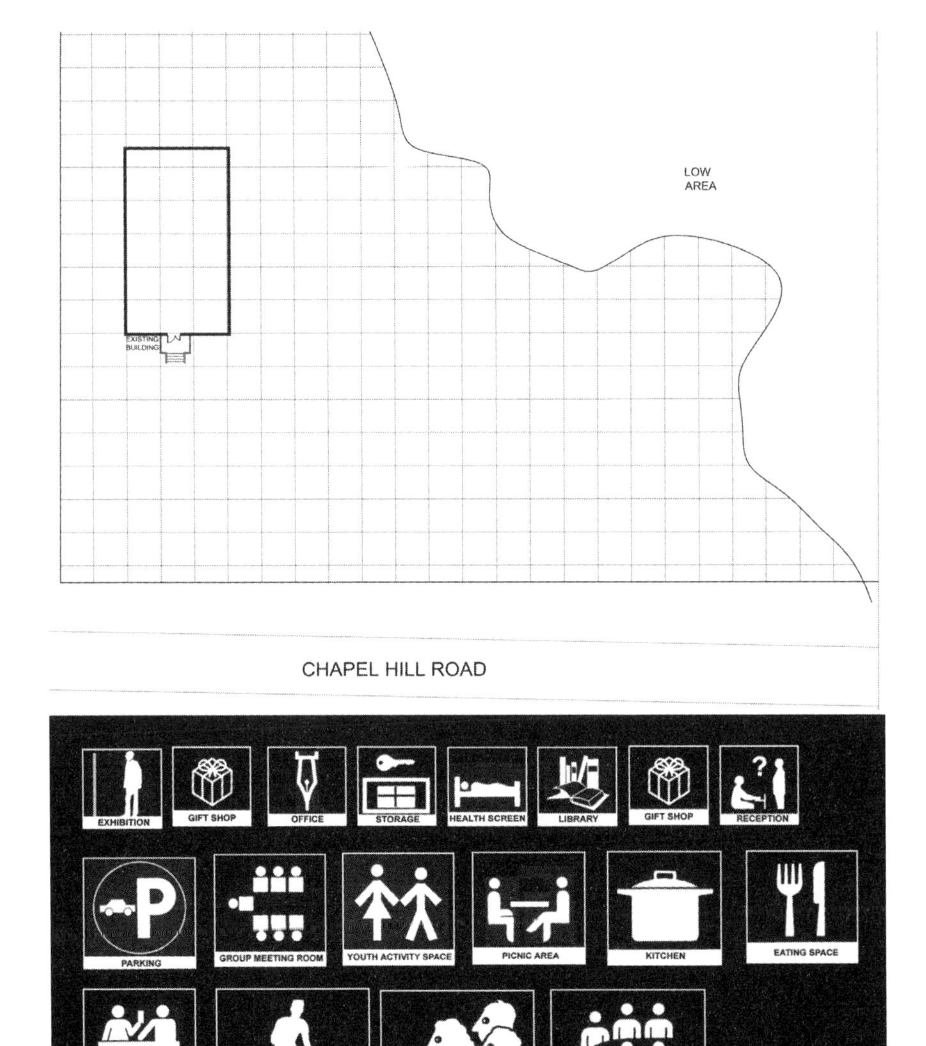

11.2. The design game prepared for the community workshop. Top: the site with the grid layout; bottom: examples of icons provided to the participants

11.3. Top left: participants playing the design game; top right: one of the participants presenting his team's plan layout proposal; bottom: one of the team's plan layouts

put on preserving the original façade of the building. The massing of the addition was set back from the original façade so as not to overshadow the historical façade. A porch, which was especially requested by the community members as a storytelling space, was also located in front of the addition to minimize its visual impact (Figure 11.5).

Following design development, a fund-raising document was developed for the SFHA to seek grants in an effort to have construction documents developed and build the proposal. The design proposal and the fund-raising document were presented to the community in the location of the community workshop. The community received the proposal very positively. The SFHA is continuing efforts to raise funds to develop construction drawings and build the proposal. The SFHA Community Center development process has enabled the community members to provide input into the programming and design development phases.

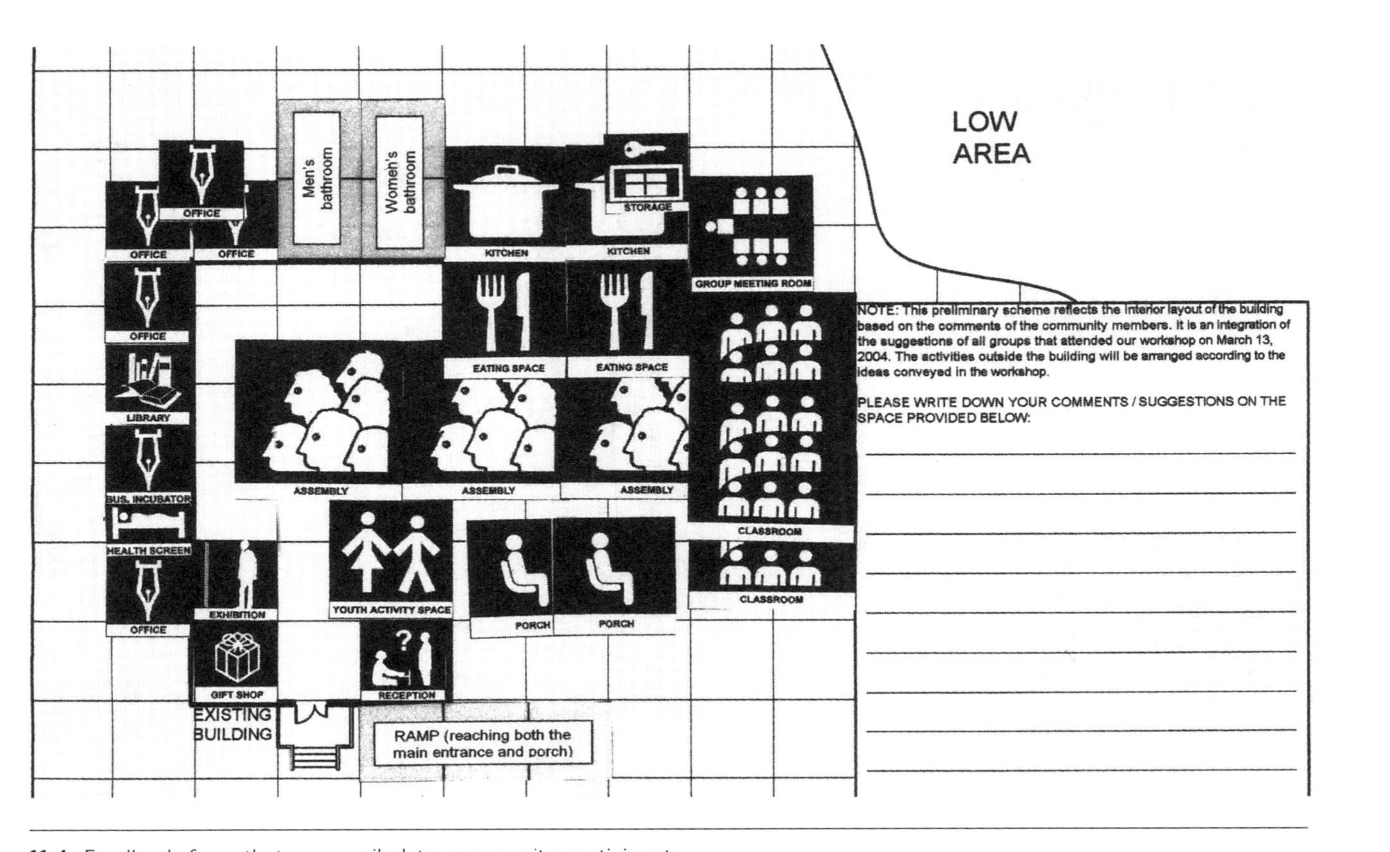

11.4. Feedback form that was mailed to community participants

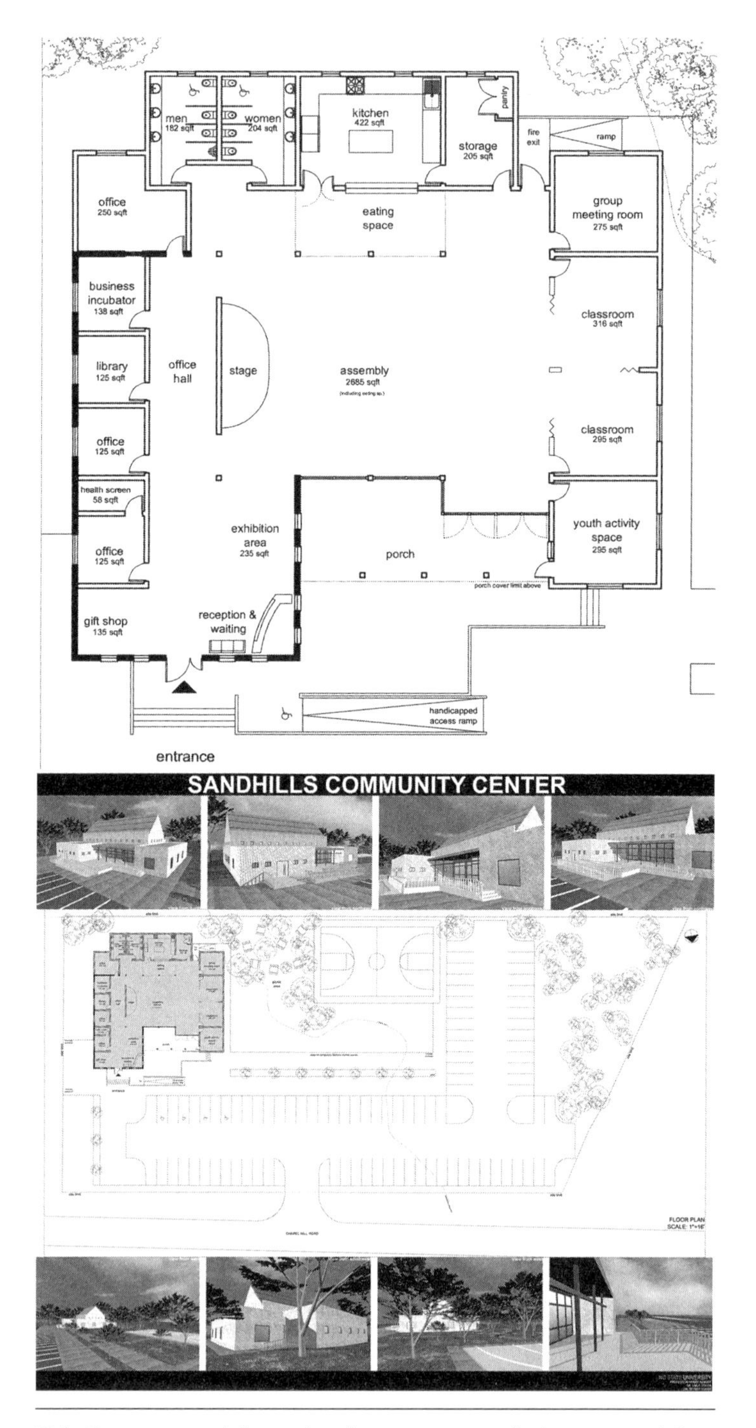

11.5. Top: proposed floor plan; bottom: poster display prepared for the community

11.5. CASE: LAGUNA CHILD AND FAMILY DEVELOPMENT CENTER, PUEBLO OF LAGUNA, NEW MEXICO

Leading group: Laguna Department of Education

Project team: Henry Sanoff (North Carolina State University faculty); Umut Toker, Zeynep Toker (North Carolina State University graduate students)

Project duration: Approximately 4 months

Project timeline:

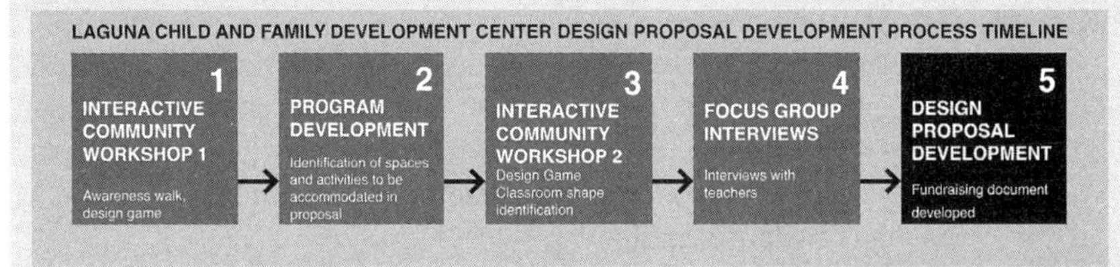

Activity formats used: Interactive community workshops, focus group interviews

Methods used: Awareness walk, design games, focus group interviews

Instruments used: Design game kits, interview instruments

The Pueblo of Laguna is a Native American reservation located approximately 40 miles west of Albuquerque, New Mexico. Laguna is composed of six villages and is home to a population of approximately 4,000 people. It covers parts of Bernalillo, Cibola, Valencia, and Sandoval counties in New Mexico (Figure 11.6). One of the Pueblo of Laguna's government departments is the Laguna Department of Education (LDoE). The LDoE oversees the educational system, consisting of an Early Childhood Program, an elementary school, a middle school, and a program named Partners for Success, which focuses on higher education, employment, and training.

Assistance to families in the Pueblo of Laguna is one of the important needs of the community (Sanoff, Toker, and Toker 2005). The LDoE provides assistance to families and their children through its programs. The community design team was approached by the LDoE to develop a design proposal for a new Laguna Child and Family Development Center. The Early Childhood Program had received a grant for the development of a design proposal for new facilities with the involvement of community members, parents, and teachers.

The community design team started the process by visiting the existing Early Childhood Program facilities. These facilities included four buildings and three portable classrooms. After the site visit the community design team started the participatory design process. The participatory design process consisted of two interactive community workshops, focus group interviews, and feedback acquisition during the design development phase.

Community members, students, parents, and teachers attended the first community workshop. After an introduction, the workshop began with an awareness walk. A rating scale was provided to the teachers for them to evaluate the existing learning spaces. This activity enabled the participants to refresh their memories about the existing facilities and familiarize themselves with the current conditions.

After the awareness walk the participants engaged in a design game that focused on play areas for children. Using a base map and icons that represented a variety of play activities, participants developed ideal play areas for children in small groups. Each group then presented its ideal play area to the rest of the participants.

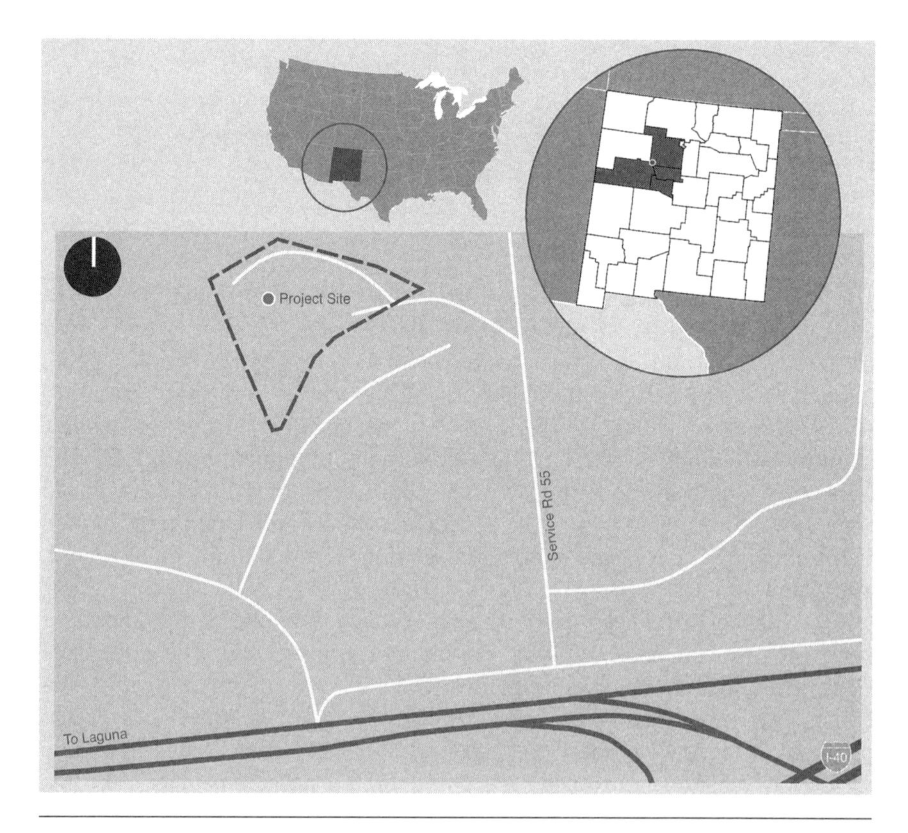

11.6. The Pueblo of Laguna and the project site

Work on the development of materials for a second community workshop started with data analysis. The community design team analyzed the outcomes of the first community workshop and developed a preliminary program for the new Laguna Child and Family Development Center. A design game with a focus on the spatial layout of the proposed building was then developed using the preliminary program. Like the design game used in the first community workshop, this design game included icons of varying sizes for activity areas and a base with a grid overlaid on it.

The second community workshop started with an introduction of the upcoming workshop activities. The same participants that attended the first community workshop were asked to form small groups in this second community workshop and develop their ideal building layouts. The groups developed ideal plan layouts by cutting and pasting the icons, as well as by drawing and writing on the base grid provided. At the end of this process, each group was asked to share its layout with the rest of the participants through a verbal presentation (Figure 11.7).

The final activity in the second community workshop focused on the plan layouts of classrooms. Participants were provided with four classroom layout shapes that are commonly found in similar facilities. After small-group discussions, participants agreed that an L-shaped layout would provide identifiable learning areas, and chose this layout (Sanoff, Toker, and Toker 2005).

Analyzing the information collected from the community workshops, the community design team started developing a detailed program for the building and some conceptual design ideas. Feedback and input from teachers were integrated into this process through focus group interviews, at the end of which the team developed a detailed building program (Sanoff, Toker, and Toker 2005).

Throughout the participatory design process a number of themes came up. First, it became clear that courtyards would be effective in organizing

11.7. Left: one of the group spokespeople presenting a layout; right: one of the plan layouts developed by the participants

the spatial layout and circulation, as well as in maximizing shaded outdoor areas. Local architectural practices, which also use courtyards for shaded outdoor areas because of the hot, arid climate, were influential in this decision. Second, it became clear that three main entrances to the building would be necessary because of the three different groups served by the LDoE: Early Head Start students (infants and toddlers), Head Start students (preschoolers), and home-based services recipients (families). The design proposal needed to specify three entrances with which the individual groups could identify. Third, in addition to educational uses for the new design, community members wanted to see indoor and outdoor community gathering spaces that could be used for community events such as local celebrations. The design proposal needed to identify an outdoor community plaza as well as an indoor multipurpose space that could accommodate community events.

Through the participatory design process the community design team developed a design proposal for the new Laguna Child and Family Development Center. The design proposal featured three distinct service areas: an Early Head Start area, a Head Start area, and a home-based services area. The three areas were organized on an L-shaped building layout, which allowed the development of three distinct entrances as required. The L-shaped layout also made possible the development of a centrally located community plaza (outdoors) and an indoor multipurpose room. Classrooms were clustered around courtyards based on the age group of students, and outdoor play areas with clear lines of sight from classrooms were developed for each classroom (Figure 11.8).

The massing of classrooms was organized so that clerestory windows would allow natural light into classrooms. Courtyards and transitional spaces between outdoor play areas and classrooms were provided with awnings to maximize the shaded outdoor areas. A multicolored scheme was chosen for the proposal to reflect the youth-oriented use of the facility. Overall, the massing strategy for the design proposal was influenced by the physical expression of local buildings (Figure 11.9).

In addition to the design proposal, a fund-raising document was developed for the LDoE to seek grants to have construction documents developed and build the design. Based on the building costs, the fund-raising document also specified a phasing strategy that would enable the LDoE to start construction without having to raise funds for the entire project. The LDoE is continuing its work to raise sufficient funds to develop construction drawings and build the proposal. The Laguna Child and Family Development Center design development process has enabled the community members, parents, and teachers to provide input into the programming and design development phases. The design proposal also received a reviewer award from Designshare.org, a website dedicated to globally sharing ideas about best practices in educational facility planning and design (Designshare n.d.).

LEGEND
A preschool playroom
AA preschool outdoor play
B early head start playroom
BB early head start outdoor play
1A preschool reception
1B early headstart reception
1C home based reception
2 courtyard
3 teacher workroom
4 head start director
5 small group meeting room
6 education coordinator
7 language / culture office
8 health services
9 isolation room
10 adult toilets
11 storage
12 janitor
13 hvac
14 mental health
15 therapy
16 early head start director
17 laundry
18 multipurpose room
19 large group meeting room
20a early headstart home based off.
20b head start home based office
21 parent activities coordinator
22 parent resources
23 adult training classroom
24 home based training class
25 prenatal office
26 transportation office
27 family services
28 parenting apartment
29 kitchen
30 multipurpose room storage
31 loading dock
32 community plaza/picnic area
33 outdoor play
34 center director's office
35 home based director's office
headstart entrance
early headstart entrance
home based entrance

11.8. Proposed floor plan for Laguna Child and Family Development Center

11.9. Top left: overall massing with Head Start entrance in front; top right: overall massing with Early Head Start classrooms in front; bottom left: classroom–transition space–outdoor play area interface and the Head Start entrance; bottom right: one of the courtyards in the Head Start area

12 Community Participation in Planning and Design

Future Steps

In this book we have provided a comprehensive picture of the past and present of the community design field. The remaining question is, what does the future of community design look like? In this chapter we consider some possibilities, many of which are tied in to fast-paced social, environmental, and technological changes.

From the time of the Industrial Revolution, urban settlements have been associated with large-scale social and environmental problems. The relentless outward expansion of urban areas, while consuming vast swaths of land, has also spurred greater reliance on mechanical means of transportation and, by extension, on fossil fuels. At the same time, fluctuations in economic conditions have driven patterns of human migration, leading to overpopulation in some areas and underpopulation in others. Such happenings exacerbate social problems. Consequently, the contemporary issues facing planning and design are complex. How might community design processes and methods be instrumental in addressing them? We discuss possible answers to this question in three categories: physical planning and design, social issues in the information age, and the environmental.

12.1. COMMUNITY DESIGN, PHYSICAL PLANNING, AND DESIGN ISSUES

Many cities around the world are compiling inventories of unused infrastructure and unused buildings. In the United States, suburban sprawl has contributed to the underutilization of downtowns and other older high-density areas. Such spaces and places include older industrial districts and buildings, as well as bridges, rail yards, and similar facilities. The adaptive reuse of these facilities can help minimize or avoid urban expansion while putting existing resources in the built environment to use. Community design processes and methods can be instrumental in furthering this trend, especially as communities become more aware that they cannot continue to expand indefinitely without jeopardizing their own future.

Since many older, underutilized pieces of infrastructure and buildings are perceived as facilities "to go," those interested in saving and reusing them are, knowingly or not, activating a newer version of what the original community designers did: grassroots movements—or the "neo-grassroots" movements of the twenty-first century. One of the best-known and most celebrated examples of reusing existing urban infrastructure and urban space is New York City's High Line, the subject of an adaptive reuse effort initiated by a neo-grassroots movement.

Originally designed in the mid-19th century to bring products into the heart of the city, what would later become the High Line was an industrial rail line terminating in Manhattan. As the peninsula became more and more active, as well as dense with people and services, the rail line was raised on a structure to increase safety and efficiency, hence becoming the "High Line." By the 1970s the line was used less and less often, and parts of the line had already been demolished. Underutilized and dilapidated, the High Line was soon left as an unused structure on a significant right-of-way in one of the most valuable pieces of land in the world, Manhattan (Eck 2011).

When the subject of demolishing the High Line and reusing its right-of-way came to the fore and was partly implemented, two local residents, accompanied by interested community members and business owners, started a grassroots movement to save the structure and convert it for reuse. Calling themselves the Friends of the High Line, the group worked with Design Trust for Public Space, a nonprofit organization in New York City composed of designers, artists, and other professionals interested in public space. Over a period of approximately 12 years, the group and its supporters successfully advocated for the adaptive reuse of this piece of infrastructure. Today, the reused portion of the structure provides its visitors with green spaces and walkways, new vantage points from which to experience New York City (Rybczynski 2010). The movement received support from for-profit and nonprofit designers and institutions, and the decision-making process resembled that of the early community design advocacy movements, utilizing common community design formats and methods of the time (Eck 2011).

Another example of community design emphasizing the adaptive reuse of existing urban facilities is the "park(ing) day." Originally initiated by the design group Rebar in San Francisco, park(ing) day involves converting one or more streetside parking spots into temporary open spaces. Paying the parking meter, volunteers convert parking spots into a green space (or something like it), with a groundcover different from the original asphalt, seating, some kind of shade, an enclosure to protect from vehicular and pedestrian traffic, and signage identifying the event (Rebar Group 2009).

Beyond its symbolic value, park(ing) day has drawn a wave of support from ordinary residents in many cities. In this form, park(ing) day emerges as a participatory decision-making and action mechanism that emphasizes the importance of open space in higher density urban contexts. The "parklets" of San Francisco (Figure 12.1) are among the signs of change sparked by community design activities such as park(ing) day.

Perhaps even more important than the role of community design in supporting the adaptive reuse of older spaces and the creation of new open spaces is its role in supporting a resource that is vital for all of us, food. It is well acknowledged in the built environment literature that sprawling urban areas are taking over agricultural land that is directly connected to the support of human life (Hester 2006). Issues beyond land use and suburban sprawl add to the problem. According to the U.S. Department of Agriculture, by 2006 as many as 4 percent of families in the United States lacked money or other resources with which to obtain food at some point during the year (Nord, Andrews, and Carlson 2004). The issue is not limited to families in the United States with food insecurity, however. Many countries around the world with fewer resources and a poorer agricultural infrastructure than the United States are facing much more severe problems. In addition, even in industrialized nations, significant resources are being spent on transporting food to urban centers.

12.1. A "parklet" in San Francisco. Park(ing) day and parklets exemplify new modes of public participation in the creation of public space.

Against these trends, urban agriculture in the form of community gardens (Figure 12.2) has been on the rise over the past decade as a way to provide affordable food to populations without wasting resources on transporting food long distances. The concept of urban agriculture entails residents of an urban area growing crops in their community using available land or even rooftops as a way to access fresh, affordable food. Community design provides invaluable resources to those who are interested in implementing urban agriculture and developing community gardens. In fact, community design approaches have been used to promulgate urban agriculture and community gardening while developing community-building efforts. Operation Green Thumb, organized by New York City's Parks and Recreation Department, seeks neighborhood revitalization through participatory urban agriculture in the form of urban gardens intended for personal cultivation (Thompson 2008). Urban agriculture through community participation is an expanding trend. It not only provides populations with fresh produce but also fosters community-building activities through participatory decision making.

While participatory decision making can help generate innovative ideas on how unused or underused facilities can be reused, it can also help educate communities that are unaware of, or less knowledgeable about, such resources. The first potential area of focus for community designers of the 21st century, therefore, is the innovative, community-initiated reuse of unused or underused urban areas, buildings, and infrastructure.

12.2. A community garden in San Luis Obispo, California

12.2. COMMUNITY DESIGN AND SOCIAL ISSUES IN THE INFORMATION AGE

Participatory community design processes and methods help people understand each other's needs and wishes and empower communities. As a natural extension of this function, community design processes and methods can help build a better sense of community. David W. McMillan and David M. Chavis (1986) have characterized the sense of community along four dimensions: (1) membership, (2) influence, (3) integration and fulfillment of needs, and (4) a shared emotional connection. Membership refers to a person's sense of investment in and belonging to a community. Influence refers to the capability of influencing or being influenced by the community to which one belongs, while integration and fulfillment of needs calls up a positive sense of belonging. Finally, a shared emotional connection refers to community members' identification with a shared past, either contemporary or historical.

In an era in which cities are increasingly multiethnic and multicultural (Castells 2004), a sense of community is likely to be especially important for the future. Through community design processes individuals can not only develop a stronger sense of belonging in their communities but can also increase their influence. By providing individuals with a voice in the shaping of their environment, community design processes help people become aware of others' concerns, in this way both influencing and being influenced by their peers. Further, through participatory decision making people are able to contribute to a shared history even if they are new to the community.

Community design processes as they have been practiced over several years are already recognized as a way to build community. The information age, characterized by advanced technologies and global communication capability, offers new means to bring together individuals from different backgrounds very easily. Two applications of the new information exchange technologies stand out: the use of social media—Facebook, Twitter, YouTube, webpages, and the like—as communication and community participation tools, and the use of such media as a data source for the community designer. The user-generated content of Internet based media provides unprecedented amounts of data previously unavailable to the community designer. The vast reach of online communications can, however, be trimmed down to the community level to support local decision-making initiatives in Internet-enabled communities.

Let us open up these two applications of IT for community design purposes and look at them in more detail, beginning with the use of social media for communication and community participation. The past decade has witnessed an explosion in the use of social media by the masses to communicate and share their experiences with acquaintances of various kinds—friends, family members, colleagues, individuals holding similar political views—as well as perfect strangers. Since this technology allows user-generated content to be shared with countless numbers of people, the Internet enables multidirectional information flow, as opposed to earlier uses, whereby users were typically limited to viewing content provided by webpage publishers. This phenomenon has distinct implications for community design. Beyond using social media to organize community design activities and public meetings, community designers can initiate and guide dialogue and promote participatory decision making. As examples, a project may establish a Facebook page or a Yahoo! group where interested parties can make comments, or community designers may use Twitter to provide updates to interested parties about the progress of a project. As digital technologies become more common, the two-way information exchange capability of online media will present new opportunities to the community design field.

The second opportunity for community design, the use of social media to capture data, may present even bigger, unexpected advantages. When not project-specific, people's contributions to social media can turn into a very detailed, expansive data source. In any project-specific contribution opportunity on social media, just as at any public meeting, it is not unexpected for positions to form and harden. In non-project-specific, voluntary contributions, however, people may simply share their observations and comments. This presents a unique, unbiased data source for the community designer able to tap into it. A simple example is the prospective redesign of a park, made available on social media for commentary and reaction. Site visitors can make comments about the park in various ways, post photographs of what they like or dislike about the park, and submit videos showing how the park is used. These comments and visual records of observations can become an invaluable information source for the community designer.

Recent research into this phenomenon by Ray (2011) revealed that social media can indeed be a valuable data source for the community designer. Through analyses of four projects, Ray demonstrated that data collected from social media sites, such as photographs and written commentary, added to the information provided by the public in community design events. In some cases, data collected from social media sources had more details than the information collected through conventional community design mechanisms.

At this point, neither the use of social media as a community participation tool nor their use as a data source seems able to replace conventional community design efforts. However, as the bandwidth—the amount of information exchanged per communication effort—of online communications increases, community designers will need to attend to the implications for participatory decision-making processes. Participatory decision making consequently gains an important role in the formation of functioning communities with these properties. Community building in the information age, therefore, is a second potential area of focus for community designers of the 21st century.

12.3. COMMUNITY DESIGN AND THE ENVIRONMENT

The world today faces many environmental issues as a result of unceasing expansion of the built environment, especially in industrialized nations. The creep of urbanization due to increased migration patterns and economic incentives (Castells 2004) has facilitated expanded transportation networks and hence has increased urban areas' dependence on fossil fuels, particularly oil, as sources of energy. The increased use of fossil fuels has in turn contributed to overall pollution problems while reducing the available supply of nonrenewable energy sources.

It is not only industrialized nations that have been affected by environmental issues. Developing countries also bear the burden, in some cases far out of proportion to their own use of environmental resources. Intense consumption of the world's resources by privileged areas has left less privileged areas with a reduced quality and quantity of water and food.

Some community designers have begun to confront these issues directly in their practice. Nabeel Hamdi, for example, a consultant and academic working with the United Nations and nongovernmental organizations, has been practicing community design to mitigate environmental stress in countries such as India and Sri Lanka for years (Hamdi 2004). According to Hamdi, the main challenge in such projects is the need to simultaneously collaborate with the local government, the economic market, and the local community. In countries where community design has been practiced for decades, stakeholders have a certain level of familiarity with the process. However, as Hamdi points out, in communities unfamiliar with the community design approach, connecting stakeholders and creating ownership in such projects often requires educating local partners about the process (cited in Toker and Toker 2006b).

Similar issues may come to the fore in relatively new planning challenges, such as responding to climate change, even in countries with established community design traditions. Because of some communities' limited familiarity with contemporary phenomena such as global warming and carbon emissions, community designers may need to take on a larger training role. It may be necessary to discuss the implications of conventional growth and transportation patterns with community members even before participatory decision-making processes can begin—and to expect some pushback. As Elizabeth Wilson and Jake Piper point out in *Spatial Planning and Climate Change* (2010, 54), "there is evidence that—whether it be promoting wind farms, controlling development of areas at risk of flooding, designing energy-conserving settlements and transport, or taking account of climate change in assessment processes—this reframing of spatial planning is contentious and difficult."

All of this presents new challenges to community designers. Beyond the implementation of community design methods and participatory decision-making processes, as new issues come to the fore, a new task of setting the context for the community emerges. Years of community design background, however, should provide practitioners with a variety of formats, methods, and instruments to address these challenges.

Community design processes and community designers can continue to take a leading role in addressing these issues, and so expand their influence. The challenges facing the field in relation to environmental concerns include educating communities in industrialized and developing countries, as well as facilitating participatory, informed decision making to confront these issues. Through developing innovative participatory decision-making methods, community designers can have a positive impact and be instrumental in contributing to better environmental practices. The third potential area of focus for community designers of the 21st century, therefore, is the natural environment and how it relates to the creation, reuse, and management of the built environment.

12.4. THE FUTURE OF COMMUNITY DESIGN METHODS

With its emphasis on participatory decision making and providing everyone with a voice, community design as a field has much to contribute to work on physical planning and design issues, social issues, and environmental issues in the years to come. In all three fields, the use of information technologies to support participatory decision making seems to be coming to the forefront.

Developments in GIS technology over the past decade have helped shape a new approach to scenario planning. Now, communities can be presented with the anticipated outcomes of decisions relatively quickly, as the outcomes are being discussed. Scenario planning supported by GIS and other information technologies under development is one of the frontiers of community design. Scenario planning can be applied to all three focus areas for community design discussed in this chapter. Physical development scenarios for neighborhoods and cities can be analyzed through rapid data analysis with emerging software. Social networks can be analyzed using social media tools to help support community development, and climate-related data can be used to develop projections of the impacts of climate change on communities. By monitoring developments in enabling technologies closely, community designers can expand their access to information and more efficiently help communities shape their future.

Another frontier community design method is visualization of the existing and imagined built environment as an aid to the community design process. Two- and three-dimensional computer-based visualization techniques have progressed tremendously in the past two decades. It is not unreasonable to anticipate that this development will continue, with applications getting ever faster and more sophisticated. Paired with the conventional over-the-board visualization methods, these technologies make the community design field visually stronger than ever. The software currently available in this area connects GIS databases with three-dimensional visualizations of building types and other urban elements such as urban furniture, lighting, and trees. By assigning proposed land uses to parcels and various properties to proposed rights-of-way, the software allows visualization of the physical implications of ideas proposed or discussed. Community designers can use these technologies to enhance the community design process and better serve the communities they work with.

Computer technologies have also greatly changed the ways in which people interact (Castells 2001). The bandwidth of computer-based interaction options has increased steadily over the past two decades. It is common practice to use the Internet for video conferencing and other forms of communication. And it is not too far-fetched to anticipate that these technologies will continue to get more and more sophisticated, with computer-based interactions becoming closer and closer to face-to-face interaction experiences. Computer-based interaction methods thus constitute another frontier of community design methods. Community designers should monitor these developments and integrate them into community design whenever they would make genuine participation possible.

Digital technologies also make possible an unprecedented amount of information exchange. This is a major possibility for empowerment of many communities, since more knowledge brings more power. Receiving the information does not guarantee better creation and management of the built environment, however. The integration of digital information consumption into the community design process, therefore, is a challenge for community designers. Community designers should monitor advances in this area and integrate into design processes techniques that enhance genuine participation. The other face of the information exchange is the vast amount of data that community designers are now able to receive from community participants, not all relevant. Sorting out the dross from the gold is expected to be a time-consuming but potentially useful task, as the new thoughts from participants allow the designer to acquire new knowledge about a project.

All this presumes a narrowing of the digital divide that now splits the world (Castells 1999; Hall 1999). Many communities around the world do not have access to online technologies and rely on conventional methods of information consumption, interaction, visualization, and decision making. The intent in integrating new technologies into community design should be to enhance the field, and enhancing the field is only possible by ensuring that no community is left out of the effort.

This book has reviewed the conceptual underpinnings and historical development of the community design field and has systematically analyzed the community design timeline, activity formats, methods, and instruments. Community design processes have been introduced and exemplified at four project scales: regional, community, urban, and site-specific design. But no formula or toolbox has been prescribed in this book. Every community, and therefore every community design process, is unique. It is the community designer's responsibility to design a timeline and develop an appropriate mix of existing methods, or be innovative with new methods, to provide the best participatory decision-making process possible. The formats, methods, and instruments of community design presented here are not exhaustive since community design is an ever-changing field and process. It is a custom-designed decision-making process based on the characteristics of a given community and problem.

No matter what timeline, activity format, or instrument is selected, the ultimate objective of community design is to ensure that genuine participation in decision making is achieved. Good design responds to people's needs, and community designers should be interested in understanding those needs and in learning for better practice. The activity formats, methods, instruments, and technologies discussed in this book should serve community design with these objectives. Only by placing people's wishes and needs front and center on the agenda can the field of community design sustain its existence.

References

Alinsky, S. 1971. *Rules for Radicals: A Practical Primer for Realistic Radicals.* New York: Random House.
Arnstein, S. 1969. "A Ladder of Citizen Participation." *JAIP* 35:215–24.
Atlee, T. 2003. *The Tao of Democracy: Using Co-intelligence to Create a World That Works for All.* Cranston, R.I.: Writers' Collective.
Ballon, H., and K. T. Jackson, eds. 2007. *Robert Moses and the Modern City: The Transformation of New York.* New York: Norton.
Bell, B., ed. 2004. *Good Deeds, Good Design: Community Service through Architecture.* New York: Princeton Architectural Press.
Berke, P. R., and D. R. Godschalk. 2006. *Urban Land Use Planning.* 5th ed. Urbana: University of Illinois Press.
Brolin, B. C. 1976. *The Failure of Modern Architecture.* New York: Van Nostrand Reinhold.
California Government Code. Sect. 54590, Chap. I, Preamble. Available at http://leginfo.ca.gov/cgi-bin/calawquery?codesection=gov&codebody=&hits=20.
Carpenter, S. L., and W. J. D. Kennedy. 2000. *Managing Public Disputes: A Practical Guide for Government, Business, and Citizens' Groups.* San Francisco: Jossey-Bass.
Castells, M. 1999. "The Informational City Is a Dual City: Can It Be Reversed?" In *High Technology and Low-Income Communities,* ed. D. A. Schon, B. Sanyal, and W. J. Mitchell. Cambridge, Mass.: MIT Press.
———. 2001. *The Internet Galaxy: Reflections on the Internet, Business, and Society.* Oxford: Oxford University Press.
———. 2004. "Space of Flows, Space of Places: Materials for a Theory of Urbanism in the Information Age." In *The Cybercities Reader,* ed. S. Graham. London: Routledge.
Curry, R. 2004. "Community Design Centers." Pp. 61–70 in Bell.
Davidoff, P. 1965. "Advocacy and Pluralism in Planning." *JAIP* 31:331.
DesignShare. n.d. Laguna Child and Family Development Center: DesignShare Projects. Available at http://designshare.com/index.php/projects/laguna-center.
Dobbins, M. 2009. *Urban Design and People.* New York: Wiley.
Eck, B. D. 2011. "A Case of Reclaiming Ruin: Beyond the Hype and Hyperbole of New York's High Line." Master's thesis. California Polytechnic State University, San Luis Obispo.
Envision Central Texas. 2004. *A Vision for Central Texas: May 2004.* Austin, Tex.: Envision Central Texas.
———. n.d. "Your Ideas, Our Region's Future." Available at http://envisioncentraltexas.org.

Faga, B. 2006. *Designing Public Consensus: The Civic Theater of Community Participation for Architects, Landscape Architects, Planners, and Urban Designers.* New York: Wiley.
Feldman, R. M. 2004. "Activist Practice." Pp. 109–14 in Bell.
Frampton, K. 1992. *Modern Architecture: A Critical History.* New York: Thames and Hudson.
Habermas, J. 1990. *The Philosophical Discourse of Modernity: Twelve Lectures.* Cambridge, Mass.: MIT Press.
Habraken, N. J. 1972. *Supports: An Alternative to Mass Housing.* New York: Praeger.
Hall, K. B., and G. A. Porterfield. 2001. *Community by Design: New Urbanism for Suburbs and Small Communities.* New York: McGraw-Hill.
Hall, P. 1999. "Changing Geographies: Technology and Income." In *High Technology and Low-Income Communities: Prospects for the Positive Use of Advanced Information Technology*, ed. D. A. Schon, B. Sanyal, and W. J. Mitchell. Cambridge, Mass.: MIT Press.
———. 2002. *Cities of Tomorrow: An Intellectual History of Urban Planning and Design in the Twentieth Century.* 2nd ed. London: Blackwell.
Hamdi, N. 1995. *Housing without Houses: Participation, Flexibility, Enablement.* New York: Van Nostrand Reinhold.
———. 2004. *Small Change: About the Art of Practice and the Limits of Planning in Cities.* Sterling, Va.: Earthscan.
———. 2010. *The Placemaker's Guide to Building Community.* Washington, D.C.: Earthscan.
Hatch, R. C., ed. 1984. *The Scope of Social Architecture.* New York: Van Nostrand Reinhold.
Hester, R. 1990. *Community Design Primer.* Mendocino, Calif.: Ridge Time Press.
Hester, R. T. 2006. *Design for Ecological Democracy.* Cambridge, Mass.: MIT Press.
Howard, E. 1898. *Garden Cities of To-morrow.* London: S. Sonnenschein. Repr. 1965, Cambridge, Mass.: MIT Press.
Iacofano, D. 2001. *Meeting of the Minds: A Guide to Successful Meeting Facilitation.* Berkeley, Calif.: MIG Communications.
Jones, R. T., W. Pettus, and M. Pyatok. 1997. *Good Neighbors: Affordable Family Housing.* New York: McGraw-Hill.
Kroll, L. 1984. "Anarchitecture." Pp. 166–81 in *The Scope of Social Architecture*, ed. R. C. Hatch. New York: Van Nostrand Reinhold.
Le Corbusier. 1931. *Toward an Architecture*, trans. John Goodman. Los Angeles, Calif.: Getty Research Institute. 2007.
Lennertz, W. 1991. "Town Making Fundamentals." Pp. 21–24 in *Towns and Town-Making Principles*, ed. A. Duany and E. Plater-Zyberk. New York: Rizzoli.
McMillan, D. W., and D. M. Chavis. 1986. "Sense of Community: A Definition and Theory." *Journal of Community Psychology* 14(1): 6–23.
Mockbee, S. 2004. "The Role of the Citizen Architect." Pp. 151–56 in Bell.
Myregion.org. 2007. "How Shall We Grow? A Shared Vision for Central Florida, Created to Help Our Region Continue to be a Great Place to Live, Learn, Work and Play." Orlando, Fla. Available at www.myregion.org/clientuploads/pdfs/HSWG_final.pdf.
———. n.d. "Goals and Objectives." Available at www.myregion.org/Aboutimyregionorgi/tabid/53/Default.aspx.
Newman, O. 1996. *Creating Defensible Space.* Washington, D.C.: U.S. Department of Housing and Urban Development, Office of Policy Development and Research.
Nord, M., M. Andrews, and S. Carlson. 2004. *Household Food Security in the United States, 2003.* Washington, D.C.: U.S. Department of Agriculture, Economic Research Service.

Peña, W. M., and S. A. Parshall. 2001. *Problem Seeking: An Architectural Programming Primer*. New York: Wiley.

Peterson, G. D., G. S. Cumming, and S. R. Carpenter. 2003. "Scenario Planning: A Tool for Conservation in an Uncertain World." *Conservation Biology* 17(2): 358–66.

Rapoport, A. 1982. *The Meaning of the Built Environment: A Nonverbal Communication Approach*. Beverly Hills, Calif.: Sage.

Rapoport, A. 2005. *Culture, Architecture, and Design*. Chicago: Locke Science.

Ray, A. P. 2011. "Planning Connected: Using Online Social Networks to Improve Knowledge about Places and Communities." Master's thesis, California Polytechnic State University, San Luis Obispo.

Rebar Group. 2009. "The Park(ing) Day Manual: A Primer on User-Generated Urbanism and Temporary Tactics for Improving the Public Realm." Unpublished brochure. San Francisco: Rebar Group.

Rybczynski, W. 2010. *Makeshift Metropolis: Ideas about Cities*. New York: Scribner.

Russell, B. 1981. *Building Systems, Industrialization and Architecture*. New York: Wiley.

Sanoff, H. 1979. *Design Games*. Los Altos, Calif.: William Kaufmann.

———. 2000. *Community Participation Methods in Design and Planning*. New York: Wiley.

Sanoff, H., U. Toker, and Z. Toker. 2005. "Research Based Design of a Child and Family Education Center." In *Proceedings of the 36th International Conference of the Environmental Design Research Association*. Edmond, Okla.: Environmental Design Research Association.

Steiner, F. 2006. "Metropolitan Resilience: The Role of Universities in Facilitating a Sustainable Metropolitan Future." Pp. 1–18 in *Toward a Resilient Metropolis: The Role of State and Land Grant Universities in the 21st Century*, ed. A. C. Nelson, B. L. Allen, and D. Trauger. Alexandria, Calif.: Metropolitan Institute Press.

———. 2008. "Envision Central Texas." Pp. 16–19 in *Emergent Urbanism: Evolution in Urban Form, Texas*, ed. S. Black and F. Steiner. Austin, Tex.: Congress for the New Urbanism.

Taylor, F. W. 1911. *The Principles of Scientific Management*. New York: Harper and Brothers.

Thompson, J. 2008. "Urban Agriculture, Food Insecurity and Sustainability: Proposing Urban Agricultural Land Use Plans for New York City." Master's thesis, Columbia University, New York.

Toker, Z. 2007. "Recent Trends in Community Design: The Eminence of Participation." *Design Studies* 28:309–23.

Toker, Z., and U. Toker. 2006a. "Community Design in Its Pragmatist Age: Increasing Popularity and Changing Outcomes." *Middle East Technical University Journal of the Faculty of Architecture* 23:2.

———. 2006b. "An Interview with Nabeel Hamdi." *Middle East Technical University Journal of the Faculty of Architecture* 23:2.

Turner, J. F. C. 1972. *Freedom to Build: Dweller Control of the Housing Process*. New York: Macmillan.

Wates, N. 2000. *The Community Planning Handbook: How People Can Shape Their Cities, Towns and Villages in Any Part of the World*. London: Earthscan.

———. 2010. *The Community Planning Event Manual: How to Use Collaborative Planning and Urban Design Events to Improve Your Environment*. London: Earthscan.

Wilson, E., and J. Piper. 2010. *Spatial Planning and Climate Change*. London: Routledge.

Wright, F. L. 1945. *When Democracy Builds*. Chicago: University of Chicago Press.

Wulz, F. 1986. "The Concept of Participation." *Design Studies* 7(3): 153–62.

Zeisel, J. 2006. *Inquiry by Design: Environment / Behavior / Neuroscience in Architecture, Interiors, Landscape, and Planning*. New York: Norton.

Index